DREAMING

UNIVERSITY OF CALIFORNIA PRESS
Berkeley · Los Angeles · London

CAROLYN SEE

AMING

HARD LUCK

AND GOOD TIMES

IN AMERICA

University of California Press
Berkeley and Los Angeles, California
University of California Press, Ltd.
London, England

First Paperback Printing 1996

Library of Congress Cataloging-in-Publication Data
See, Carolyn.
  Dreaming: hard luck and good times in America /
  Carolyn See.
      p.   cm.
  ISBN 0-520-20482-4 (pbk.: alk. paper)
    1. See, Carolyn—Family.   2. Women novelists,
American—20th century—Family relationships.
3. Substance abuse—United States.   4. Family—
United States.   I. Title.
PS3569.E33Z464   1996
813'.54—dc20
[B]   95-46872
                                                CIP

Manufactured in the United States of America on
acid-free paper.
Book design by J. K. Lambert
9 8 7 6 5 4 3 2 1

FOR
MICHAEL DORRIS
AND MAUREEN

Why should the narrative be continuous?
Why not write the story in self-contained scenes,
like a play . . . an album of snapshots? . . . With
the eyes of friends, we look deeply into their
faces, reading, in times' cipher, everything that
is written there.

               —Christopher Isherwood,
               Lions and Shadows

ACKNOWLEDGMENTS

I am indebted more than I can say to Ann Godoff, Anne Sibbald, Linda Kamberg de Martinez, and Jean-Isabel McNutt, for bringing this book into being.

To Healers and Friends: Marina Bokelman, Dorothy Anderson, Noel Lustig, Crystal Pritchard, Brian Murphy, Harvard Gordon, Sara Mitchell, Jackie Joseph, Joan Weber, Nancy Stone, Beryl Towbin, Sasha Stone, Gretchen Kreiger, Buzz and Kristin Kreiger, Tracie Reid, Virginia Wright, Karen Stabiner, and Larry Dietz.

To Family: Richard See, Stella See, Richard, Alexander, and Christopher Kendall, Tom, Jacqueline, and Michael Sturak, Mary Sturak, Chris Chandler and the entire Chandler family, Bob and Lynda Laws, Susan and Jordan Espey, Alice Espey Heidseck and Ralph Heidseck. To Katharine Sturak, Jean-Pierre Mignon, Yara, Eloise, and Marius. Special thanks and love to Lisa See Kendall and Clara Sturak, angels in my eyes. To Maureen Daly for being so brave. And to John Espey for his steadfast sweetness, affection, and good heart.

In Memory of: George Laws, Nell and Bob Laws, Klein and Ada Ault, Red and Ted Tedford, Wynn Corum Laws, Jim Daly, Charlie Lentz, Jim and Solveig Andrews, Eddy See, John Sturak, Michael Sturak, Bob and Helen Turner, and Anne Cox.

In a class by herself: Kate Daly.

CONTENTS

We've spent the last three hours—my daughter Clara and I—looking through the pigskin chest that holds about seventy-five years of
family photographs. I need some for this book, but I don't want to go
through the chest alone, or for too long at a time. I guess it might be
like that in every family: if the pictures remind you of sad times, you
feel sad all over again. If the pictures bring back something joyful,
you feel an emptiness because that time is gone.

We're looking for stuff from the old days; we know it's in here
somewhere. We seem to be groaning and sighing a lot. Then Clara
rocks back on her heels. "Aaah," she says. "Oh God!" She hands it
over. "Pay dirt," she says.

And there's my Aunt Helen, the cruelest person I ever knew,
dressed up to beat the band. My mother, dressed up too, looks
straight into the camera. Aunt Helen's got her arms around my little
half sister Rose, who's about thirteen years old, already wearing mascara, one of the things that would get her into so much trouble down
the line.

"OK! That's it!" Clara says. We close the chest, get up from the
floor, move creakily over to the couch. "How can you keep doing
this?" Clara asks, and then, "I know I shouldn't, but I could really use
a glass of wine." I open up a bottle and we tell each other, as rapidly

XVI | CAROLYN SEE

as possible, the story of Uncle Bob, so drunk (but who wouldn't be with that *bat* for a wife?), unfurling his napkin through a candle flame on Thanksgiving and setting himself on fire. Or Uncle Bob sitting next to Clara's dad on another terrible holiday, when something like *Godzilla Meets the Undersea Monster* was playing on TV and as Godzilla crushed an aircraft carrier, Uncle Bob earnestly said to Tom, "I guess this reminds you of the old days?" Because Tom had served on a carrier. And Tom had to laugh.

We tell these stories fast because we know them so well. Then Clara sighs, and sighs again. "Poor Rose," she says. Clara's done her good deed, helping me with this, so she goes home.

I take the bottle and my glass and go out to the patio, which overlooks miles and miles of Topanga Canyon and the mountains beyond. It's so beautiful out here! I need it, because most days, working on this project, I feel like I've gone fifteen rounds with the champ, and the champ has generally won. I pour a second glass. I'm pretty much the only one around here who drinks anymore.

I've been writing a history of how drugs and drink have worked in our family for the last fifty—actually it turned out to be closer to a hundred—years. In varying degrees, it's history seen through a purple haze. It's full of secrets and chaos and distortions, and secretly remembered joys. I'm beginning to think it may be the unwritten history of America. Sometimes it's hard to be American—to live, and work, and love—and not be disappointed by the results, the discrepancy between what we wanted and what we got. It's so easy to slip into easy answers to the question of what has happened to us: the exhortations of Norman Vincent Peale, or AA, or "Just Say No!" And the equally easy rhetoric of "I'm just no good, that's all, so I'm going to get loaded and stay that way the rest of my life." I want this book to fall like a plumbline down through four generations, tracing that history of drugs and drink, depression and divorce. I just want to take a look at it, see how it works. Refrain from judgment. But of course I can't refrain from judgment.

My family on both sides is very "old" in America. We've been here since before the Revolution. How lucky for those starving peasants—to make it out of England, Ireland, Scotland, over here to a land of unimaginable opportunity. The trouble was, they *were* starving peasants, so they really couldn't imagine the idea of opportunity or dream. It took about 14,000 drinks for them to calm down. I began to see pretty early that this was also going to be a story of climbing— or drifting—out of the underclass, into the working class, and into something upper-middle or beyond. From the beginning, as far as I can make out, "dreaming" in our family meant either the opium that my grandmothers used—for medicinal purposes—or buying that "lovely" home, starting the new business, getting married, publishing a book. Getting high, going up, in this society.

As a child, listening to family stories, I'd think: "If we're so old, why aren't we rich?" Later, my mother would echo this to me: "If you're so smart, why aren't you rich?" Now I know the obvious answer. I wrote the draft of this introduction in the British Library, and when I got tired I went out and looked at the illuminated manuscripts next door. What beauty, what focus, what intelligence, what hard work! But for every learned monk, there were thousands of other Joes out in the fields toiling and sickening and dying. My family on both sides belonged to the toiling and dying types who made it over to America.

And once in America, people divided once again: you could say they became the poor and the rich. The losers and winners. The artists and scientists. If they were countries, they'd be Ireland and England. The former have a particular set of belief systems. They are prone to dreaming, wool-gathering, calling in sick. They lose the deeds to their houses and cry easily. They are often eloquent and intelligent, but they succumb to melancholia, drink, and drugs. The latter? When they hear about clinical depression, they say, "Oh, everybody gets discouraged sometimes." They do not see the abyss. Maybe in their world the ground is flat and safe. Maybe it's a golf course.

This is partly the story of a family finally getting enough of the abyss, getting terminally tired of psychic and emotional free fall, and trying with all its collective might to at least consider breaking through to the world of peaceful afternoons at home, whole months going by without a fight, with nobody nodding off in a restaurant or throwing up on the rug. That's been the struggle of our family for perhaps twenty of the last fifty years. The truth is, we still live more or less in both worlds. My family is full of disappointed lives, of "potential" not lived up to. Of folks who were dealt lousy hands (and played them badly, too). But they took the cards, cracked open a bottle of scotch, and made that material glitter as much as they could. And then, when it felt right to them, one by one they stopped drinking, or the drugs they used went out of style, or their lives pleased them so much that drugs and drink didn't seem to be a problem anymore. Out of the abyss and onto the safe green lawn.

———

The heart of my story is what happened to my half sister, Rose, who left home when she was sixteen, hung out with the rest of us for five uneasy years, then disappeared into the world of hard drugs for another twenty. For us to find each other again, to be sisters again, has been one of the sweetest things in my life. Rose's story alone guarantees that this history can't be chronological. In Californian terms, she lived in a parallel universe.

Life lived by a few dozen people isn't like a novel. You can't stick a love affair or a betrayal or a deportation into Chapter Six and be done with it. I'm happy about these photographs, the ones from the pigskin chest, and I ask the reader to look at this book as a family album. Here are these little girls, so happy! Here's a man, he's in disgrace, because there's only one picture of him left in the whole world. There's a side of the family where for two generations there are no pictures of men at all. Here are some parties: the people *look* happy, but take another look, and then another. Here are some wedding pictures; some marriages didn't work out, but these others— they have to work out; there's so much riding on them, so much love. And these moments last through time.

So, some of these chapters aren't precisely chronological. The ones on acid and on divorce overlap, because the years my second husband and I were dropping acid and getting divorced overlapped by about six months. The chapter on "hanging it up"—becoming a respectable citizen—and "the embarrassing Californianness of it all" overlap because in our particular case becoming respectable paradoxically meant going to some pretty silly seminars. And the main part of Rose's story comes before the story of how we met again after twenty years—partly to keep things as chronological as possible, and partly to say to readers who have lost people they cherish to the hard-drug world: don't worry! You may still get them back again— sit down for long hours on a balcony beside a lagoon and talk about the things you missed, piece the past together again.

I said I've tried not to be judgmental, not to intrude on events, just to write them down. But sometimes I can't help it, sometimes I have to call time out and talk about what's happening. Sometimes the photograph, the telling of a story, isn't enough. What's behind the story? I may bend your ear for a while, but I won't take long, because I hope these characters speak for themselves.

I've changed some names. Rose has criminal friends out there: I don't need some irate speed-dealer coming after her *or* me. Rose's name is changed to protect her privacy. There aren't any grown-up pictures of Rose here. Friends of my mother's get their names changed; they're kind and good, they need their privacy protected, too. (And my own name has changed—from Carolyn Penelope Laws, or "Penny," to Carolyn See, with another last name, Sturak, tacked on for a while.)

Finally, I see that I've organized this book around husbands and children and marriages and weddings—girlie things. If I were a guy, I might structure the last fifty years around war and science—Hitler getting his doctors to invent methadone in World War II, scientists in Switzerland bending over an experiment and seeing a suddenly psychedelic world, or giant cargo planes flying out of Vietnam chock-full of heroin headed for—well, headed for us. But I'm not a guy. Besides, our family's attitude toward war was aptly summed up by my dad: in World War II, dizzy with relief that he was too old to be drafted, he announced, "I go, after the women and children go!"

So my method is skewed by many things, including the fact that through at least two of these chapters I was in something of a purple haze myself.

—

Every writer has a voice in his or her head, chattering along, writing the bad review of what's getting written. Since reviewing books is one of my jobs, that voice can get rowdy. The first thing it says is *"Who cares!"* I answer stoutly, "They'd better care, because I bet three quarters of the nation's families have a drunk uncle or a drugged-out kid, or parents who drink a few too many martinis around the pool. They've got cousins and uncles who can't hold a job and watch daytime TV."

And I hear voices that say with fastidious distaste, "But this is so California-*trendy*! Luckily we don't behave like that here in Ohio, Montana, Maryland, New York." My mother's folks came from upstate New York and my dad's from Texas. My parents journeyed here to shed their pasts. A lot of Americans do that. I know it's embarrassing to be from California, but here's the other side: this state is the repository of America's dreams; it is to America what America is to the rest of the world. If some of those dreams are tacky or inappropriate, that's part of what I'm writing about.

And talk about being a product of the times! If this is 1967, we must be doing acid, right? I have to admit it: our whole family tried as hard as it could to be "different" and ended up being exactly like everybody else. We ate tuna casseroles in the fifties and painted everything chartreuse and dark green. I named my elder daughter Lisa and thought I was the only mother in America to think of it. We were unwitting slaves to every fashion. When I gave up acid and smoking joints to become a responsible mother, the rest of the world was changing too, only lots of them went over to cocaine. It seems to me we're the same as everybody else—discouraging, but there it is.

And why don't I just come out against demon rum once and for all? Why don't I endorse AA with all my heart and pitch out this glass of white wine and switch to Snapple? Because I can't and I won't. To write something for or against drugs and drink just adds to the mountains of material for or against them. The American manifestation of this is so much bigger than any set of opinions about it. Drugs and drink in this country go to our philosophy, our conscience, our finance, our government, our pleasure principle.

Personally, I believe that the government, consciously or not, uses every kind of anodyne to keep the middle and lower classes tranquilized, depressed, and dysfunctional. But I can't prove it, and I may be wrong. I can only show how drugs and drink have played out— like a pachinko game—in my own family. And hope the compact mirror I'm holding up to America isn't too flawed.

Finally, as a reviewer, I'd have to wonder about the narrator here. Who is this woman, who in spite of sporadic efforts to be profound, seems to care most—in her youth—about the next drink, and—all through her life—about the next party? It's true I've never much appreciated the literature of depression so fashionable through this century. I think if your life has been depressing, you don't need more of it. You need celebration and happiness, as much as you can get. With a margarita or not, it doesn't matter.

The sun's going down now, over the Canyon. The stars are out and I go back in. There's no point in being afraid of my aunt Helen—or any of the rest of them. She's dead now. She made history the only way she knew, and maybe she's pleased to be in a book. I feel better. I've had two glasses. I try to limit myself to that. Unless there's a party.

PART I

Alcohol had an incomparably larger place in
the lives of the proletariat than it did among
the bourgeoisie. . . . workers do not drink out
of sheer exuberance; they drink to cast off
the misery of their lives for a few hours. In
every age, even in the Middle Ages, alcohol
has to some extent been a "cure for cares,"
"for what ails."

—Wolfgang Schivelbusch,

Tastes of Paradise

Turn off your mind, relax and float
downstream.
It is not dying, it is not dying.
Lay down all thoughts, surrender to the void.
It is shining, it is shining.

—John Lennon and Paul McCartney,

"Tomorrow Never Knows"

1. ORPHANS

My mother, Kate Laws, and me, "Penny."

The year is 1940. The place is Eagle Rock, a working-class—but very pretty—suburb of Los Angeles. The address is 5212 Townsend Avenue, one block up from Colorado Boulevard, at the end of the Five Car Line, an open-air trolley that makes it an easy twenty-minute ride into the City of LA. We are halfway up the block between Colorado and Hill Drive, which borders chaparral-covered hills, where rich people live.

The house is pale-yellow painted wood, a small but inviting California bungalow with a wide front porch. A fence runs by the driveway, smothered in Cecile Brunner roses. The backyard is small

but well tended, with a nice green lawn and the world's biggest walnut tree smack in the middle. My dad hasn't exactly built me a tree
house, but he's hammered wooden rungs into the trunk and built a
little table into the first big overhanging branch. You could say I've
got a tree *table*. A wide hammock goes from the tree to the side of the
garage. The neighbor in back has a dovecote, so that every morning
you wake up to the sound of palm trees rustling in the California
breeze and the coo and hoot of a hundred doves.

The time is just a little before four o'clock in the afternoon. My
mother has picked me up from St. Dominick's Elementary School.
We've stopped off at the Safeway to shop and I've run around in the
aisles, so she's beating the living shit out of me. I stand in the backyard holding my skirt up so she can get easy access to my legs. She
crouches down in front of me, pulling switch after switch off a convenient hedge and using them until they break. She's breathing
heavily and her cheeks are pink. She's smiling. She's beautiful.

After a long time she rests. She can't be said to lose her temper
because she's already lost it, but she loses something more. "Get that
look off your face!" She's panting with exertion. I don't and won't get
that look off my face. (There's another reason I can't get that look off
my face and she knows it and I know it. I've got a birthmark, something I've already begun to think of as a map of North and South
America, on my right cheek. It's purple, with a fingerprint of dark
blue at the bottom. So I can't get that look off my face.)

I raise my chin and look right at her. Whatever she can give, I can
take. She knows it and I know it. She pulls another switch from the
hedge, peels the leaves off with one skinning gesture of her left hand
and whales away at me again. The roses shimmer behind her, and
the sky above is a deep afternoon blue. I breathe hard and squint.

Finally, as she must, she gets tired. "All right. Go to your room. Think about what you've done. Wait until your father gets home."

I walk slowly, showing as much freedom, as much contempt, as I possibly can, across the soft green grass, then down the driveway—where once I saw, after my father left for work in the morning, a run-over, flattened-out frog, all his red guts spilled out from his mouth—until I get to the back steps of the house. Once I get there, I begin to run, and run through the house—through the back porch with its wringer washing machine, through the spotless square kitchen with the oilcloth on the table, the dining room with fruit on *that* table, and my mother's needlepoint on all the chairs, past the clean little living room with a pink-flowered couch and a green-flowered carpet. I turn into the hall and head for my room, full of sparkling bungalow windows, freshly waxed hardwood floors, and twin beds with freshly washed chenille bedspreads. There's a night table. There's a bookcase full of children's books. It's a pretty room.

Because I go to Catholic school, my father has made a little shrine for me, a kind of birdhouse for statues which he's hammered up above my bed. There's a statue of the Virgin there—actually two, one about eight inches high of pink and blue ceramic, the other, two inches high, of glass. There are a couple of others made of soapstone, a material that tastes sour to the tongue. Sometimes I pray to the Virgin, or hope that I really have a guardian angel, but on this afternoon, I could be said to be praying to the Devil. I want my mother dead, and the whole lot of them dead—the kid who got me in trouble in the store, the nuns who give me grief down at St. Dominick's, my mother.

I know she won't "tell my dad when he gets home," because I haven't done anything. She does this—and always has, since my very earliest memory. If we're supposed to go to the zoo on a Saturday afternoon and it starts to rain in the morning, she'll knock over a glass of milk at breakfast, accuse *me* of doing it, and say, "OK, we don't go to the zoo this afternoon." It's so dumb, because *she* knows and *I* know that: A) it's raining, and B) *she* knocked over the milk. I get blamed for shifts in the clouds and movements of the moon. My only weapon is that I'm on to her, and she knows it and I know it. I could go to my father about all this. But he works hard all day, comes home at six-thirty, I'm in bed at eight. And he plays golf on the weekends. Besides, he's always joking around.

The only clue I have that he knows is that once my mother promised me that he'd spank me and he did. Then he lost his own temper and told my mother *never again.* He plays the ukulele and tells jokes. My mother beats me until she's ready to drop. The truth is, she hates me. The other truth is: I'm not too crazy about her either. The contest is and will be: who's stronger? I know the answer, even though I'm six. I know I'm right, too. No contest. This doesn't cheer my mother up any.

In my room, I sit on one of the twin beds and look out the window. It must be close to five by now. I can hear Mother getting dinner ready. It's all so self-contained. She'll be scrubbing potatoes with an awful scrub, or snapping string beans with an awful snap. She'll be slicing beets to make her pickled beets. She'll be peeling a clove of garlic to put in her French dressing. She'll shake the living daylights out of the dressing in its big mason jar and put it on the kitchen sink right next to Daddy's bottle of scotch and her bottle of Hill and Hill Blend. We use jelly glasses for everyday and mother will, in the middle of cooking, pour out half a glass of Hill and Hill Blend, toss it down in one gulp, make a terrible face, pour a belt of tap water to chase it down, then go on cooking.

When I come out, I set the table, under my mother's careful eye. Then I go into the little living room to wait for Daddy.

He's always glad to see me. He walks the block from the end of the Five Car Line and so he always comes in smelling of fresh air, and tobacco, and scotch, and good wool. He's careful about his clothes, and he's handsome. He acts as if seeing me, coming upon me here in the darkened living room—because it's dark by now—is the greatest thing that's happened to him since *last* night.

We go into the kitchen, where Mother is working. He hugs her, but she's got other things on her mind: "I took the whole stove apart today, piece by piece," she'll say, or, more often, "I didn't sit down once. I didn't sit down all day!" Or sometimes, "I took Penny out shopping, and we were dressed and out of the house by ten o'clock. I don't think you can call it shopping unless you spend the day doing it."

My father wants a kiss. He dances around the floor. He works in advertising now. "I'm the backbone of the agency," he says. "Milt and Bernie always say that." He's the only gentile in an all-Jewish ad agency. He's from central Texas, with a high school education and a love of literature. He wants to be a writer, but now, in 1940, coming out of the Depression, he likes his job. The Weinstein Agency carries "The Pep Boys"—Manny, Moe, and Jack—and Daddy swears that he's the handsome guy in the middle of the logo—*Moe,* with the mustache and the big ears. My mother once persuaded me to write, in colored chalk, "My daddy is out of shape and has big ears," on the sidewalk in front of the house.

By now we're at dinner. The levels of both the bottles have gone down considerably. It's the kind of thing I didn't notice then; I only remember now, or find out later. My father is cheerful as always. Only every once in a while will he say things like, "Sometimes, when you go away from home they give you a party, and you're gone for six months and when you come home you think it will be some kind of big deal. But you come home, and they say, 'Oh, it's you, George. How's it goin'?' You've been gone for six months, and they haven't even noticed." Or, "Sometimes when you get up in the morning, you're so lonely and down that you can't think of a reason for getting up, but you do get up. And then it gets better."

Usually he talks about his childhood in Oakcliff, a suburb of Dallas, Texas: the Methodists singing, "Will there be any stars in my crown?" and the Baptists answering back, "No, not a-one. No, not a-one."

My part of the night is getting done by now. I have to be in bed by eight. From seven-thirty to eight we listen to the radio: *I Love a Mystery*. "The Decapitation of Jefferson Monk—a new Carlton Morse Adventure Thriller!" My dad gets a kick out of this show. He gets a kick out of anything. He gives it his best shot. My mother, exasperated and bored, insists I finish my potatoes and beans and halibut. She generally makes a dessert—apple brown betty with Grape-Nuts.

Mother turns in the same time I do. She's sick to her stomach; she has a headache, she feels "as if rubber bands are snapping" inside her head. She pulls the covers way over her shoulders, but leaves the bright lights on. She loves to go to sleep in what looks like broad daylight.

When I get up at night to go to the bathroom, I'll see my mother in bed, and if I look out into the other side of the house, my dad will be sitting at the kitchen table reading the newspaper, or out in the living room in lamplight, reading a book. Mark Twain, or James Branch Cabell, or Herman Melville. Maybe, around one, he'll go to bed. Both bottles will be empty. New ones will be up on the sink the next morning, as Mother, in a bad mood, squeezes fresh orange juice, pours a tablespoon of cod-liver oil into me, and fries up bacon and eggs.

Where's the sex in all this? Well, there's a six-year-old masturbating furtively in the front bedroom, but things aren't as bad for Dad as they seem. He will tell me when I'm twenty-five that he had a new, a *different,* woman every day of his adult life. This story may not be completely true but there's truth in it.

If weekday life seems a little too lonely, angry, heartbreaking, weekends are a horse of another color. Kate and George love to party. Dad used to be a newspaperman, working city-side for the *Daily News,* the cool paper of the day, and his friends are still hard-boiled newspapermen and their wives. Their names mean something in Los Angeles in the forties. Matt Weinstock, who writes a column for the *Times.* Erskine Johnson. Gene Coughlin, a freelancer who's always getting a cover story on this magazine or that. One wonderful woman journalist, Virginia Wright, drama critic for the *News,* always gets us free tickets to the circus. Virginia and Hugh, her businessman husband, don't come around much, but we spend some Sundays on their yacht.

Our house fills up on Saturday night. The dining-room table gets covered with green baize, and the sideboard opens up to reveal packs and packs of playing cards, poker-chip holders that look like lazy Susans, and a wonderful collection of shot glasses with goofy sayings on them. A clutter of ashtrays—all Catalina pottery—little jars for matches, and jars of cigarettes. My father, party doll, attacks the big chunk of ice in the icebox with a dangerous ice pick, cracking off jagged shards to slip down in tall glasses.

No fancy cocktails for this crowd. Just bourbon and scotch, and water and sometimes soda. The ratio of liquor to water is about fifty-

fifty. There's plenty of laughing and shouting, but nobody throws up. The whole idea is to hold your liquor, to "do it standing up," to be a hard-boiled newspaperman—or his cool, alienated wife. To be handsome, to be pretty, to play poker well, to stay up late.

On Sunday morning, Daddy gets up and puts away the chips and the glasses. Mother vomits every twenty minutes, groaning. But she stays in pretty good spirits. They talk about who lost what and who won what; about how Gene Coughlin came in late and his wife wouldn't speak to him and no one else would either, and how Gene went around and around the table dejectedly, hoping someone would make room for him, but nobody would. "I just want to be part of the family circle," he mourned, but he didn't get to be that night, and the sentence passed into the language of the group, ironic and resonating.

Around four o'clock Sunday afternoon, my dad goes into the back bedroom carrying a scoop of vanilla ice cream basted with a couple of tablespoons of Hill and Hill Blend. If it's before four o'clock, Mother can't keep it down. If it's after four o'clock, she can. About four-thirty—if it's winter, the sun will be slanting through the glass curtains, turning the living room rosy pink and lemon yellow—here comes Mother! Daddy laughs. I like it! I poured some of the drinks last night, *I* was part of the family circle, last night and again today.

Other weekends we'll hop in the car and make the hundred-mile drive from LA up over the Cajon Pass to the high Mojave Desert, where mother's half sister Helen lives with her husband, Uncle Bob. Victorville, by the beginning of World War II, is swamped with young soldiers and their wives, living in back bedrooms, or hotel rooms, or even garages rigged with electric lights. Uncle Bob served in World War I. He was an air ace until he fell out of his plane and got a silver plate in his head. On top of that he got a good dose of mustard gas, so (I'm told pretty often) he's not what he was when Aunt Helen married him, which is why they tend to live in property owned by his family, and why Aunt Helen works as an insurance agent in this godforsaken little town crawling with scorpions and centipedes and rattlers and tarantulas—but which still has the greatest fresh air and the most wonderful number of stars in its night sky.

Aunt Helen and Uncle Bob live in a grim little motor court on the outskirts of town, but Aunt Helen is joviality itself when we drive up there. "Hi, Hi!" is her invariable greeting. "Let's have a short snort!" Or, as variant: "It's Toddy Time!" Daddy doesn't mind this kind of family trip. He hates Aunt Helen, but he kind of likes her too. He used to go out with her. When she heartlessly stood him up one night in the deep past he took immediate revenge by taking out her much prettier younger sister, Kate. Listen, no hard feelings, at least not until further on into the weekend. Uncle Bob drifts about, silver-haired and courtly, always wanting to talk about "the British Isles," but nobody takes him up on it. The whole bunch are mean to him, but he blows it off with quiet dignity. He's done what they will never do. He stands still and takes their bad manners, with a cocktail in his hand.

The drinking starts on Friday night and the atmosphere is festive. Sometimes the men jump off a garage with a beach umbrella as a parachute. Sometimes they sneak a veal chop into another person's coffee. When this happens, the person with the veal chop in his coffee will solemnly remark, "You floored me," and then stretch out flat on the floor.

Kate and Helen ricochet with energy. What they love to do is sit down together at the upright piano and pick out "Nola" or "Kitten on the Keys." On Sundays, no matter how hung over anybody is, everybody (Kate and George, Helen and Bob, sometimes my cousin

Anne and always me) has to dress up and go to mass at St. Joan of Arc Church. But mostly they drink and play cards (bridge up here in Victorville) on a folding card table, with bridge cloth, bridge napkins, scoring pads of every variety. I'm locked out of the house for hours at a time while they play, out there in the hot little tunnel of the motor court. Once I get some revenge. When I'm nine or so I've been to see *For Whom the Bell Tolls* with Ingrid Bergman and Gary Cooper, and as we sit outside to catch a little afternoon breeze— again, with matching cocktail napkins and coasters and drink trays painted with sleeping Mexicans—I pipe up, commenting on Aunt Helen's new haircut, "Gee, Aunt Helen, you'd look just like Ingrid Bergman *if you weren't so old and fat!*" Even my father gets mad at me that time.

But there are fresh Sunday mornings in Victorville, when my mother wakes me early and we walk on down through the scruffy little town to the railroad tracks, turn left and hotfoot it to one of several truckers' coffee shops under huge green cottonwood trees. We have French toast and a stolen good time, until we have to go back home to Aunt Helen's scrambled eggs.

Everybody knows there's a dark side to this. My father has a story he likes to tell about a reporter friend of his named Ed. Before Daddy was married, he and his reporter friends used to go over to each other's parties. When Ed came over, he always got drunk in a big hurry and then threw up on the floor, broke some dishes, put his fist through the wall, and so on. When the time came for Ed to hold a party at his house, Daddy and a friend named Phil devised a plan. They sauntered into Ed's house, downed about a bottle of scotch each. Phil threw all the highball glasses against the wall. Then he turned a bowl of potato salad over on the floor. My father staggered to the window and pulled down some drapes. Then he decided he needed a cigarette, and, taking out his lighter, reeled over to another set of drapes and the highly flammable, absolutely mandatory glass curtains that fluttered between them. Ed got the point. "OK, boys," he said quietly to his drinking buddies, as his own wife wrung her hands at her trashed house, "I'll lay off. You lay off too, will ya?" Daddy loved the story.

Drinking meant a chance to turn over the rocks of daily life and see the crawly stuff underneath. It meant a chance for my Aunt Helen to tell her daughter she was "homely as a mud fence," and triumphantly repeat, as Cousin Anne sat weeping, "Well, you *are*, you *are*! It's best that you know the *truth*"—Helen being enthusiastically seconded by my pie-eyed mother: "It's the truth, Anne. Face it now. Get it over with!"

Back home, my dad's friends were fun because they were supposed to be. My mom's friends aimed to be respectable and genteel. My mother had met a fellow mom down at St. Dominick's Elementary, Mary Sheehan. Her husband, John, had been a victim of the Depression: he pumped gas. Their little California bungalow, only four blocks away from us, was crammed with her mother's good late nineteenth-century furniture. The walls were covered with family pictures. (My family didn't have any pictures of their parents around at all.) Mary Sheehan, dressed in long, rustling silk hostess gowns, waited every night for her husband to come home. She served them both red wine in crystal glasses, poured from a crystal decanter. It really came from two-gallon jugs of very dubious rotgut under the kitchen sink. There might be as many as six of those jugs, ranging from full to empty.

My dad made fun of the Sheehans, but Mary Sheehan, for five or ten years, was my mother's soulmate in Eagle Rock. (Because they were friends, Molly, their daughter, was my friend.) Molly and I spent afternoons together, spent the night together, learned (more or less) how to keep house from each other's moms. But Aunt Mary had a rich sister, Aunt Pete. She and her husband, Uncle Pat, patronized their poor relatives dreadfully. When Pete and Pat visited, Aunt Mary would implore my folks to come over.

Pete would be decked out in heels and a knit suit. Pat would be in business wear, in contrast to my dad's writerly tweeds and Uncle John's gas-station work clothes, or freshly ironed white shirt. They'd bring their own bottles (as would my folks), and a horrid frivolity would begin: "Penny! Molly! Why don't you two act as bartenders so we can all sit and talk?" Molly and I would check out Aunt Pete's makeup—her bleached hair and store-bought hairdo. Her penciled eyebrows. Her bright gash of lipstick.

Then we'd line 'em up; highball glasses with plenty of ice, fill them three-quarters full with scotch (or, for my mother, blended bourbon), tip in a little soda, put the glasses on trays with salted peanuts and ashtrays, and scoot politely around the living room handing out these bombs. Within forty-five minutes, five out of six adults would be reduced to blubber. My father would be conscious, irritated, but drinking right along. Mother, Aunt Mary, and Uncle John barely held their own, but Pete and Pat, the two fancy pushovers, would disintegrate before our eyes.

They'd begin a sentence. Then begin again. Aunt Pete would begin to sweat an awful sweat. Uncle Pat might remark, "Wuh, wuh." Molly and I would pipe up girlishly, "Oh, would you like another?"

"Wuh."

When my father drove my mother and me home, he'd ask her what she could see in those people. They were so . . . *not* what he wanted to be. Mother would have one of her rip-roaring hangovers the next morning and sometimes my father might meanly tease her:

"Oh, wouldn't you want to take just a little glass of *wine* for your condition? I think I have some of it, maybe a *vat* of it out back."

But just the mention of any kind of alcohol would send her groaning to the bathroom, and he'd relent, hop down to the grocery for vanilla ice cream, open up a fresh bottle of Hill and Hill, because their weekend life was full of banter and teasing and acting silly. Acting silly against a wall of sorrow.

—

The truth was: every time my mother squeezed up a fresh batch of orange juice or ladled cod-liver oil into her daughter or did a batch of laundry in the washing machine, or cut a little posy of Cecile Brunner roses to put in a cut-glass Fostoria vase, she was reinventing the wheel of domestic civilization. We had no pictures of her family around the house because she hated her father, who had lived long enough to raise three grown children and then died drunk in a snowdrift. (I have never seen his picture: there are none, anywhere.)

Mother's mother was a second wife of three. (Aunt Helen came from the womb of some woman somewhere, but there were no pictures.) Mother's mother married beneath her, some Irish dude, the man with no pictures, then quickly came down with TB. The husband seemed not to care, and my mother, little Kate Sullivan, learned housekeeping this way: you change your mother's sheets every morning because of night sweats, and then you roll a series of funnels made of newspaper, twisting the end at the bottom, and line them up along your mother's bed. During the day, you hold the newspaper for her as she coughs up sputum, then fold over the top and take it out and burn it. That way you control, to some extent, the germs that swarm through the house.

Mother's grandparents lived in upstate New York. Her grandfather was a hunting guide and according to the custom of the day drew most of his daily wages in whiskey, which added to his he-man reputation, but didn't make the family fortune. Mother's grand-mother fed the family from the farm, and fifty or sixty years later my mother remembered a dish of new potatoes and fresh peas cooked up in fresh butter, with cream straight from the cow. "There's no way you could get a dish like that now, ever."

At her own parents' house, all was poverty and squalor. The Sullivan family moved from Saranac Lake (famous for curing TB) to Pasadena, California, and back again. Her father couldn't hold a job, and for years at a time the family lived on tea and toast three times

Greatgrandmother
Clara Moxley.

a day. An imaginative mother might have thought to buy some vegetables, but this mother was on her back, coughing and dying.

Though Mother's half sister had yet to come in and rescue her, Mother did have a full brother, close to her own age, Art. Art grew up lazy, selfish, sluggish, and insolent. He once announced to his mother that he was going out and didn't know when he'd be back. She, weak and bedridden, propped up on pillows, said she didn't think that would be a good idea. Art, who was about fourteen, raced across the room and slapped his mother across the face as hard as he could. My own mother, little Kate, stood watching. She ran, got on her bike, and raced to where her father was spending the afternoon. "Art's hit Ma!" she announced breathlessly.

"So?" her father answered. "What do you want *me* to do about it?"

The tea-and-toast story, the Art-slapping-Mother story, the newspaper-as-sputum-cups story, were all anyone could ever get out of my mother about her childhood. By the time her mother had died and her feckless father married again (all unaware of his last drunken evening to come and the inviting snowdrift that would so easily usher him into the next world), my Aunt Helen, a smart, abrasive typist, would have moved in. When Helen realized that no one cared enough to buy Kate a dress for her high school graduation, Helen spent her own money to do it. (Kate was beautiful by now. Her high school sweetheart, Rohmer Grey, son of the novelist Zane Grey, would come over after school with jars of olives and adoringly watch Kate eat them. The family was still too poor for olives or anything else except the infernal tea and toast.)

Helen got her half sister an office job after she graduated from high school. They lived at home (not terribly welcome souvenirs from previous marriages) while they saved up money to get an apartment together. As they left home in the morning dressed for work, they'd see their brother, Art, unshaven, slovenly and hung over, slumping in a rocking chair on the front porch. When they came home at twilight, there he'd be, with a little more beard on his chin and a little more liquor in him. The girls made such cruel fun of their brother that fifty years later, as a retired Navy man in San Diego, old Uncle Art, unshaven and half drunk, seeing his sister Kate for the first time in decades, slunk out on the lawn to meet her, wouldn't let her into the house, and kept two vicious dogs between them.

That was how the girls addressed the world, to make pitiless fun of it, as my grandmother coughed her way into oblivion, and my grandfather (and mean, scarcely acknowledged uncle) drank their way to death and failure, respectively. The girls made mean fun of all that they saw. Helen got married, had a kid, dumped the kid and her husband, still laughing. Then Aunt Helen snagged Uncle Bob. Kate married the handsome, funny George. After a nightmare of drink and poverty and hard feelings, the younger sister's luck might turn. George would take care of her, and he was funny. And he was cute!

But to look in that direction was to find another family irrevocably bruised and hurt. Another grandfather so mysterious and disgraceful that his name was hardly ever mentioned. My father wrote down a family history in his late seventies, when he knew he was dying. He didn't write it for me, but for another Bob, my half brother, his beloved baby boy, whom he'd had—with his fourth wife—when he was sixty-nine. It is full of brave paragraphs: "Your grandfather's father, your great-grandfather, was named George Washington Laws. He was a wealthy young man and bought a great deal of fine farmland north of Dallas. He owned slaves, but so did every prosperous Southern family in those days . . ." Then he fast forwards to the very end of the nineteenth century, writing of his own father, Robert Headsperth Laws, and his cousin, Leander Beaumont Hughes: "They went to a party out in the country one night, and met a girl named Catherine (Katie) Bowlin. They were acting smart alecky, and having a good time with the country girls, and Katie Bowlin went home that night and told her mother 'Tonight, I met the two biggest fools I have ever known.' She ended up marrying both of them!"

Daddy clarifies this for my little brother: "She married Mr. Hughes first and had two girls by him, Lavinia and Ada. . . . After Mr. Hughes died, my mother married my father, and they had three children, Penelope (Nell), Robert H. Junior, and me, George N. Laws. Bob died in 1918, Nell in 1933 or 34. All this is in the Laws' family Bible that Penny has." Daddy ends his account, which he must have

My paternal grandfather,
Robert Headsperth Laws, Sr.,
b. 1860, d. 1922. This is his
only surviving picture.

"Little Georgie," my dad, his older brother, Robert Headsperth, Jr., who would die at nineteen from typhoid, and their favorite sister, Nell, who died in her thirties from TB.

known would have been his last written message to his little son: "My grandfather Laws was wealthy and he left my father a lot of money which he failed to hold on to. But he left me a legacy of love and respect, a memory of courage and integrity."

Oh, Daddy! As always, as full of shit as a Christmas goose, but so kind. There is only one surviving picture of the man who lost the family money and left "a legacy of love and respect, a memory of courage and integrity." He gambled the money away on riverboats; he killed a man in a gunfight. When his house burned down, he managed to save only the family Bible and a few drawers of clothes. He drank a lot, with very good reason, and smoked cigars, and when the doctor told him to give up drinking and smoking, he said he would rather die, and did. There's no clipped obituary of him in the family Bible and the entry of his death shows only a month, not a date.

I grew up on stories of little Georgie—my dad—growing up in Oakcliff, playing with his brother Bob and his older sister Nell in a modest home attached to a huge backyard. There were tire swings and a dirt fortress with tunnels. The Laws family had kinfolk for miles around and were city fathers of Dallas. There was a Laws Street in town, named for his grandpa and a Record Street named for the family of his grandma's family, Martha Record.

My dad's mother made pies and set them out on the veranda, where armies of little boys out to play could come and snitch a slice. She'd save the bacon and biscuits from breakfast—"wraparound bacon," Daddy called it, soft enough to wrap around your finger: everyone in the family detested crisp bacon. Shadowy in those stories were the stepchildren from that previous marriage to Leander Beaumont Hughes. Lavinia (the family pill) must have married early. Aunt Ada, Daddy's half sister (*rescuing* half sister, it would turn out), told her own story of coming home from a date, kissing a beau on the front porch, and hearing her stepdad's voice imploring my father—a toddler at the time—to "pee for Papa, Georgie. Come on, *pee* for Papa!" All seemed cozy, cheerful, pastoral.

My dad had a second layer of stories: because of family setbacks, he went to work very early for cousins named Red and Ted Tedford. They ran a bootlegging establishment and hired little Georgie to walk bottles of hooch across town in a baby carriage under a pretty blanket. Later, at picnics, George and his brother and cousins would watch the pretty young ladies to see if they could catch them sneaking off into the bushes to relieve themselves. Some hardy young girls could last eight hours, giving rise to a phrase that survives in our family to this day: to have a "picnic bladder" is to pull a window seat in a flight from LA to Sydney or Frankfurt and never have to disturb the person between you and the aisle.

At dances in the park, young couples whirled on summer nights on a raised bandstand and dance floor. Small boys, my father among them, would scramble in the dirt for change that fell through the cracks. You could divide the boys, Daddy said, between the ones who looked down for change, and the others, who looked up, because many proper young girls, on steamy nights, wore their voluminous skirts and petticoats, but left off their bloomers, because it was too damn hot.

My dad loved the ladies. In high school, he and his pals would travel out to a local home for wayward girls. Drunk, they'd cry up into the darkness, "Oh, wayward girls! Why don't you come on down? We're so lonesome here!" Some of them did.

My father played the ukulele, and when I was small, he'd play every single verse of "That Strawberry Roan," or "I Wish I Could Shimmy Like My Sister Kate," or "Thousand-Mile Blues" or even "Give Me That Old-Time Religion." He made sure I read the complete works of Mark Twain. He bought me a copy of *The Jungle Book*. Before I was ten I'd had James Branch Cabell quoted to me until he ran out my ears. And Daddy turned me on to C. S. Forester. "Read the Captain Horatio Hornblower books," he told me, "and you'll be ready for *Moby-Dick*."

So when, as a kid, I thought of my father, I thought he was the fun one, and he was the one who loved me. I knew to stay away from my mother; I thought that mothers hated their children and their lives, and dads had the stories and the fun.

Here's what really happened to my father. Some of this I found out when I was forty, working on assignment about my dad for *Esquire*, since he had decided, at the age of sixty-nine, to take up the writing of hard-core pornography. (He would publish seventy-three cheery volumes in about seven years and spend his last three in clinical depression.)

"So, Dad!" I said on the phone, with my list of questions in my hand, "whatever happened to *your* Dad? I don't seem to remember."

My father burst into tears. I'd seen him tear up sometimes (when he saw the Watts Towers he got tears in his eyes from what one man can accomplish with nothing but concrete, bits of pottery, and a vision), but I'd never heard or seen him really cry. He sobbed like a kid. He was seventy-one.

"OK, well then, how about your sister? I know Mother met her once . . ." After ten minutes I had to get off the phone and hope that his fourth wife could get him back together.

When my grandmother Kate married Robert Headsperth Laws, she had already been married and had those two daughters—the pill, Lavinia, and Ada, who would grow up wild. Katie had been saved at the age of twenty. She was a good Methodist, a young widow, and those years must have been hard. When she married Robert Headsperth, she was thirty, a little old for bearing children, and not exactly in the pink. Ten months later she had her first child, Nell, (the "Beth" of the family, the one everyone loved). Two years later they had Robert Headsperth Junior and three years after that, my dad, Little Georgie.

Little Georgie grew up hearing his mother in the bedroom late at night screaming at her husband to leave her alone. (Later, my father refused to have children with his first wife, because he had learned— all too well—that sex after children was untenable and unbearable.)

Nell, the beloved favorite sister, contracted TB early on. Lavinia jumped ship and got married. Ada began screwing around in an effort to emulate her rakehell dad instead of her devout, morose stepmother. The whole family contracted malaria. My father remembered that when the children were sick and the stench over-

My paternal grandmother, Catherine "Katie" Laws, who shot herself, with Baby Nell.

powering, his mother would roll up a great swatch of newspaper, light it, and run through the sickrooms, leaving a trail of smoke behind her to purify the air.

It was a disorderly household. When Bob was sixteen and my dad thirteen the boys were fooling around, roughhousing with guns. Bob shot my father just above the heart. "They sat me in a rocking chair and stood in a circle and cried," my father said. "I was fixin' to die. I'd never known a man to get shot in the chest and live." But he did live, and carried the bullet in his chest until his death. Nell's TB got worse. My grandfather drank more and more. Some people said he was a monster. But the one who got the monstrous last word was my grandmother Kate, who, at 5:45 A.M. on 18 July 1916, after a hellish night with her husband, went into the bathroom and blew her head into a million pieces with one of the family shotguns. She left a blistering note indicting her husband for unmentionable sexual practices (though it may have been no more than forgivable desire to sleep with his wife). It fell to my father to discover what was left of the body. George was fourteen. His mother, who had threatened to "cut it off" if she ever caught him masturbating (this, the kind of single, disturbing phrase that might slip out between endless accounts of church picnics and the correct way to make cold fried chicken), had disposed of her own head instead.

The family stayed together, shakily. There was no money for anybody to go to college. On the Monday after Bob graduated from high school, he went to work in the Sanitation Department (a fancy way to say he would work in the sewers of Dallas). On his first day underground he cut his finger. Three weeks later he died of typhoid. Nell was sent down to the border, to El Paso, to the nearest TB sanitorium. After George graduated from high school, he went down to be with her. My grandfather was left to consider a life that from absolutely every point of view had turned out to be a failure. His stepchildren detested him. His own children viewed him with alarm. His wife had despised him with all her heart and mind and soul. Weeping, he would record her death in the family Bible: "So sweet

My dad, George Laws (far right) posing with the staff of a small Southern Californian newspaper. Note the laundry behind them.

so good God took her for his own—she was to [*sic*] pure for this earth any longer—" But he defended himself, too: "a sad, caring loving husband." Then he died.

Consider then, what happened in LA in the early thirties, when George Laws, a darling, hard-drinking newspaperman with one unpublicized marriage already under his belt and a ukulele under his arm, came out to California and met two cute and zany office girls, half sisters named Helen and Kate, who, drunk on freedom and sometimes bad whiskey, typed all day and partied all night.

George already had a friend out in LA who'd gone stone blind from bad alcohol. George worked city-side on the night shift of the *Daily News*: he'd seen the seamy side of life. He saw a man who'd been making love to his vacuum cleaner and gotten caught. Wretched and naked, the guy sat on the side of the pulldown bed in his one-room apartment, every physical part of him shivering and shrinking, except for the one part that counted. At first George huddled with the other news guys and made silly remarks, but then he couldn't stand it anymore, picked up a blanket and slung it across the guy's lap.

George courted Helen. Who can say if they had sex? But I think of my father and I think of my Aunt Helen. If one thing is true about both of them, it was that they didn't hold back when they were older, so why should they have held back when they were younger? They were both tough customers in their way, and that one night, Aunt Helen stood George up. He came to the apartment and Helen had already gone out with someone else. Kate, eleven years younger, barely out of high school, answered the door. Then . . . she asked him in, and he, with his hat on his head (probably with a press pass in the band) and a newspaper folded around a bottle of scotch, came on in.

No one could have warned my mother. She was smitten, bamboozled, knocked silly with love. The only men in her life so far had been her father—an unemployed and unemployable drunk, her brother, also an unemployed and unemployable drunk—and Rohmer Grey, who watched her eat olives and asked her over to the Zane Grey mansion on Catalina Island, but he was out of her league: part of a regular family who not only fished and hunted but did things like sit down to dinner together. Here was this . . . George, whose one supreme talent in life was to make silly jokes, to turn the lead of daily life into gold, and what if it was fool's gold? You had to take a chance sometime. My mother fell, she jumped, she dove into love. The poor kid didn't know any better.

My father knew better. He had a high IQ and one failed marriage. He was already putting away a bottle of scotch a day. He was lucky to have a job of any kind in the Depression, but he nourished a keen sense of disappointment even in his professional life. All through his childhood he'd been tabbed the "smart" kid. In a different world, George might have been the fortunate one in this family; the first since the War Between the States to succeed.

But here's the other thing that Daddy must have known: he was an orphan. His brother Bob was dead and Nell would die within the year. Nothing stood between him and the relentless requirements of life except two half sisters. (Make that one. Lavinia loathed him, and he returned the compliment.) Only Ada, hard-drinking half sister, was there to protect him from the world. The lovely little lady he was preparing to fall for was an orphan too, with just one hard-drinking half sister to look out for *her* interests. Really, Kate had no defense at all. And there she was, looking up to him with fanatical love and total vulnerability.

Suppose you could send someone back to lay a friendly arm across my dad's shoulder and have that someone say: "George! You're an *orphan*, Babes! You had to help scrape your mother's brains off a bathroom ceiling. Any fool can see that besides being bereft and needy and all that, you can't be too crazy about women. Your mother left that terrible note: she hated men and you're a man. Ergo! Therefore!" But George would have shaken the friendly arm off his shoulder even if the friendly presence had gone on to say: "Doesn't it even bother you that your mother's name was Kate, and this girl's name is Kate? Don't you think there might be a lot of booby traps on this particular road to love?"

The people who'd heard about Freud by then were not people Kate and George hung out with. Kate and George were starlings getting sucked into the jet airplane of life. Clueless. Besides, George was somewhat swacked. And along with my mother's winsome, childish, lonely face, she had a twenty-two-inch waist and a thirty-

eight-inch chest. She was a knockout. So if he did think about anything, he might have thought: here's a chance to get some of the love
I was so sadly deprived of by my mother, and get some of that terrific sex I'm going to be spending my life looking for. This is the
chance of a lifetime!

But after about six weeks of marriage my mother hated sex. My
father lost his job and had to take his pregnant wife out to places like
Flagstaff, Arizona, where thunderstorms and tarantulas terrified her.
She wept and pleaded to be taken "home" to LA. George took Kate
down to El Paso to meet his dying sister, Nell. Kate took one look at
her, remembered her own mother dying of TB, and fainted dead
away. No one could think of even the lamest excuse, and Nell died
a few months later.

**Grandmother Sullivan,
who died of TB when my
mother was twelve. (But
where are the pictures, or
even the names, of my
greatgrandfather and
grandfather?)**

Christmas Eve of 1937, when I was three years old, Kate and George put up a nice tree in their little house. They were dead broke. In spite of that, they'd managed to buy me an enormous doll, Marilyn. You could feed her from a bottle and she'd wet her pants. It—*she,* Marilyn—was the greatest thing I'd ever had in my life and for a long time I thought of that as my favorite Christmas. Because, what a great doll! But my dad had to go to the hospital on Christmas Eve. When we went to visit him, the nurses made a big deal about Marilyn, and I couldn't have been more pleased.

My mother and I stayed an hour or two every day for ten days, and joked around with the private nurse who was always in the room. Daddy was in a great mood, even for him, and he had the nurses in stitches. After a while—I'd say when I was five—mother told me he'd had "a nervous breakdown." Then she said they'd had the twenty-four-hour nurses to keep him from taking a dive out the window, because he'd had a couple of guns at home and tried to kill himself that Christmas Eve. Then it came out that he'd tried to kill all three of us, but not very hard. He'd ended up with his head in my mother's lap, sobbing that he couldn't take it anymore; he had to die.

After the ten days he was home again, full of jokes, working pretty hard. They both worked as hard as they could—my father spending some Sundays putting together enormously complex Pep Boys ads, pasting up pictures of batteries and floor mats and jumper cables, laying down illustrations with pungent rubber cement, then, if they didn't fit, unpeeling them again. Mother did laundry and fixed balanced meals. They got smashed every night.

Each one of them, lonely as the loneliest Eskimo at the very top of the North Pole, went on with it. The little house in Eagle Rock was the cleanest possible house. My father went on working. There was no question of them having another kid. When World War II came, my mother signed on as an air raid warden and my dad joined the bomb squad. We enlisted our dog Mike in the dog army, where he was promptly "killed in action." We tore up sheets and practiced bandaging each other at night. *I* was happy, but what did I know? We didn't see the insides of many other houses.

My father went into the mail-order business—Betty Co-Ed—selling "V-for-Victory jumpers" to factory girls who'd never had money to spend before. He laughed about orders from "Rose and Tuberose Wong," and someone who wrote: "Dear Betty Co-Ed, Please worry about this order." When he decided he was going to write some short stories and put a desk in their bedroom, my mother went into her fiercest mode: she sat up in their double bed with me by her side and said, "Look at Mr. Big Man! Mr. Big Man's going to write now!" She thought he was getting too smart for her and he was.

Meanwhile, he planted a victory garden. Mother bought Fostoria and pretty flatware. Daddy bought a beautiful square piano that took up half the living room. Daddy played golf on the weekends. Mother played golf on the weekdays. Again, if a friendly presence had moseyed in and asked the eight-year-old how things were going—as she poured out staggering half-and-half highballs for the yelling journalists in the dining room and the poker chips rolled, and some woman always ended up sobbing—the little girl would have answered: everything's fine. My dad loves me so much he even wrote me a letter pretending he was Snow White—because I liked that movie so much. My mother can take me or leave me alone. She locks me outside when Daddy's not home, but I can take it. I've got some friends at school whose mothers can't stand them either. Big Deal!

The birthmark on my cheek temporarily ceased to be an issue. My mother found me a thick gooey compound to spread over it called Lydia O'Leary's Covermark Cream. It made such an uncompromising statement people must have been afraid to ask about my cheek. And the Breakdown went into the memory- (the *non-*memory) file where my grandmother's shattered head lived.

Maybe forty years later I asked my mother if she hadn't been scared that Christmas Eve when Daddy was waving his gun around and crying, and she'd called the cops and then the hospital. "Nah," she said scornfully, "that wasn't anything! He'd had too much to drink, that's all!"

My mother, Kate Sullivan Laws Daly.

*S*ometime in the summer of 1944, at an extended poker party up by Big Bear Lake a hundred miles from LA, four journalists (my dad among them) and their devoted wives took to discussing what they would do with their lives—if they could actually do what they wanted. One yearned to journey to the south of France to study Provençal. One craved to be right there in Berlin when Germany fell. My dad knew he could write the Great American Novel. Another wanted to travel around the world. (They were all saved from these lofty goals by the women and children in their collective domestic entourage.) The wives, perhaps sensing this, tactfully said

George Laws as a hardboiled journalist. What a charmer!

that they *had* everything they wanted: just to take care of their wonderful husbands and bring up their kids to be healthy and happy.

But when my mother's turn came, she was dealing, and she didn't even look up.

"I want to drink and play cards," she said.

My father took a look at his wife through the clouds of cigarette smoke and the noisy banter of a twelve-hour poker game. Although Kate was still very beautiful, he found her wanting.

George had already moved that big newspaperman's desk into the back bedroom of our little home. He began to write Westerns for the pulps.

My mother still drank and had terrible hangovers. My father still drank and held his liquor.

Then the man who owned our house in Eagle Rock decided to sell it. A friend of my father's had a Spanish-style house with a picture window in Silver Lake on the Micheltorena Hill he wanted to sell; my dad decided to go for it. And while I just want to stick to the facts, I have to ask, what relationship did this simple-seeming move have to do with the chain reaction of stuff all through the country—even as the atomic bomb went blooie in another part of the world—that would cause our family to begin to blow, and blow, and blow, and not begin to settle itself back down again for another forty, fifty years?

World War II.

More money than usual.

A generation still pridefully "lost" from the last war.

People moving *up*, through the middle class.

People moving *around*, because of money and the war.

The bottle in the cupboard.

The bottle in the cupboard.

—

My mother hated our new house with a passion I couldn't figure out. Even though it had a picture window and a view so magnificent you could see a glittering ribbon of the Pacific thirty miles away, she wept every time she picked up a broom—quiet, bitter tears. They only had one party there that I remember, and my father, mean drunk for once, chided a journalist who had become more successful than he.

We lived on this big hill, and there didn't seem a way to meet neighbors. Silver Lake, then, was sort of in downtown, sort of out. There was no community that you could see. They hated the new church. They didn't belong to clubs. Then there was a vacation over Labor Day weekend, just three weeks after the Bomb dropped; my mom and I stayed alone in a sad little cabin at Balboa Beach. My father came down on Sunday afternoon. They talked inside as I sat outside on the steps. When he left that day he walked right over me without saying good-bye.

Back in those days, 50 percent of marriages didn't end in divorce. Edward Teller hadn't even begun to think about the unthinkable.

The next night, when dinner was ready and my mother gloomily banged away at pots and pans in the kitchen of this unloved house, the phone rang. It was my father, who told me to relay the message to my mother that he wouldn't be coming home anymore, and no thank you, he didn't want to speak to her, I could just relay that message to her, and he'd be calling me later.

—

Kate was a woman in her middle thirties, who hadn't held a job since she was eighteen, who had only a high school education, whose husband would "give her the house"—which meant she had to keep up the payments. He would pay child support to the tune of fifty dollars a month. Sometimes these checks, made out to my mother, were signed by women's names—Sara Kaplan, Wynn Corum—members of his platoon of girlfriends who were willing to pay his wife for the pure pleasure of his company.

My father took his revenge on the woman who'd called him *Mr. Big Man* when he'd tried to write, and had his revenge, as well, on the highstrung woman back in Dallas who'd blown her head all over the bathroom ceiling.

My mother cried quietly for the first three weeks. Those twenty-one days were unbearably painful. I would come home alone from the seventh grade in a huge public school where I knew no one, climb the Micheltorena Hill with dread, come in through the back door, and walk down the long "Spanish" hall to my own room, where my mother would be lying in my bed. She couldn't bear to go into the room she'd shared with George. She would have spent the day crying.

When things got worse, they actually got a little better. Mother had the beds changed around, so that my twin beds went in her room, and I moved in there, so she wouldn't have to spend the nights alone. She went to business school for ninety days and got a job working for an insurance broker, whom she loathed. She took a look around this house she hated and assessed what her fourteen years of marriage had left her. A kid with a birthmark.

Which is when she began to really shout, "Get that *look* off your face!" Which is when she began to say, "If you don't like it around here, why don't you go live with your *father*!" Which is when she began to scream, usually whirling freshly laundered bedsheets around her head, "You've got to take *shit*, take *shit*, take *shit*!" Which is when I stopped getting any sleep for about four years, because once she saw I was asleep, she'd begin to scream, and scream, and scream all night, and smash so many pieces of costume jewelry it's amazing she had anything left (except I still have one gold locket of hers). Which is also when she came home with a bottle of bourbon a night, and walked straight to the kitchen sink, poured off a full jelly glass and flung it down in one chugalug, gasped, made her signature horrible face, held the glass under the faucet for a water chaser, gulped it, poured off another jelly glass of bourbon, and did the same thing again. She fell asleep, by six-thirty if I was lucky, so that I could cook a dinner for myself, get my homework done and my clothes ironed for the next day. That way, I might be up and out of the house in the morning before my mother. But about nine or ten every night she'd wake up, sizzling with a terrible energy. It was like living with an earthquake, watching books and wristwatches and hairbrushes and occasional stockings swirling and crashing around the bedroom we shared, but it was reassuring too. She screamed and howled and raked her nails across her face, but she was coming back, beginning to resemble the woman I knew.

My mother took in a boarder for companionship, some ditsy lady she'd met at the bottom of the hill on Sunset Boulevard in a friendly dive called the SOS Bar. Jackie Lary lived downstairs, in my father's old study, with nothing but a mattress and a huge picture of herself, a portrait, very flattering. She washed her wooden coat hangers in the kitchen sink, to my mother's disgust. She made Kraft Dinner with onions in it. She wore no underwear, preferring airy "ventilation." She brought around a distracting set of boyfriends, one with the startling name of Jonah Pimper. Jackie threw a party once, and one person, *one person,* came. So if I'd ever entertained the hopeful idea that we three females were not alone in the world, that was put to rest once and for all as I watched all the radish flowers I'd made and all the pickles I'd sliced just sit there, while the one man who'd blundered in plotted desperately to get out of this living death house while there was still time.

—

I knew that school was the only way out. I practiced smiling in front of a mirror. My mother had brought me that Lydia O'Leary's Covermark Cream. My dad, always the class act, took me down to Perc Westmore, who made up Hollywood beauties for a living and advised me kindly that sometimes the most gorgeous women were the least memorable. (He mentioned someone, a great beauty, and he must have been right, because I can't remember her name today.)

Every night I wrote down a list of ten people, five boys, five girls, that I was going to force myself to say hello to the next day. "Hi!!" I'd blurt in the halls of Thomas Starr King Junior High, and they, startled, often answered back, "Hi!" In the seventh grade I made two real friends. One, Margie, had a bookie for a dad, who went to jail. Her mother was a raving drunk, worse than mine. And a girl named Georgia, who cut off our friendship with a devastating phone call: "Do you have any idea at all how much people hate you? How much they laugh behind your back at that pathetic smile you have?"

Well, of course I had an idea! I might have been pathetic but I wasn't dumb. "What course of action," I might have asked bitchy little Georgia Brown, "do *you* suggest I take? I'm eleven years old and friendless, entirely alone in the world. The one person I depend upon hates me worse than snakes. The one person I love is gone. We're very poor now, so I can't buy friendship. So what do you suggest, Georgia? I've got my list of ten people in my hand. I'm going to pretend that things are *cool*, Georgia! I'm going to say hi to Kenny Smallwood and Bruce Willock and Jimmy Johnston and Morgan Morgan and even Marc Marcus if I get up the nerve. Then I'm going to say *hi there* to Beryl Towbin and Joan Wilheim and Nancy Stone and Jackie Joseph and even Donnetta Dehan if I get up the nerve. And if they hate me, Georgia, well, it can't be worse than the flying costume jewelry that zooms across the bedroom I share with my mother here at home, or the sound of retching late at night, or the pitiable single women who hang around this house now, the aging typist with the tapeworm, or the lady who only owns a mattress and a portrait of herself, or the single men—rootless bar bats who end up in this house crying and shouting and swearing and vomiting from dusk to dawn. I'll tell you something, deceitful, vicious Georgia Brown! I don't know what I want out of life, I'm only eleven, but THIS IS NOT IT!"

—

Then, thank God, my mother's looks and "you-bother-me" ways did her some good down at the SOS Bar. She snagged a well-meaning contractor who was making a living putting up badly built tract houses south of what was then LA. Charlie Lentz had a broken nose from playing college football, tremendous biceps and triceps from pitching in to help his laborers, and a bottle-a-day scotch habit. He came up every night for almost four years, with a bottle of scotch and a bottle of bourbon in his arms. Sometimes he took us out to dinner to flossy places—one particularly fancy Hollywood hangout where Esther Williams sat on one side of the room, and on the other an irate wife picked up her entrée and hurled it at her husband, who sat in quiet dignity as waiters wiped his face with the finest linen napkins. He was clearly a victim of demon rum.

But during the forties it was still cool to drink. People went to see *The Thin Man,* and they thought it was a *comedy,* not the story of a couple of childless drunks who solved murders because they didn't have a life. (And when Paul Henreid lit those two cigarettes and gave one to Bette Davis, they thought he was *romantic,* not an ad for lung cancer.)

From my point of view, life started to normalize a little. My mother still began the night with two enormous slugs, then passed out for an hour or so, but Charlie hung out with her during this process. A few new friends—hard drinkers all—began to come around as my mother began a new, monstrously unhappy life. When my dad had gone, he'd taken the books, the records, the pictures, and the fun. These new people were a boring bunch of bad drunks.

Charlie stayed through it, even the terrible visits to my mother's sister Helen in the high desert, where the grown-ups referred to me as "Probby," short for Problem Child, and spoke at length of the terribleness of George, and many tears were shed. Charlie bought my mother a suede jacket and me a charm bracelet—the very height of fashion in its day.

Every night, as my mother wept or snored or screamed, I did my homework and made phone calls. Charlie held my screeching mom in his burly, boring arms, bearing the burden of being the man my mom didn't love. (Thank God for these surrogate dads, these strangers who come in off the street and act as grounding wires in houses where the misery level is so high, *so high*, that, properly harnessed, it could make trains run and airplanes fly.)

"As soon as you're eighteen, you're out of here," my mother said daily, in her lucid moments. "If you think you're getting anything more than that out of me, forget it. Because as soon as you're eighteen, you're out of here. If you think you're getting anything more than that out of me, forget it." (Drunks are nothing if not repetitive.) But since I was twelve by then, I took that as a sign of hope. Six years! Anyone can stand six years!

I took academic courses, even in junior high. By the end of eighth grade, my incessant *hi there*s earned me an invitation to Donnetta Dehan's birthday party. I'd lucked into a cadre of four girls, two desperately poor, two quite rich. The rich girls—Joan and Nancy—had us over to their houses and lent us their clothes. The poor girl, still my best friend, lived alone with her drunken single mom who was wilder than my mother but far less mean. I made up the fourth.

(Jackie, my friend, might not have thought so. Her mother stood hopefully by while she developed rheumatic fever, urging her to get out and play.) But when she was in a good mood Jackie's mom laughed a lot.

From when I was twelve to when I was sixteen my whole purpose and goal was to turn myself into a rock, a stone, an army tank. When my mother said I was like my father, I said nothing. When she said if I wanted clothes I'd have to work for them, I borrowed clothes from my rich friends. When she said men would know I'd be an easy lay because of my birthmark, I duly noted it. Everything my mother did I watched and thought about. Scorn was my career. When, once, she screamed at me about not doing the dishes, saying that I was lazy and irresponsible, just like my father, I lagged out to the kitchen and began, as slowly as possible, to wash the hated things. Suddenly, Charlie was beside me. "The trick is to do them fast and hard," he whispered. "It's only ten minutes if you do them that way." After that, I did them fast and hard. When, once, my mother let me over-sleep and be late for school, so that I'd "learn some discipline," I was up after that before she was, *every day*.

When you're trapped in a nightmare, the urge, the perverse urge, is to see how and when you can make it worse. My mother was beginning to find life a little dull. After three years, a plain divorce wasn't enough to warrant her twelve-hour wingdings, and we were running out of breakable stuff. She'd had a kind and faithful man who'd stuck by her four years while she freaked. Charlie kept taking us to places like the ballet and the Ice Capades and Rams football games and the track. Once my mother won eighty bucks off a two-dollar bet on a nag named Alpha down at Del Mar. So what if all the crying and screaming and vomiting and rolling around in agony on the floor had been inappropriate behavior? I don't believe she could let that happen.

Events came to my mother's rescue. When I was fifteen, Charlie developed angina. The man was in terrible pain. It was disorienting, really, sitting at the dining-room table watching someone holding back the tears, and for once it wasn't my mother. For Kate, this state of affairs got old mighty fast.

Every Tuesday night Charlie and my mother drove me to a YMCA club in the basement of a Presbyterian church, where I relentlessly pursued my social agenda. They whiled away the two hours drinking at a nearby bar, the Windsor, far less raffish than the cozy SOS. A few weeks after Charlie got sick, my mom dressed up the way she did if she and Charlie were going out. "If Charlie comes by, tell him I went out," she said.

I gave her my usual look of scorn and went back to the book I was reading. She'd sold the house, bought a spiffy new car for cash, had money in the bank that she spent on herself. She could go to the moon as far as I was concerned.

When Charlie came by with his bottles of scotch and bourbon, I realized, by his look, that something was truly up. Whatever was going on, he hadn't been informed.

"Can I come in, anyway?"

"I don't think so," I stammered. "I don't think she'd like that."

I went to bed and was woken up around midnight by someone banging on the kitchen door. I went out and saw Charlie through the screen, jimmying ineptly at the door with a crowbar.

"Charlie," I cried, "don't do that, please! You know you shouldn't. Please, Charlie, go home." He walked away and I went back to sleep.

My mother woke me up later, sitting on my twin bed. Moonlight streamed into the room, lighting her face. She looked happier than I'd ever seen her.

"Charlie tried to kill Jim! He waited under the stairs and hit him across the head with a crowbar! It's a miracle he isn't dead!"

"*Jim?*"

"The man I went out with tonight. I met him at the Windsor Bar! I've called the ambulance! Jim's in the hospital now! I've called the police. But Charlie ran away! I've told them where he lives."

"*Jim?*"

"He'll be all right. They said just a half an inch higher up and he'd be dead right now!" Her teeth chattered with excitement. She couldn't stop grinning. She crossed and uncrossed her legs, her nylons rustling, her high heels trim and smart in the moonlight. She finally trotted back into the living room, calling up her friends, telling them what happened.

The next day, drama or not, my mother went off to type, and I went to school. Old *Jim*, whoever he was, stayed in the hospital recovering from his concussion. When I got home from school the phone rang. I was hoping for a call from a cute boy and was disappointed and nervous to find that it was Charlie on the phone.

"My mother isn't here," I began, but he interrupted me. "Penny, I want you to know I'll always love you and I'm glad I knew you. I want you to be a good girl and do what your mother says."

"Well, sure, Charlie," I said awkwardly. He had hung up. By six o'clock that night they'd fished his body out of the Pacific. My mother was peeved beyond words.

The next day she was going to bring Jim home from the hospital. He would be spending the night so she could nurse him. I thought it might be smart to spend the night away from home.

A man sat at our shiny dinette set—Mother had sold our wooden table with its hand-done needlepoint-covered chairs—looking straight ahead into blank nothing. A purplish bruise spread from his temple above his ear down across his jaw. His head had been shaved, haphazardly, so in some places he was shiny bald, in other places his gray hair had been unevenly cut, sticking out at all angles. His whole head was covered with stitches. His face was an unnatural, clammy gray. His eyeballs were sick pink, and his baggy cheeks just hung there. He may have had a concussion, but it was a hangover he was feeling now. He wore one of those terribly unattractive sleeveless ribbed undershirts that left his white shoulders and arms exposed and barely covered his slack little paunch. But it was his *face* that made the stone impression. He looked like a sewn-up corpse, Frankenstein's monster, a dead guy.

Mother introduced me, in a butter-wouldn't-melt-in-her-mouth tone. I must have said something, but he couldn't talk or move his head. He picked up the coffee cup in front of him (our best china), and his hand shook so badly that half the liquid spilled. Mother poured him a little more. Very slowly, he bent his butt-ugly head down to the cup and sucked at the coffee. Mother gazed at him fondly. I went into the bedroom and called up a girlfriend. I knew I was looking at a prospective stepfather, but I just couldn't believe it.

Within a couple of weeks we drove up to Victorville, where mother proudly exhibited this vile specimen to her horrified half sister. My Aunt Helen made some tactless remark, and my mother had a high-heel-clicking tizzy fit. She drove Jim and me on up to Las Vegas. Mother dragged her comatose prize up before a justice of the peace, married him, rented a very cheap motel room. They consummated their really gross union, while I kicked pebbles around in a weedy vacant lot. Then we drove home to LA, passing up Victorville where my aunt fumed, to a new life.

Mother's aim was to sober this guy up and start him practicing law again. I didn't get it at the time, and I don't get it now. My first objection: he was such an *ugly* dog! How could my mother, so beautiful, and who set such store on looks, tie up with someone who *never* looked any better, but only looked worse, worse, and worse?

Second: Jim was mean as a snake. He insisted my mother stop working—which she did with alacrity, but that meant they had almost no money. Broke again! We moved into the second floor of a decrepit duplex out in Glassel Park, close to the railroad tracks. We had gone from nowhere to *ultra*nowhere. My mother had sold off, broken, or given away anything that reminded her of my father, so everything pretty that we ever had was gone. Jim moved in with a set of law books and several jars of Durkee's dressing, which he said went well with fish.

I kept the twin-bed set, had my own books, some pictures from my dad, and put together the only good room in the house, a fact that did not go unnoticed by crazy Jim. I "ran away" a couple of times, but only got as far as Jackie's. (During this time, when I was only in the tenth grade, I was asked to a senior prom, and my mother, from nowhere, found the money to buy me a dress.)

By this time she was pregnant, and sick as a pig. She'd been married to Jim maybe three months. She threw up and threw up and threw up. She drank grape juice and ate crackers. Jim came home every night, and when he drank, boy, he drank! He played in a different league! He threw his shoes around the house. He passed out cold, falling straight forward from his heels, so that his forehead hit the floor and he got another concussion. My dad got married again about now. At fifteen, I could look at the future and think: *three more years.*

During this time, when my mother complained of the agony she was going through, I answered carelessly, "Well, it's your own fault, isn't it? You didn't have to get pregnant!" If she'd had the strength, she would have killed me. Jim, drunk one night, insulted my father, and I stood up so fast I turned over a chair. I was made to apologize, but left an unwrapped and very used sanitary napkin in the bathroom, out on the tub where he could get the message. When I had a canker sore, he suggested I apply alum, which produced such pain that I screamed, "I know you're trying to KILL me!" When they had company, I borrowed a leaf from my mother's book, holed up in my room, and cried like a banshee for hours at a time, so that their guests couldn't hear themselves think.

Every day I stepped smartly out to school, where I was in the Scholarship Society, worked on the school paper, and was a devoted member of the drama department. My friend Jackie's mom had gone to work for a flossy clothing store (Matthews, of Beverly Hills) which she cheerfully stole blind so that Jackie might have her own extensive wardrobe. Of our two rich friends, Joan and Nancy, Joan's mother gave us many dinners, and showed us a life of fine art, beautiful books, and drawers where clean underwear was stacked in perfect little piles. Nancy's family was generous to a fault, inviting us all out to their perfect Malibu Beach house, where we lolled in the sun and threw parties and necked with cute boys, and stayed in a perfect French-provincial guest bedroom about twenty feet away from the Pacific.

It wasn't as if we hid our poverty and chaos, Jackie and me. It was a question of two goodhearted teenaged rich girls, Joan and Nancy, doing pure good for no reason I could think of. What Joan and

Nancy's mothers felt or said, I had no idea. But I knew when I stepped out of my own door I was free until I came home, and even at home there was the phone. I lived for the weekends too, when my dad came by to take me out.

My mother got further and further along in her pregnancy. She lost weight all nine months, because she'd adopted a policy of not eating at all. One night in May, when I was sixteen and in the eleventh grade, sitting in my room typing a paper, my mother opened the door. She was smiling. "The baby's coming," she said. "Jim's driving me to the hospital." The old lush hauled himself out of his chair and drove her on over.

The next day, I had a baby sister, Rose. Jim had seized an opportunity (when my mother was in the hospital and I was in school) to find all my baby pictures, all the snapshots of my mother, my father, me, and burn them in the family incinerator. My mother, home now, weighing ninety pounds and crazy as a loon, wandered through the house in a nightgown. She accused me of stealing Mallomars from the refrigerator. She made Jim steaks and gave herself and me chipped beef on toast. Jim went, walleyed and hungover, to work every morning, came back, drank two bottles of whiskey, and the shoes began to fly.

One morning, when Rose had been home less than two weeks, my mother sat down at the breakfast table and looked at me spitefully. "You're more like your father every day! You still have that *look* on your face! You're going to have to live with your father. If *he* won't take you, you'll have to go out on your own. I can't stand the responsibility anymore. You'll find out what life is really like! Because I can't believe he'll ever let you in."

As I remember it, I got up, balanced my books on my hip, and left the house without a word. At the bus stop, at a pay phone, I called

Daddy and told him what was up. He too was newly married, living in a one-room apartment with twin Murphy beds, but he said he was delighted and I really think he was.

For the past five years I'd been putting friends in place around me, and at school, my friends, in proper horror, devised a plan. We went to a grocery store after school, picked up cardboard boxes, found a boy with the meanest expression and the biggest car.

He drove me home that afternoon. My room opened directly off the living room. We went in the front door and made a sharp right. I packed my two straight skirts, my three blouses, my two pairs of Capezio flats. My books. My pictures. We scooped up everything in fifteen minutes flat. The whole house echoed and sang with frightfully bad energy. My mother, I knew, was in the back bedroom, either lying down with a headache or ready to spring into action; to kick me out of the house full of righteous rage, so sure had she been that my father wouldn't take me.

She never came out, though. The boy, a nice guy named Harry, gestured with his handsome head. Time to get in the car, time to go. It couldn't be too soon for me. But before I left, and this is no bullshit, I took my scary-looking rescuer into the dining room, which opened onto a little outdoor side porch.

"My sister," I whispered. *"Rose."*

And if I had been older or smarter, I would have phoned or written or called a social service or the police. *"Take care of the kid!"* I would have said, *"because the shit around here is certainly going to be hitting the fan!"*

But I wouldn't even hear that expression for ten more years. And the little doll-thing all wrapped up in its pram with a mosquito net over it, a baby with a thousand-percent crazy mom and a dad whose veins ran pure bourbon, didn't carry any genuine reality for me.

When we got to the apartment over on Melrose Avenue, my dad helped us with the boxes. My new stepmom, Wynn, gave me a monster hug. Everyone was laughing! They gave Harry some coffee and cake, and then he went home. I talked and talked, giving my side of the story. There was still a month left of school. We figured out logistics. How could I get over to John Marshall High? They'd manage it. Wynn piled on one of her abundant, delicious meals. She was tall, hefty, redheaded. She glowed in the yellow lamplight, and so did my dad. They kept putting their arms around me. We told silly jokes. We stayed up until maybe one o'clock. They were in AA, almost-founding father and mother of that wonderful organization, and in their colors, and their smiles, their goofy jokes, they seemed lighter than the actual air.

Late, late at night, they pulled down their Murphy beds. (Because they were technically more poor at that time in their one-room apartment than my mother and Jim.) They'd fixed up a bed for me on the couch, no more than six feet away from where they slept. I knew this had to be a big stretch for them, for Wynn in particular, but nothing in their jokes, their embraces, and their firm resolve to say nothing bad about my mother or even her husband, gave away their concerns, or worries about what might happen in the future.

One day at a time, right?

Three weeks later, after school, while I was—as always—doing my homework, as relaxed and happy and shook-out as when you step off the most horrid rollercoaster ride in the scariest amusement park, the phone rang. I was sitting at a tiny desk in a little dressing room, next to the upright Murphy beds. Behind me, in the bathroom, Wynn had scribbled *I love you* to my dad in lipstick on the mirror. I answered the phone. It was my mother, crying. "Oh, please come home, you can come home now, I don't care about the others, I don't

care about anyone but you, oh, please come home, you can do anything you want, you can have anything you want, because I *hate* the
others, I hate the baby, I hate Jim, I hate them, hate them, hate them!
So you can come home now and come home right now!"

I took a look around the tiny apartment, the life-sized naked
photo of Marilyn Monroe, my dad's desk, where he had written his
pulp stories, the books from floor to ceiling, the cozy clutter, the
matchboxes, the little pewter mouse, the brass ashtray made to look
like the palms of two hands outstretched . . .

"Oh, gee, I don't think so. I don't think I could do that," I said, and
hung up on her.

My dad and his AA wife, Wynn Corum Laws.

To go back a little in time: when my dad left, he left my mother and me the house and the square piano. He took the matched set of Mark Twain and the California watercolors by Edwin Botsford. The beach scenes—the landscapes. He took a watercolor of himself by Don Masefield Easton. He took his desk. He took the records, books, and fun.

In the first year after the divorce, every Saturday or Sunday he'd come over and take me out. He was not one of those dads who evaporate or flee the scene. He insisted on never saying a bad thing about my mother, and this alone made these afternoons and evenings a total treat.

In my eyes, and in his own, he was a man-about-town. In Hollywood, we'd take in a matinee and once on Hollywood Boulevard we encountered the Great Gildersleeve. My dad was back in advertising, and during the days of Jack Benny, Fibber McGee and Molly, Fred Allen, my dad would place his affable self in the wings where they staged these shows. When a joke occurred, an applause light would go on and my dad would step forward, waving his arms, coaxing laughter from the audience.

Fun! That's what he had, or appeared to have. He took me to Scandia and the Brown Derby. He took me to Chinatown, often. He bought me pastries and Chinese rice-pattern teacups. We had our

My dad and me on a "date" after the divorce. I was twelve.

picture taken by "Charlie Chan." The picture that survives shows a cardboard cutout of a drunken rake holding an outlandishly large cocktail glass, with a scantily clad nymphet perched in it. His head is in the hole where the rake's should have been and I'm in the nymphet's. We thought we were having fun, but the picture, when it got developed, showed two human beings in surprising misery.

My father was still marginally in the mail-order business, so my clothes, when I had any, came from leftover fantasies of Rosie the Riveter, who was rapidly running out of disposable income. For a while I had gabardine suits with bolero jackets, circle skirts with poodles on them, headbands with studs. I wore these strange clothes when I went out with Dad. Once, in Chinatown, on a weeknight, when almost no one was there, he let his veil of cheer slip just a little. He said something like: "What's it all about, Penny?" I realized with dismay and surprise that Daddy was a bit drunk. Something in the hang of his lips, the trembly way he spoke, made me think he wasn't as happy as I thought, or as he said.

My dad had bought into the twin myths of the journalist who could drink the world under the table, and the novelist who *had* to drink to unleash his demons. He, like my mother, still had at least a bottle-a-day habit. The difference is that while my mother tore up the furniture and screeched, my dad kept his scotch in a drawer at work and paid the janitor to take out the empties so that his coworkers wouldn't know.

They did know, though. Once, in the parking lot of Scandia, after a long and alcoholic lunch, my dad stood under the porte cochere, swaying slightly, waiting for his car to be brought around. He overheard one of his Jewish colleagues saying to another "*shikker*," a word which even my Texan dad knew meant *drunk*. He was mortified, but not enough to stop drinking.

He took me to writers' parties, where men actually did wear tweed jackets with leather elbow patches, and leaned their elbows on mantelpieces and talked about literature. I would stand in these gatherings and soak it in. People having fun. People making jokes.

Daddy began to go out with many women. They were big and flashy and towered over him. He *loved* that. He'd stand back and admire them, point them out. They were naïve girls, trying to make it in Hollywood. They blushed under his attention.

Then my father changed his life. He'd decided to stop drinking, my father said. (He didn't tell me why.) He joined AA. One night in 1949 he took me to hear Peggy Lee at an AA fund-raiser. That night she was exquisite. She wore brown suede and belted out a song: the theater was packed with insanely happy people.

> The window she is broken
> And the rain is comin' in . . .

Waves of elation radiated through the room. Positive energy! I didn't even know how to name it.

> But if we wait a day or two,
> the rain will go away, and—
> We don't need a WINDOW
> on such a sunny day!

After the benefit, my dad drove me on over to the Hollywood Roosevelt Hotel, which was then a hangout—not the bar, no, *not* the bar, but the coffee shop—where crowds of intense people hammered out the AA program. What if you didn't believe in God, what about that? Because these were mostly intellectuals, agnostic by nature, fed up to the gills with organized religion. But the *Book* just said a power bigger than yourself. That could be a *bus*, you know?

They drank twenty cups of coffee at a time and, wired out of their minds, denounced people who weren't in the room for every possible crime. Infidels who did their Fifth-Step work with members of the opposite sex! Who took sleeping pills to go to sleep! Who took pain pills to get rid of pain! Who destroyed their anonymity by telling people they were in AA! The *nerve*! They laughed like crazy and told stories of what they used to do—how much they used to drink.

Those people in AA in the late forties and early fifties can be said to have reinvented American narrative style. All the terrible, terrible things that had ever happened to them just made for a great pitch.

The thing was: you could change your life. You could remake your life. But you had to go by the Book. And although this new, sober, moral, honest organization was aggressively classless (no heads, no directors, no dues, no bosses), a natural hierarchy began to form. How could it not? If you had a boring pitch, you didn't get to give that pitch at an AA meeting very often. AA was small, then, no more than 2,000 members in LA. You could have almost known Bill W.

One afternoon, my father had a new and different woman in the car. She topped off my dad by the two or three inches he liked, and she was hefty. There might have been a hundred and sixty pounds to her, but she didn't mind. She had girlish breasts, a porpoise torso, and a face that was astonishing in its beauty. Wynn Corum had translucent skin with a tiny dusting of freckles, Katharine Hepburn cheekbones, bright red hair, turquoise eyes. She was a knockout, and she knew it, and dressed like a chorus girl. She could do that because even though she'd gone through four husbands and had a flock of stepchildren, and had done jail time for drinking, she was sober now, and she had known Big Bill Wilson, who, along with Dr. Bob, had envisioned this extraordinary organization. Indeed, she would say often, she and Bill had been a mighty item. She'd come within a hairbreadth of becoming the First Lady of AA. Bill was married, unfortunately, but he did put her story in the second edition of the Big Book, under the section "They Lost Nearly All," and even now, to go into an AA meeting and remark, "You know that story, 'Freedom from Bondage,' about learning to forgive your mother? My stepmother wrote that," is to ensure free coffee for the rest of your natural life. Bill and Wynn had struck a hard but loving bargain, she would tell me often. He wouldn't, couldn't marry her, but he'd put her in the Book. My father, though nice, was her second stated choice.

Daddy didn't hang out with journalists anymore. He knew sober people. When, because I moved in with them, they felt they had to buy a house, an AA banker arranged a no-collateral loan, and wealthy AA matrons showered Wynn with cast-off furniture. But Wynn and George also liked the poorest and craziest of the poor and crazy. In those early days their closest friends were an ex-skid-row bum and his ding-a-ling wife, Mabel and Booker, wow!

Mabel, if I remember correctly, had been a showgirl. Booker had been nothing but a drunk. At the rowdy dinner parties my stepmother threw—dozens of people rocking with laughter, outshouting each other—Booker would insist that the easiest thing in the *world* to be was a wino, that living at the bottom was just like living at the top. He had been a beggar, and a good one. His never-fail gambit had been to take out his handy glass eye, expose his red and weeping socket to the public at large, and whimper until he'd collected enough to "buy a new eye." When he got enough to buy a gallon of muscatel, he'd pop his eye back in, drink up his gallon, snooze on the sidewalk until he woke up. Booker had lost a few IQ points along the way, but he was kind, and full of joy.

Wynn and Mabel were fast, best friends. Together, they'd managed to sleep with most of their known world. Mabel's marriage to Booker was, I believe, her fourth; Wynn's marriage to my dad, her fifth. They waited tables now, to make their share of everybody's living, they spent time together and bought fancy underwear.

At one dinner party, when Wynn and my father were still living in the one-room apartment with the twin Murphy beds, there had been a long and goofy dinner at which Wynn served one of her masterpieces—nothing but a ham hock, new potatoes, onions, and pounds and pounds of string beans, which, by some alchemical trick, turned after about six hours of simmering into the most fantastic food anyone had ever eaten. Giddy, wired on caffeine, they ate until they were dazed—thus proving that money or booze were the last thing you needed to worry about, you could live on string beans and love. They filled up the little living room, telling stories of when they had been drunks: my stepmother with tears in her eyes from giggling, recalling World War II, when she'd married her third husband because of his army captain's uniform; how she'd met him on leave and they'd gone to the Top of the Mark in San Francisco, put down five martinis each, and then been escorted to their dinner table, which had the very best view. Wynn, perfectly blotto but gorgeous, wore a dress of ivory silk that had a hundred ivory-silk buttons down the front from neck to hem. The maître d' seated Wynn, and took off her coat as he did so. This movement ripped off all her ivory buttons, leaving her in only the skimpiest of lacy lingerie.

Husband number three was lost in the view of the city and the Bay, while Wynn and the maître d' stayed locked for what seemed a gin-soaked eternity . . .

I'm laughing, my dad is on the floor howling, Mabel is in hysterics, Booker is hiccuping, the others groan helplessly, and this goes on for hours in the golden lamplight, until my dad decides he has to go to bed, and tells them, but the guests don't pay attention, so with great fanfare and silliness he begins to take off his clothes, reappears in his pajamas, pulls down one of the twin Murphy beds, and slides on in, pulling the covers up to his nose. *Then* they break it to him that he's promised to take one of the AA people home—because everybody was broke then, nobody had a car, they were all just one step up from the gutter. They break it to him that he has to *get up* and take someone home, and start to howl again. A dozen grown-ups, and one very relieved kid, laugh with the abandoned sense of being saved from a terrible illness, or a life-threatening car accident: we are alive! We're here, in the present. We're sober, we're alive, we're OK. We understand that we had "an obsession of the mind coupled with an allergy of the body." We're in the clear as far as disaster is concerned because we've turned our lives and our minds over to the care of God *as we understand him.* And as for that Notorious Fifth Step, the one where we take a moral inventory of all the wrongs we've ever committed, and then go through it with another person (of the same sex, please, to avoid possible complications and indiscretions), all of the people here are doing pretty well as far as the Fifth Step is concerned.

Except, you know that Ninth Step, the one where you make amends, except where it would do more harm than good? I never heard my father apologize for leaving me and my mother. I did hear him say that he had to leave or else he would have "gone mad," and

I understood that completely. When he said it, I bought it, because I loved him, and I was so grateful to him for taking me in, and being such a sport about it. But later, I did think, well, if it would have driven *you* mad, and you were a grown man with a job and a car, and a way to get out of the house, what did you think it was going to do to *me*, a kid, and before you left, my mother hadn't even gone crazy? But I never got the nerve to ask him that, although he lived to be seventy-nine, an old-timer, very respected in AA. But he was an alcoholic, you know? So it might not have occurred to him.

George and Wynn were in great demand for double-pitching. They went out maybe five times a week, and I often went with them. What a high it was: "My name is George and I'm an alcoholic . . ." "*Hi*, George!"

My dad was Wynn's opening act. He couldn't help but be funny, giddy, frivolous. He talked about his crazy sex life, his naturally low mind, his evenings with chorus girls, and he'd tell about how he'd developed this wacky persona to cover a naturally sorrowful and even suicidal temperament. But such was the power of his jokey performance that even as he spoke of plotting his own death, the friends of Doctor Bob and Bill W. were rolling in the aisles.

Then he deferred to Wynn, whose tale was hair-raising, and in another time, might have been perceived as a tale of Ur-feminism— a story of a powerful woman constantly blindsided in her lifelong quest for an identity. Wynn's mother had deserted her in order to go out and live a selfish life. An unloving grandmother reared her in strict poverty. She contracted typhoid fever and hovered between life and death for about ninety days. All her hair and (though she would not admit this) her teeth fell out. When she recovered at about age sixteen, with beautiful new red hair and a set of dentures stuck in so firmly that no one saw her without them, she began carving out a career as a femme fatale, and started drinking to bridge the gap between the grim hash-slinging reality she was born to and the golden mirage of American romance she yearned for.

As she herself told it, she thought the clear and simple way out was to marry money. She was beautiful, and so she did. That marriage didn't work; who could have said why? In her pitch, Wynn put it down to the fact that she was full of resentments, an alcoholic through and through. In her long conversations with me, she said that the guy was a jerk, not worth knowing, that when she spoke with him she felt more alone than when she was alone. But there was also the fact that she came directly from the underclass. Perhaps his family made it hard on her.

Wynn's second husband was a bandleader and she sang for the band. (Wynn might have been the best American I've ever known. She bought the line that money could finance her American dream, then, when that didn't work out, she went for glamor as a viable alternative. She lectured me on how to apply moisturizer correctly, she gave herself pedicures and slept in socks with her feet greased in castor oil. She still sang, with a highly doubtful vibrato, all the old tunes she sang in her second husband's band.) But the drinking had got out of control, she'd say with great dignity in her pitch, and she'd do things like come to parties stark naked.

When World War II came along, Wynn embraced patriotism, and married that third husband. The war and its excitements carried them through, but peace brought back the dread reality of the everyday. The captain turned out to be a schlumph in a business suit, and Wynn was still a waitress working for pocket money, with a serious, serious drinking problem.

Wynn had one last female dream to fall back on: the typhoid had left her unable to have children, but her fourth marriage would be to a widower with a flock of kids. She would surround herself with domesticity. She would keep house and cook and wash and iron. She would make a home. Except that the widower had been having sex with other people for many years, she said, and didn't see why he'd have to quit now.

You *could* say, "She lost nearly all." You could also say that—given even a BA degree—she could have "done something amazing with her life." Accidents of time and place and disease and education and alcoholism kept her from it. In AA, Wynn finally found a place worthy of her energies. She took her knowledge of money and glamor, her patriotism (which had turned into right-wing mania), her love for home and family (which manifested itself now in my father, and me, and the new little home they would buy), and wrapped it in the crackling approval of God Himself. Years later, I'd call her up to say hello. I'd call her just to hear her voice, because she'd done everything in her power to hold her nutty stepdaughter in some kind of loving balance, though it hadn't worked out too well. But Wynn, when I called her, would always say:

"Oh, Penny! I *told* God to have you call me up today."

So I never got any of the credit. Maybe she never knew that there were people who would call her because they loved her entirely on their own, without any bullying from God.

——

When Wynn, George, and I moved from the one-room apartment into a little bungalow in the San Fernando Valley, our fourth roommate, God, began to throw his weight around; to take up more than His share in the house.

Three people tried as hard as they could to make a family. My father worked, and once again gave up his ideas of writing. My stepmother began to try to redeem her mixed-up, teenaged step-daughter.

I needed clothes. She bought me a green-and-black fake satin cocktail dress with a plunging neckline. She bought me mascara and eyeshadow, and tried to get me to apply it to go to school. I was in my senior year. We needed Capezio flats, long gray wool straight skirts, starched white blouses, cashmere sweater sets. Wynn bought me acrylic sweaters with sequins on them. I was in the same bind I'd been in with my mother. Before, I'd walk to school in a straight skirt and blouse, get to school, find a friend, and change into a better version of a straight skirt and blouse. Now I had a large collection of puffy rayon skirts and nylon see-through blouses with beads on the collar. I'd wear one of those outfits to school, find a sympathetic friend, change into a straight skirt and blouse, live out the day, change back into my nylon clothes, take the bus home, dump my uneaten healthy lunch into the trash, where Wynn—with God's help—would always find it.

I'd come in as a bankrupt: my own mother didn't want me, that was bad enough. I was by definition unloved, but beyond that my mother and her husband were alcoholics, unregenerate and shame-ful. Wynn would never bad-mouth them directly, but her opinion of alcoholics who didn't choose to turn their lives and minds over to the care of God pretty closely paralleled what a Methodist minister might think of the Devil himself.

My mother, to justify our poverty, had drummed it into me that fancy clothes were common, that noticeable jewelry was common, that cosmetics were common. When Wynn took a look at our new bungalow and decided she was going to give it "window treatments," I was appalled. When she looked at the kitchen, and decided that what it needed was black wallpaper on the ceiling studded with cabbage roses as big as human heads, I was stunned. She made up a room for me, without asking me what I wanted. She put pale green flowered wallpaper on the ceiling, and carried it down three or four inches onto the walls themselves, cutting out patterns following the flowers. It was hideous, scary, and full of well-meaning. She had already painted the pure white stucco walls chartreuse. And sewn up slick taffeta rayon bedspreads in flowery chartreuse and green.

She talked to me for hours, as she Scotchgarded couches, and made sandy yogurt. She told me about her life and my dad's life. She advised me never to have an affair until I was married. She told me to let God into my life. She told me never to work harder on the first day of a job than I was ever going to work. She bought me every kind of makeup to conceal my birthmark. She gave me interminable lectures on picking up after myself, and I passed them on to my own children and stepchildren and students: "Always pretend a detective is after you, and he's standing in the house looking for you. There should be *no trace* of you *any*where."

The only currency I had to defend myself with was snippy disapproval. Faced with this, and intense longings that she must have at last realized she was not going to satisfy through AA, Wynn began to zone out. She bought twenty-seven toby jugs in unfinished plaster, and packed them on top of the kitchen sink. She would paint them, she said, and fill them with twenty-seven kinds of homemade cookies. At one time she had five separate couches in the backyard, waiting to be reupholstered. (My friends would come over and snicker.)

Wynn took on more and more in AA. I had moved in with them in May 1950. After six weeks, we moved into the bungalow in July. By September, Wynn would be on the phone five or six hours a day and far, far into the night. Had someone "slipped" and not admitted it? Was aspirin a "slip"? Had someone used his or her name to gain glory, thus violating his or her anonymity?

She spent entire days making elaborate checkerboard sandwiches, slicing loaves of bread lengthwise six times in two directions, taking them apart, filling up the holes with pureed avocado, thickened sour cream, lime-and-chive puree, wrapping the whole reconstituted package in wax paper, refrigerating it for twenty-four hours, and slicing it down into a checkerboard pattern for recovering alcoholic ladies. God help them all if it didn't look like a perfect checkerboard.

Wynn began to get on my case about my birthmark. She knew it would go away if I prayed every day, and turned my life and mind over to the care of God. But my life and mind were the only things I had. I yelled at her. My dad shivered. Wynn began to wallpaper the dining room, staying up until three in the morning to do it.

On Thanksgiving, my dad and Wynn gave a dinner for thirty-two recovering alcoholics. Booker and Mabel—that sweet wino and his jolly wife—weren't much in evidence now. The people coming to dinner were bankers and their wives, businessmen; movers and shakers in this classless organization. Dad and Wynn weren't speaking. They had cooked the turkey in one of those freestanding portable ovens so popular at the time. The turkey had to be lifted up and out of the oven. They dropped it. The guests were already seated, having drunk their "mulled wine" made from tomato juice and orange juice heated with cinnamon. My father and Wynn looked at each other over the steaming bird. Without a word, they hauled it up off the floor and onto a waiting platter. I desperately swabbed up the greasy linoleum. Five minutes later, Wynn was talking to God again, offering up a particularly effusive grace which asked forgiveness for "every drunk who has slipped," and every soul, however misguided, who refused to let God into his or her heart. And yet, I have to say it, that was the best Thanksgiving I'd ever had. And those checkerboard sandwiches were great. Wynn was doing the best she could. Everyone did.

By early December, Wynn had signed up to bring Christmas presents and a Christmas program to a mental hospital. She was just supposed to help the drunk ward, but once again her impulses tripped her up. She would be bringing hundreds of shoe boxes full of toothbrushes and razors and toothpaste and aftershave and the Big Book; sewing kits, and cologne, and rouge and powder for all the ladies, drunk, nuts, or whatever. The house was a jungle of shoe boxes. She put me in charge of the program. Plenty of paranoid schizophrenics got to hear me perform a dramatic declamation as the Prince in Shakespeare's *King John*, while my friend Beryl danced *en pointe*. You never saw such a bunch of depressed crazy people.

Wynn kept waiting for thanks that never came. She told me that my father was weak, that she was too much woman for him. She complained to him (with reason) about my insolence. She told him he wasn't following the Program correctly. That hurt, and he yelled at her. I was astonished. I had never heard him raise his voice before. All he had ever done before was leave. So why didn't he leave now?

He couldn't leave. First, he had me to think about, and, because he was a decent man, he had to stick around until I graduated from high school. (The assumption was that I would get a job typing. Wynn said I didn't have the discipline or confidence to be a waitress.) Second, Wynn had the clout in AA. She was the one in the Book; he was only her opening act. She always had the moral high ground. Her enemies became "dry drunks," or they had "slipped" and wouldn't admit it, or—most difficult to fight against—they were still "harboring resentments." "You're harboring *resentments*!" the poor woman would scream at me. "I am *not!*" I'd desperately yell back.

"See? That just *proves* it!"

Third, by New Year's Day, Wynn had taken another tack. Secure in her own sobriety, she'd been giving out kisses fast and loose, finally settling in on Phil P., one of the handsomest, sweetest (married) men in AA, very close to Big Bill, one of the oldest timers. Phil P. was tall, so tall that he stood on one step of our front porch and Wynn, taller than my dad, remember, had to stand on a step up from Phil to get in convenient line with his lips. At parties, they stood in broad daylight on the front steps, hugging, kissing, stopping traffic, and effectively becoming the center of attention—since all the people at the party, hearing of this commotion, managed to find an excuse to come in or out of the front door, just to check the scene. What a sight they were, Wynn and Phil, with their astonishing good looks and their sweet murmurs! And how utterly immune to criticism. Their Programs were in perfect order, they were absolutely above reproach.

It drove my father almost bats. Wynn had preempted his ace in the hole, his philandering, the only thing that managed to keep him sane. Here was Wynn, using his own stuff against him. She had God and country on her side, and now she pulled out the old sexual glamor to put him in his place.

His pitch at meetings became more clownish, hers more pious, sexy, high-flown. By March, because the stress in the house had become intense, I told my father I'd be leaving right after high school graduation. We sat in my garishly overdecorated bedroom. Daddy had come in to tell me to be kinder to Wynn, more respectful, something like that. I did have some strong resentments by then. Wynn had railed that I should get a job; I was not only Godless, I

was lazy, lazy! But I absolutely refused to get a job until after I graduated. They would *not* get rid of their responsibility until I was out
of high school.

As I sat at the frilled dressing table Wynn had made for me—
chartreuse taffeta gathered and tacked all the way around—I registered his look with sorrow. He was the human I loved most in the
world, he had always been kind to me, and he was so relieved that
I'd be leaving he couldn't see straight.

"Well," he said, "you'll be leaving home when you're seventeen. I
guess that's not so bad. I left home when I was eighteen. Are you
going to be a typist? Maybe you can work up to stenographer."

"I'll work part-time," I said. "I plan to go to college."

He sat on one of my slippery twin beds, slouching, his hands slack
between his knees. "That takes money . . ."

"Don't worry," I said haughtily. "I won't take any money from
you. I'll work my way through."

He told me he loved me, and then got up and left the room.
Regret, guilt, and misery showed up about equally in his face. But I
heard him out in the hall telling Wynn that I'd be leaving soon, and
his tone was light.

Wynn gave me more advice about the outside world: "Always buy
modern furniture, because people on a budget can't afford antiques,"
and lectured me some more about my birthmark: "Always blend
your base makeup into the area between your eyes and your ears.
That's a patch of skin that you almost always miss."

I had been a fanatic about school, piling up A's, getting the lead in
the senior play, winning the journalism award, and in my third year
at Marshall there wasn't one prom I'd missed. It was my ambition to
go to my own senior prom with the student-body president, but he
was going steady. I wished on stars like a maniac, and the girlfriend

of the *vice* president had to leave town. I ended up going to the prom with him. Only a month to go before I'd be out on my own.

—

Alcoholics Anonymous does that one wonderful thing: if people want to stop drinking or doing drugs, they can. AA does a second wonderful thing: for people who are aware of the abyss and worry about it, the outfit builds a wonderful suspension bridge made of the sweetest consolation in the world—the pitch, *the story*.

AA can be said to have worked for my father and Wynn. Although they would divorce, neither of them would ever take a drink again. But the organization never addressed my father's smoking—he was a three-pack-a-day man, and wrote enthusiastic newspaper columns about smokers' rights up until he died from lung cancer. It never addressed his addiction to women, which broke a lot of hearts, including his. Once, when my dad was old and in a funk, I asked him what was wrong. "I'm thinking," he said, "about the general sadness of things." (For after a long, pleasure-filled life, George succumbed to heavy depression and died in wretchedness.) Still, he never took another drink.

Wynn got cancer within a year after I left—cancer of the uterus— and when her uterus went, so did their sex life. Wynn, with characteristic energy, seized the chance that cancer gave her, and became chairperson of the regional American Cancer Society. Just as she had in AA, Wynn rose high in the organization. She made another gallant run at a rich and prestigious marriage, but she struck out. AA couldn't fix the fundamental fact that she was a hard-luck girl from the American underclass, with a snowball's chance in hell of any dignity, respect, financial security, recognition.

But here's the other thing: my father wanted, above all else, to write. My first and second husbands wanted, above all else, to write.

All I ever wanted was to write. But guess who really got to be the writer? Who's the one in our family who has actually changed, improved, transformed thousands of lives? The woman who wrote "Freedom from Bondage" under the section "They Lost Nearly All" in the AA Big Book. The girl who lost all her teeth from typhoid when she was in her teens, who slung hash way up into her forties, and who died a cruel death from cancer when she was way too young. She couldn't have done it if she hadn't "lost nearly all."

The night of graduation day in June 1951 I didn't go home and I didn't call. The next afternoon, when I knew neither of them would be in the house, I went back, put some clothes in boxes—leaving in my coordinated closet many of the things that Wynn had picked out for me. I would go to live for six months with my poor but cheerful friend Jackie, and her rowdy, drunken mom. After that I would live alone, in five-dollar-a-week furnished rooms, having a pretty good time until I married at twenty. Daddy and Wynn would stay together for about five more years.

Across the San Fernando Valley, in a newly purchased three-bedroom house, my sister Rose was growing up in hell.

**My half sister, Rose, daughter of Kate
and Jim Daly.**

fter I left my father's, I saw both sets of parents every other
week, taking the streetcar long distances from Hollywood out into
the Valley. I saw my father and Wynn for a treat. Now that I was out
of there we got along again.

I saw my mother for Rose. I had the idea that I could "save" Rose,
do for her what Wynn and my father had done for me.

Rose, as a baby, would have heard the sound of men's shoes crashing around her crib. (My mother told me that Jim still threw shoes.)
She would have spent days and nights listening to my mother
scream and cry. Often, when I went over there, Kate's face would be

swollen to a solid pink slab. During those years, Mother was on a particular kick: "Every day, every day for the rest of my life, I'm going to have to get up, fix breakfast, and get Jim to *work*! Then every day, I'm going to have to take care of *her*. Tell me. Tell me! What's the use of living? Because every day for the rest of my life . . ."

Mother had moved out of Jim's room and slept in the same room as Rose. She had stopped eating again and weighed in at under ninety pounds. When the doctor told Jim to stop drinking, he switched from scotch to vodka. For a few weeks, he really did stop drinking, deciding on maybe twenty or twenty-five Bromo-Seltzers a day instead. They turned him blue and made him so weird that everyone was sneakily relieved when he went back to vodka.

Poor Jim! He must have been a bad man at heart, and married my mother in the certain hope that he could bully her, fling his shoes around, throw up on the rug, lose his driver's license and his job, and generally fill the role of asshole the way he had in his first marriage. He might not have been playing with a full deck. He spoke in the cryptic ways of the stone-drunk. He'd peer with glassy eyes at my mother and then remark, "If I were a gopher, I'd gopher you." Whenever he saw me, even after he'd burned my baby pictures, he'd sigh and say, "Ah! Penny's from Heaven." To Rose his signature words were, "You're my little princess."

Jim wouldn't join AA, he said, because he was "a professional man." He was doing great if he remembered to say, "If I were a gopher I'd gopher you."

Jim developed heart trouble. Looking like some badly drawn science-fiction beast, he'd sit staring at Lawrence Welk on TV, and the terrible pain of angina would overtake him. "Quick, Kate, my pills!" He'd sit there, turning bluer than his usual shade, his face straining to show expression. Mother would stay sitting, then, regretfully, she'd get to her feet and saunter into the kitchen, where she kept his pills along with an avocado seed she'd been trying to sprout. Sauntering still, she'd wander back into the living room, and drop the bottle of pills into his lap.

Now, the voice of reason and a kazillion years of therapy suggest: why didn't Jim keep his pills in his own pocket? Why didn't Mother, on the other hand, saunter out to the kitchen, go on out the back door, get in the car, drive out for an ice-cream soda or a couple of double martinis, and come back in four hours, when the chances of finding him dead would be greatly increased? The answer is that she needed him alive to support her and Rose, and more important, she'd finally found a man who was as awful as her wildest dreams.

Why didn't the visiting eighteen-year-old stepdaughter waitress, her tip money securely weighting her right pocket, a couple of semesters of community college already in her accomplishment bank, rush forward, wrest the pills from her mother's clenched fist, open the damn bottle up, and put a couple of pills into Jim's hands? Well, he was a person I wouldn't have minded seeing dead; I also wouldn't have minded seeing him die in front of my eyes.

One afternoon I went out after school to visit my mother and sister. I'd bought Rose a gift of a frilly navy-blue organdy dress, and little socks to match. It delighted me beyond words to buy extravagant gifts and negligently toss them in my mother's direction (a bit like those fabled pills, I see now), and in the toss was the silent insult: "I'm just eighteen, I'm working my way through school. *I* can afford things for her, what's the matter with you?"

Mother was out in the backyard, hanging up spanking clean sheets, making them snap so that they'd hang perfectly. She was smiling, and her cheeks were pink.

"Where's Rose?"

"I was hanging up the laundry and I turned my back, *just for a minute,* and she upset the basket. She ruined a whole load! I whipped her with a coat hanger and she ran into the house and under her bed. I had to do the whole load over again. I'm going to have to leave this out overnight." (She hated to leave clothes out overnight, saw it as one of the many marks of a bad housekeeper.)

"I have a dress here for her. And some socks."

She marched into the house and the spotless bedroom. "Rose! Penny's here. She's got something for you. Come on out and try it on."

Nothing, not a sound. Mother picked up the coat hanger, a wooden one. "Come on! Come on out!" She poked under the bed, as if she were rousting a rat. "Come on. I'm going to get *mad* if you don't come out!"

Not a sound.

Irritated, but still smiling, mother moved the twin bed into the room. "You can't stay under there all day!"

Rose moved with the bed, staying out of reach.

Mother finally put her head level with the floor. "I see you under there! You're going to catch *hell* when you come out, pal!"

"Well," I said, "I've got to go now. I'll see you next time, Rose."

———

Around this time Jim would drive into the garage, note down a few sentences in a diary my mother would find later, cross the lawn to the kitchen, and hit the cupboard for a drink. Then into the living room, where Rose, safe now, would dance into his lap. He'd turn on the television, and yes, it would be Lawrence Welk. My mother would go out to the kitchen to fix dinner: lamb chops, baked potatoes, frozen peas, those biscuits that come in a carton that you bash against the sink to open.

My guess? Mother never said much during these evenings. She put Rose to bed at eight, but first she went out on the back porch, clenched her fists, pulled her hair, ground her teeth, and sobbed.

As Rose turned four or five she was given tap lessons. She fell in love with the Mouseketeers. She performed in Saturday-morning television amateur hours and brought home trophies.

"Rose can have anything she wants," Kate would often say to me. "She's beautiful, and her rich cousin is going to take care of her education. She can have anything she wants." I would have been jealous hearing these words, except for the tone in which they were said. To Mother it was monstrous that anyone on earth should get what they wanted.

Jim loved his little girl. He paid for those lessons, he doted over her trophies, he watched her dance in front of him. In every other respect, he played the garden-variety monster.

Kate, her new husband, Jim, and Rose.

Jim, almost chair-ridden by now, would sit silent and drinking through dinner, and after dinner take some verbal revenge. One memorable evening he suggested to us all that his wife was a lesbian and having an affair with her sister and that I had been working as a hooker instead of as a waitress to stay in school. My boyfriend got to his feet and said shakily to Jim: "Stand up and fight like a man! You can't talk about my girl that way!"

"That's right," Jim said. "You'd hit a cripple. Go on. I can't stop you."

Rose watched television all through this with focused intensity. She lived in the set. Between the set and the constant assurance from her dad that she was a princess, Rose was getting through. She stayed out of her mother's way. She only saw her for an hour in the morning, two or three hours at night, and dancing on Saturdays, church on Sundays.

"Don't believe everything our mother says," I told her one day when she was seven.

"Oh, I don't," she replied. And that was the end of that.

——

One fall morning, my mother got grumpily up in the gray chill and clattered out to the kitchen to make breakfast for two of her least favorite people. She was stopped by the sight of the television test pattern, and the top of Jim's sewn-up head showing above the back of his easy chair. He was dead as a trout. Mother called a priest and then went in to get Rose ready for school. She took eight-year-old Rose over to a neighbor's house while the priest held Jim's dead hand and said, "You've gotten a little sick, Jim. It looks like you're going to have to go to the hospital."

Mother called Jim's nephew so that he could arrange for the funeral. Then she called me.

When I got to the house, Mother was dancing in the driveway, that curious skipping dance that she only performed when she was seriously enraged.

"He's . . . he's . . ." In each hand she held a little red book bound in limp leather. "Diaries!" She gasped. "He's left *diaries*."

Every day in dozens of limp leather, five-line-a-day diaries, he'd faithfully—if subjectively—recorded his feelings about his nine-year marriage.

Another terrible scene with Kate.

Kate beat Rose again. I don't know what to do.

Kate broke four plates—our best china.

Life with Kate is unbearable. I only stay for my little girl.

My mother was hopping mad. She couldn't stop hopping. I began to laugh, and she did too. "Come *on*," she said. "We'll *burn* the son of a bitch!"

Kate started up a fire in the incinerator with yesterday's trash, and with boundless, snapping energy began to rip the little books to shreds. She burned them and burned them until they were all gone, and then she tore up the cardboard carton they were in and pushed that in too. "The lousy son of a bitch," she said.

Mother told Rose that her father was dead. The little girl cried and cried.

Within weeks, Mother had decided to move up to Victorville, to be with her half sister. "It's not like I have anyone down here," she said to me. "It's not as if *you'd* do anything to help me out." She sold the house, took Rose out of school, and moved the two of them up to the high desert, in with Aunt Helen.

—

It made sense that Kate would move to be with the only person in her life who had always "been there for her," in the greeting-card vernacular. My mother's needs were not particularly financial: Poor Drunk Jim had been insured and had a pension, and there was Social Security for her and for Rose, but Kate had been locked for nine years in a passionate tug-of-war with a deadly enemy and now that enemy was dead.

Victorville, in our family, was the equivalent of Grandma's house. It was the provincial hideout, the place that wasn't the city. It came into our family by coincidence, when Aunt Helen married the World War I air ace with the silver plate in his head. But was it coincidence or fate or *what* that made people call it, in the Great Depression and later, *Liquorville?* Was it fate or *what* that instead of a little town with rolling green meadows and a church with a steeple, Victorville was a town of scorching sand, boarded-up houses, tum-

Aunt Helen and Uncle Bob in Victorville, with Rose. (Uncle Bob dressed, as usual, in suit, tie, hat and probably gloves in the 110-degree heat.)

bleweeds passing through front yards, with, for years, just one restaurant (and bar) called The Green Spot, and a bookstore full of paperbacks called The Happy Booker?

Aunt Helen had run here from her first marriage, leaving her daughter behind in New York. When Helen snagged Bob, who had a position in this town, Helen sent for her daughter but didn't meet the train. Instead, she sent Uncle Bob, who, totally at a loss about what to do with a twelve-year-old, took her into the nearest bar and bought her a brandy. She drank it right down. And my mother had sent me to Victorville to spend two summers after the divorce—with Aunt Helen.

The other side of Victorville was that there was something wonderful walking home from swimming all day, just one step from sunstroke, something wonderful about my wild-eyed aunt coming home from work in her high-heeled shoes, sitting down, waiting for Bob to fix them both highballs, while she tossed her vigorously permed hair and said, as she always did when she first saw you, "Hi, Hi! Let's have a short snort!" My parents had once called her, behind her back, "Mrs. Victorville," because she wore long dresses and belonged to civic organizations. But when the sisters got together, beware.

My Aunt Helen took the position that anybody who gave my mother any trouble was the enemy. She hated her niece, little Rose. (She couldn't stand me either.) By the time my mother moved with her daughter up to this desert town, the fix was already in. Helen saw that Kate bought a house just two doors down from her so that Helen could keep an eye on Rose. War money had made it possible for Bob and Helen to buy one of Victorville's first postwar houses. It had two bedrooms, a sleeping porch, a garage that turned into a den. In one of the stunningly bad decisions of her life, Helen had decided to decorate it in native yucca wood, so the furniture seemed to twist and writhe beneath you. Two doors down, my mother bought a house built to the exact same plan. The main furniture was a huge television set. Rose danced alone after school in front of this set, rocking out to *American Bandstand* so steadily that she wore a hole in the rug, and caught hell for it.

My mother worked as secretary of the junior high school, so every teacher knew, when Rose came in, that they were dealing with a criminal, a deviant, a crook. Mother told them so.

Rose happened to mention, one day when she was ten, that a man had followed her home from the swimming pool. I was there at the dining-room table when she said it. I knew she was making a big mistake.

"Did you lift your skirt for him?" my mother screamed. "Did you *touch yourself*? He wouldn't have done it if you hadn't done something. Did you talk to him? Did you ask him home here? How do *I* know what you do after school?"

"No, no, no, no, no," Rose protested, in tears.

"Are you lying to me again, then? Is *that* what's going on? To get attention because your sister's here?"

"No, no, no, no! There was a man. But he stayed across the street."

"Did you lift your *skirt*?"

"No, no, no, no."

"I'll have to call the police. *Again*."

"No, please!"

But mother was already on the phone. She had done this with me when I was a kid, but down in the city nobody paid any attention to her. Up here, she was Mrs. Victorville's sister, and the fix was in. At the age of eight, until the time she was sixteen, Rose was labeled incorrigible.

My crime, my participation in this, was paralysis. I was terrified of my mother. I could only wait until she had downed her Hill and Hill Blend and then try to console Rose in the way my father had consoled me, say that there was another world out there, and tell her that she was—in my eyes—a swell kid.

My mother had a field day with Rose.

Even after Rose disappeared out of Victorville at the age of sixteen, she remained a town legend, like Deadwood Dick or Jesse James. By this time my mother was getting a little on the old side, and her cronies, once so loyal in her defense, were on the old side too. Aunt Helen had moved away. (The story, always furiously denied by her sister Kate, was that Helen had killed somebody in a drunk-driving accident.)

As she got older, Mother collected flocks of spinster friends and widow friends named Verna and Wilma and Edna and Thelma. At some point, when I was divorced, and maybe forty—I got a call from Edna. They'd all gone out to the Fairgrounds to see the Royal Lipizzaner Stallions. (Check it out! Is someone around here saying there isn't *progress* in this world? The Royal Lipizzaner Stallions prancing around out there in the new Victorville Fairgrounds, when thirty years before there hadn't been anything but tumbleweeds and The Green Spot?) My mother had had a seizure. We'd better come up to the hospital.

I took my older daughter Lisa, who was twenty by then, along for the ride.

We found Kate snoozing comfortably, a wooden stick taped to the wall in case her teeth clenched in another fit. One of her friends, Verna, was there with her. Verna told us all about the Royal Lipizzaner Stallions.

"Oh, your mother, poor thing, the Royal Lipizzaner Stallions were just coming out and making their first turn around the stadium when

Kate fell over. I don't think she even got a glimpse of the Royal Lipizzaner Stallions. Because your mother, poor thing, she's had such a hard life, having to raise that terrible child, that criminal child, all by herself."

I'd always more or less liked Verna. She was one of Aunt Helen's old drinking buddies. When Helen would say, "Hi, Hi! It's Toddy Time! Let's have a short snort!" Verna would always reply, in pure delight, "Oooo! Let's *do*!" (But once she got in trouble with the girls when she said that *just once,* she'd like to lie down next to a man again. Not for the sex. Just for the affection.)

"All that stealing!"

Once Rose had snitched my mother's credit card, caught a ride to the next town, and bought my mother three blouses for Mother's Day. Mother had called the cops and had her booked for theft. Luckily, since Rose was still a juvenile, it wouldn't stay on her record forever.

"And that mouth of hers!"

It was true. Rose had a mouth. When someone—and generally speaking that meant Kate—bad-mouthed her, Rose, without hesitation and with great, heedless courage, bad-mouthed her back.

"And she'd never do her homework!"

Lisa and I began to shift in our seats. Here was Kate Daly, deprived of her glimpse of the Royal Lipizzaner Stallions, out cold in a Victorville hospital. We were there to do what a family does; stick by, stand by, but we hadn't counted on Verna. We weren't up for it.

"Once, your mother told Rose to go on into her room and do her homework. It was seven o'clock! Time for her to do it!"

A two-bedroom house, on Forest Street, on an unlovely road full of tract houses that seem barely to perch on the sandy ground. If it's seven o'clock, Mother and Verna will have already put away at least one bottle of Hill and Hill Blend. Rose will have dawdled through the dishes, talked on the phone. The last thing on earth Rose would ever want to do as a teenager would be her homework. And at seven o'clock? *Why?*

"Kate told her to go to her room and get started. Kate knew what was up! She grabbed my arm and we went out the front door, around the side of the house and stood right there as Rose climbed out the window!"

The hospital sighs. The air, though comparatively cool, seems to heat up. The television set, bolted into the ceiling, is dead.

"Well, *you* know Kate! She wrestled that girl right back in through the window. I ran around to the front and came in by the front door. By that time Kate had Rose back into the hall. That girl was *screaming*! Kate closed the door from the hall to Rose's room and to her own room and the bath. I closed the door from the hall to the kitchen and to the living room. There was nowhere that girl could go! There were two of us, you know, so we got her down pretty quick. Your mother sat on her stomach and I got ahold of her head—you *know* how Rose always felt about her hair—I put my fingers into her hair and got a good hold of her and banged her head on the floor until she stopped screaming and then she stopped struggling. Kate got up and opened *one door* off that hall—the one to Rose's room, so she could do her homework. Then she went outside and nailed the window to Rose's room shut. That girl! She gave your mother *trouble!*"

Mother woke up. "I missed the stallions," she said.

We stayed about fifteen minutes, and then said we had to get on the road back to LA. Outside, the air pressed down. Hot? You don't know hot until you've been in Victorville, Barstow, Adelanto, at three-thirty or four on a summer afternoon.

"Wow," Lisa kept saying. "Poor *Rose!*"

The Green Spot had burned down. Now the place of choice was a big motel on the outskirts of town close to the hospital. The Green Tree had a coffee shop and nightclub and gift shops and Indian jewelry displays. By this time busfuls of European tourists came on through to eat three-egg omelets and buy souvenir bolo ties. The nightclub was closed, but another bar, chilled to 60 degrees and thick with cigar smoke, was doing a land-office business.

Lisa and I ordered margaritas. "My God," Lisa kept saying. "Poor Rose. Jesus."

I know we had two rounds and we probably had three.

I was feeling pretty low by that time, but I knew we had to get on the road home. But before we got up, bracing ourselves for the wall of dry heat that would suck those margaritas from our skin before we even got to the car, we saw two old geezers, rustling and creaking in front of us, making their way to the door.

"I'd like to take you home with me right now, *and do whatever!*"

"Oooh! Let's do!"

"Whatever I like. Whatever you want!"

The old people made their way to the door of the bar. They both had cigarettes, dangling. The guy wore a baseball hat. His pants were huge on him, and he shuffled.

"Whatever you like! We've got all afternoon to do it."

Nobody else even looked up. They'd heard it all before.

The door opened and a bar of mighty sun slashed in. The old guy took a breath and heaved the lady up in his stringy arms. It didn't seem hard. The lady was dead-thin under her pants and overblouse and hairdo and earrings. He held her like Rhett Butler himself and said, "Let's go back to my place."

"Oooh," Verna said delightedly, looking like tobacco-gin death itself, "let's do."

Lisa and I watched them go.

"God," she said. "Jesus Christ."

———

When Rose and I sit down now to talk this stuff over, or spend long hours on the phone reconstructing the past, she doesn't remember all of it quite that way. As long as her father was alive, she says, she grew up happy. "I remember the kitchen we had in that house in the San Fernando Valley. There was a real feeling of—family. I had my cat, I had my dog, Shawnee. I was close to that dog! I'd be playing on the floor with him and I'd eat the food off his dish, and Mother'd be on the phone with the doctor to be sure it was OK. . . . We had *neighbors* in the house next door, and we had boysenberries in the backyard and once Mother made plum jam. It was great, it was wonderful.

"At Christmas my dad would step in the ashes in the fireplace and walk over to the Christmas tree so it would look like Santa had been there, and they'd take a bite or two out of some cookies. In fact, when a little kid broke the news to me that there wasn't any Santa, Mother got mad at her.

"I don't remember them fighting, I don't remember them drinking. Mother drove me everywhere. She drove me to tap-dancing lessons and to Brownies and I went to school at Saint Patrick's Elementary. At tap classes we worked up some little routine, there were three of us, I was in the middle, and we went on some Saturday-morning television thing and won first prize. Daddy said I grabbed the trophy. Then after that Mother actually took me to a Disney audition for something. There were a million kids like me. We didn't make it, of course.

"Daddy took his religion very seriously. Once we were driving to mass and I was in the front seat with him and I asked, 'Why does it always smell so funny? What do they call that funny-smelling stuff?' He reached over and smacked me. 'It's incense,' he said. 'It's sacred. Don't ever make fun of it.'

"And the only other time he spanked me was when I crossed the street without asking, to play with some friends and they couldn't find me. That was the worst, my father being mad at me. He spanked me really hard. When I came home, I had to sit in a chair in the middle of the living room for hours. I was in deep shit that night.

"And, no, I have no recollection of them fighting or being drunk when he was alive. And I don't remember her being physically abusive. She'd shake me a little, but only when I was bad. And I remember when you brought Lisa over to spend the weekend when she was real little. Mother thought that was great. And I remember another time when you came over for the afternoon and she cried after you left. She said she missed you. I'm going to say that the only strange thing I remember from when my father was alive was once our cat caught a mouse and Mother chased them outside, but later, after it was dark, she took a flashlight and the two of us went out back, so she could show me how the mouse was still alive and the cat was still torturing it.

"So that's what I remember! Until one morning, when I was seven and a half, my mother came in the room and didn't get me ready for school. She was medium grouchy, and she said, 'Just put on your robe and slippers and go next door to Mrs. Davis.' There was only one way out, through the living room, and as we went through we passed my father's chair and she said don't look, don't look! So, of course, I looked and I saw him in the chair. I got a pretty good idea of what was happening during the morning because all the cars were coming and going. Finally, she *finally* came over and looked me straight in the face and said, 'Your father's dead.' She didn't let me go to the funeral and she never took me to the grave. She'd always say, 'Get somebody else to take you.'

"And then it began to set in with me that there were just the two of us now. She began sitting in his chair. All my friends, all my Brownies, all that was over. All my tap lessons were over. We couldn't afford it, she said. We couldn't afford anything. What I found out later, and I mean *really* later, was that my father left all his money to me, in a trust fund. She had to show a man named Mr. Ford receipts for all the money she took out, like for my dental bills and my clothes. She couldn't spend money on herself. It was all for me.

"I'm going to say it was early spring of 1958 when she moved us both up to Victorville to be with our aunt Helen. And for a while we actually had to *live* with Aunt Helen? I'll always remember the smell of that horrible den! And all that yucca furniture. It was *so* hot. And that lifestyle she had. Like she'd come home from work and they sat down and drank and bullshitted from five-thirty to about eight-thirty and so if you got dinner at nine you were really lucky. I had to play outside a lot. They were always sending me outside. There were absolutely no kids to play with. Everybody was grown. Nothing but adults. So when we got our own little house just down the street, I was happy, but mother was bitter, bitter. She was a working single mother, coming home to nothing but a kid. Oh, she had her girlfriends. They played poker every once in a while. And when I listen to Oprah Winfrey now I see that things certainly could have been a lot worse. I mean, Mother didn't bring any *men* around! She was so lonely, so lonely.

"But Aunt Helen! She was the ringleader! As bad as Mother got to be, Helen was worse, much much worse. You know how Mother hated snakes and sometimes my father used to torture her, when she'd be in the kitchen and he'd be watching TV, and a snake would come on *Wild Kingdom* or something? He'd call, 'Kate! Oh, Kate! Come on out and watch! Perry Como's on, and isn't he your favorite singer?' And Kate would come out and see the snake and scream? Well, once the phone rang over at our house, and Aunt Helen went over and picked it up and got this surprised look on her face and said in a real important, low voice, '*Kate*. It's *George*. Calling for you.' And our mother's face just lit up with joy. It's the only time I ever remember her ever looking like a real woman. But, of course, it was nobody. It was just Aunt Helen being mean.

"I decked her once, I did. Knocked her glasses off and sent her falling back into a chair. We were standing in my mother's kitchen, *our* mother's kitchen. Mother was out back, watering something in that shitty little backyard in the desert. You know how she was always trying to get things to grow? Well, Aunt Helen said something bitchy about Mother and I couldn't take it, I decked her. I'm surprised they never told you that, the Ungrateful Rose hitting her dear Aunt Helen!

"I never hit Mother. But I remember a time when she was trying to strangle me. She had me over on the bed and her hands were around my neck and I was beginning to get really scared so I put my feet into her stomach and pushed her off me. It was really more like self-defense.

"Then Aunt Helen killed somebody in a drunk-driving accident. He died and she had to spend some time in the hospital. Mother said, 'She's in the hospital, but she's OK.' Then Helen came home and sat on her couch. She had to have a sedative. Mother made fun of her for that. *She had to have a sedative!* Then she said to me, 'Oh, this man died. But don't talk about it.' It never got into the papers.

"Mother wanted me to be declared legally incorrigible. But I *was* bad! I was really *bad*! I took Mother's credit card! And I took the car without her permission and drove down to San Bernardino so I could look in the stores. I smoked pot under her own roof. And there was one day in junior high, two other girls and I pulled three fire alarms in three separate periods. So we had all the kids in school standing out on the lawn three separate times in one day. That was a felony offense. It *was*, really.

"But if Mother had ever taken me *shopping*, like mothers are supposed to take their teenaged daughters, maybe I wouldn't have taken the car and the credit cards. I was trapped, you know? I was trapped in Victorville. I never even had a bicycle. She said, 'You'll ride out in front of a car and get run over.' "

My mother, Aunt Helen, and Rose. It makes me sick to look at this picture.

Right now, in present time, Rose sits in a kitchen drinking coffee. It comes to me that I don't remember too many bad things before my dad left, and maybe that's comparable to Rose remembering her early childhood as OK. Our mother made plum jam. It doesn't seem possible, but anything is possible, and the biggest example of that is: here I am, sitting at a kitchen table with Rose. She's forty-five now, and plump. But—as with anyone in any family—I can see past the middle-aged lady to the little girl in tap shoes, to the sad little kid, twelve years old and fooling with mascara, to the forever-laughing madcap zany seventeen-year-old whose favorite pastime was the True Diet, so she was svelte, and always giggling. Her favorite piece of clothing was a white feather boa. Rose, the giddy goofball! My little sister.

"You know," Rose says, "Aunt Helen liked to slap people. She'd slap you for your elbows on the table, she'd slap you for a wrong word. She'd even slap her grandson when he was sixteen, and came in the house with a new date. Why'd she have to use such violence? Sometimes, later, much later, when Mark and I had jewels and drugs and money in the house, we'd keep guns, but we never had to use them. I hate violence!"

Richard See and I cut the cake at the traditional Chinese wedding banquet.

There is such a thing as the time-bomb theory of existence, that all of us are wired like a string of Chinese firecrackers, that explosions wait in all of us, and we're just as surprised as everyone else when they go off.

After I moved out of my dad's house, my sense of anger was so strong that at some level I couldn't even feel it properly. I blamed Wynn and I blamed AA. Because Wynn and the organization she put so much faith in had the absolutely enraging habits of always being right and always having it both ways. Wynn had been wickeder than anyone and now she was better than anyone. When Wynn had sent away for a correspondence course for me in speedwriting so I could make my living as a secretary when I graduated from high school, I gnashed my teeth and cursed God and Wynn and my poor dad. All around me I saw reasonably raised daughters putting together wardrobes to go to college. There was a "normal" world out there, but not in my immediate vicinity.

So that, beginning with the day in June 1951 when I moved out of Daddy and Wynn's house—and for the next three years, when at twenty, I married for the first time—I may have felt loneliness and desperation, but I also had the most amazing days of relief, peace, pride, and elation. Put another way, according to the time-bomb/Chinese-firecracker theory, my fuse was burning quietly along but I was between explosions.

I lived with my girlfriend Jackie, who lived with her own single mom, Belle, who drank and laughed and took us to all-you-can-eat buffets, where, with purses lined with wax paper, we'd load up on chicken—enough for a week. The three of us lived in a one-bedroom apartment in Atwater Village, down by the Los Angeles River, close to Griffith Park, a blue-collar section in the middle of nowhere. Ah, the relief of it. The wonderfulness of that first summer! Jackie worked at a refrigerator repair shop, I worked at an insurance company, where I typed the words *Arthur K. Rowe* all day long at the bottom of form letters. I paid rent to Jackie's mom. I was free.

We were so unknowing about the world that when Jackie got accepted at Occidental College, a flossy private school, she went over there to sign up and was flabbergasted when they asked her for five hundred dollars for the first semester's tuition. So we both took streetcar and bus over to City College, where we enrolled as drama majors for two dollars and fifty cents a semester.

The campus was layered with thick fog on our first day, but the place shivered with energy, excitement, the euphoria of poor kids actually getting to live out their dreams. Everyone was going to be a doctor or a lawyer or a businessman or a dress designer or an actress or a professor or a writer or a director, and it was going to start right now, right here! That first day I met a boy who is now chairman of a fine English department, but then he'd come from a home where they'd chained him in closets. Jackie, who would have her own television talk show, had not come from your average stable home. But good things would happen, and we knew it.

So to take a class where you learned pantomime was great. To learn the difference between horsts and grabens was swell. Even to take a look at a cheap reproduction of *Les très riches heures du Duc de Berri,* was a revelation.

My first conscious happy moment since the time my father left my mother—which was only a matter of seven years, but it seemed longer—occurred across the street from City College in a shabby little patio behind a burger joint on Vermont Avenue. I had taken up with a kid named Dick Jones, who ran track but always wanted to run gracefully so he hardly ever won. He came from a family of prison guards, whom I would never meet. He was taking classes in comparative religion and beginning a collection of rare books, most of which he shoplifted. He played Ravel's "Bolero" for me. And "Pavane for a Dead Princess." He read Kenneth Patchen to me, and I *still* love Kenneth Patchen! I had gotten a night job as a waitress at Van de Kamp's, a huge coffee shop out on Wilshire. I took classes in the morning, and I would need to take the bus to work at about four. But here, in this sunny patio, Mr. Jones and a friend of his and I sat out under a pepper tree and the sun flickered through it. They chatted along about Zoroastrianism and how those folks put their dead bodies out on walls and the vultures picked the bodies clean. Two more hours of peaceful discussion stretched in front of us. I was dressed in black—the total beatnik—because there was no one to tell me God wouldn't like it or that no one could stand to live with me. Indeed, Mr. Jones was pressing hard to live with me; we would split the expenses, be partners in scholarly poverty, he soldering aquariums, I waitressing.

I looked across at their two sweet, unconcerned faces, their own beaming sense of being alive in life, and watched the pepper tree and the sun and thought: "Wow! I'm happy." It had nothing to do with love—I don't even remember if Mr. Jones and I ever used that word—but only freedom and peace. You could live like this! You could learn in the morning, rest in the afternoon, work at night, stay up late, read Kenneth Patchen.

——

I was already, by spring of 1952, a connoisseur of furnished rooms. I'd lived in a nasty boardinghouse with pitiful single women, presided over by an elderly lady who hung on to her own breasts all the time. I'd lived alone in a house behind a house where a would-be rapist followed me home, but I scared him as much as he scared me. I'd lived in a studio apartment filled with roaches. Once Daddy and Wynn visited me at one of these places. They praised me for my independence, looked around, and left. After they'd gone I sat on my bed—I lived in a little gallery above a driveway in an eight-by-ten room—and I saw a ten-dollar bill on top of my stack of schoolbooks. Wynn had scrawled a note: *I thought you could use this.* I knew the ten came from her own tip money.

Dick went out looking in Hollywood, in places close to public transportation. He found a pretty hotel just off Santa Monica and Vine, about three blocks away from the all-night Hollywood Ranch Market.

The Brevoort Hotel housed a lot of hookers and seedy men, but it was a pretty place—three stories, white stucco, tiled roof, French windows that opened out, and in the back courtyard a few dilapidated bungalows where Gary Cooper was said to have brought his secret friends. And a swimming pool, empty, dotted with refuse and leaves. Mr. Jones insisted on twin beds, so we could study more easily. What a good idea it was! We would spend some nights crammed into one bed, but just as many others propped up in our own separate islands of light, working, thinking, whatever it was we did.

It was a big room, with those two twin beds floating in it, a little table with two chairs, a writing desk, a place for Dick's trunk. The rent was $21 a week; we each paid $10.50. We got maid service and a great deal of sweetness from the people behind the front desk. We must have looked to them like Hansel and Gretel—so young and dumb.

Our lives were isolated. We got up early every morning, ate breakfast at a coffee shop on Vine, took the streetcar on Santa Monica to Vermont, walked down to our classes, met for lunch at the College Grill, where we ordered scallops and string beans, took the streetcar home, rested a few hours, went off to our night jobs, came home by eleven, and went to sleep.

I had Thursday nights off and we took the Melrose bus to the Coronet Theatre, where we saw Kenneth Anger's *Fire Works,* or *Inauguration of the Pleasure Dome,* or *Un Chien Andalou,* or *The Sex Life of the Rhesus Monkey.* If a movie was French and had Louis Jouvet in it, we saw it. On Saturday mornings we walked up to Hollywood and played records at Music City and had cheese omelets.

On Sundays, I'd take the streetcar out to the Valley, one week to see my dad and Wynn, one week to see my mother and Rose. They never, in fourteen months, asked where I lived. Daddy and Wynn would greet me cheerfully, and fill me up with food. I imagine I was taking the opportunity to remind my dad he had a daughter out there. He told me again and again how proud he was of me. He just didn't give me any money, and I didn't ask for it.

Every other week I went to see my mother. Now I *was* showing off, standing around with my (invisible) curled lip. Because every day I logged in class made me different from the dog-family in this house. Even though they didn't ever notice the difference, I noticed the difference. I had *Un Chien Andalou* under my belt, and my mother would never see a foreign movie. And I was earning my own living and would never again have to hear her say, "As soon as you're eighteen, you're out of here, that's where my responsibility ends!" Because I was eighteen, I'd been out of that house for two years, and when I woke up in the morning I never fixed breakfast for anyone— I went out to breakfast, one fried egg, bacon, and hash browns, and I always left an enormous tip, because since I worked for a living I knew how important that was. I went to see my mother to remind her that you could get out—if you had the courage, or if someone had been imprudent enough to kick you out.

Dick Jones and I lived in hardworking suspended animation for fourteen months. We only quarreled twice and once it involved alcohol. Dick got sad about something and brought home bottles of cheap red wine from the Ranch Market. "I bet you won't drink this," he said, "because you don't dare." I got mad and took his dare and drank two bottles of red wine. I woke up with the first crashing hangover of my life, throwing up every twenty minutes, while Dick looked on, bemused.

I called my dad and asked him what to do. He sighed and said, "Don't *ever* drink red wine if you're going to get drunk. Drink vodka and don't *ever* drink mixed drinks, they're murder." But he didn't ask me why I'd gotten drunk, or where I lived.

The Van de Kamp's life was fun. Another place full of young kids on the brink of (in their minds) amazing adventures, a future just out there, hanging in air like a glossy ball. Every night from five to eleven, sometimes Saturday afternoons from twelve to five, I and fifty other girls sailed in to take our place at this gleaming food factory. Older women groaned that if you could hold on at Van de Kamp's you could work anywhere.

We waltzed into the place wearing uniforms of teal-blue cotton with plunging necklines and wide lapels of dazzling white. We had name tags that displayed our last names (Miss Laws, I was named, for the four or five years I worked there), white rubberized plastic aprons that tied around our waists. You scrubbed them down with bleach to achieve the dazzling cleanliness they were looking for. On our heads we wore hand-folded hats of "Dutch" lace that made our customers laugh. Miss Nace, our exasperated supervisor, who trotted around the place in four-inch heels and an iron corset, could strike dread into any girl with the sneering words, "Fix your hat!" Older, sobersided waitresses made secondary livings fixing hats for the uncoordinated teenagers who couldn't do it. The trick, they said, was to soak the lace in heavy heavy starch, paste it to the refrigerator, let it dry, peel it off, fold and pin it like an intricate flying diaper. Then, never work too close to other girls on the floor, or you'd have a hat accident.

On the floor! In many ways working at Van de Kamp's was the best job I ever had. You knew you could never go hungry. You always went home with money in your pocket. And there was a moment, at five minutes to five, when you sailed out on the floor, full of energy and giggles, when you were filled with well-being. The restaurant was *huge*, bigger than a church, done in those oddly soothing blue and white Van de Kamp's colors. They'd done something pretty daring with the lights, so instead of being harsh and fluorescent they were indirect and cool. To your right as you whirled out was a place where they sold baked goods; to your left, perhaps six looping counters that seated twelve customers to a loop. And then, for *miles*, clusters of booths. Seventy-five cents an hour to work the booths, eighty cents an hour to work the counters, because the tips, in theory, were less at the counter. (Except that the counter waitresses had their own highly devoted bachelor clientele, who would order prime rib, the waitress would charge them for an Enchilada Americana, and their devotees would tip them the difference.)

Van de Kamp's! I met my first gay guy, who'd been a skating partner of Sonja Henie, and made sundaes now. And an older waitress, who'd lived through the Dresden bombing and said it had been *much* easier than California earthquakes. And a wonderful salad man named Orlando T. Hungerford. I saw an extramarital affair unfold before my eyes as the main chef began to bang one of the many waitresses. Van de Kamp's couldn't fire the guy, since he could dish up two hundred entrées at once and often did. His wife came to work and huddled in the back with Miss Nace, looking needles at the rest of us: don't mess with my husband! She stood by the door to the parking lot, where all the sex and smoking and loitering and drinking went on. Her husband straightened up, but another waitress, unmarried, unimaginably old to us, in her thirties, did it, got pregnant, and was given a baby shower by all of us, with a cake, done up by the management: WELCOME LITTLE STRANGER.

One night as I went on my shift, I saw a little tiny girl with a nice white chest that totally filled out her uniform in the way the management must have pined for. She wheeled around station twenty-eight, carrying coffee, taking in the whole vast place with a pleased and whimsical gaze. She met my eyes and I knew, with a sense of extreme pleasure, that we would be friends.

Teresa was here in town because she was following a recalcitrant boyfriend—one of Gerry Mulligan's many drummers—who was just on the verge of getting her pregnant. She was a jazz freak, turning a lot of us on to Gerry and Chet Baker and Warne Marsh, Lennie Tristano, Lee Konitz (even though those last two were still in New York). Didn't we know that jazz was *changing*? Thanks to Teresa, a lot of us found ourselves on double dates at the Haig or Shelley's Manne Hole or Whistlin's Hawaii, a low bar, where one night a week, the usual South Seas Bruisers went away and the place filled up with somber young couples in black who listened to Red Mitchell; huge, reflective Leroy Vinegar plucking a bass that looked small next to his big body. And Warne Marsh would play the most beautiful saxophone in the world. Teresa would smile.

Warne Marsh was on heroin at the time, as were Art Pepper, Chet Baker, and a few more. It stretched out their sweet notes; it stretched out their speech. We once brought Warne a turtle from a dime store, a baby thing the size of a silver dollar. He peered at it a long time, then ventured: "Just . . . how . . . big . . . will . . . this little fellow . . . grow?"

Because of Teresa, I decided to work five to two in the morning, instead of tame five to eleven. At eleven the vast majority of good girls went home. As the lights went down, we became an after-the-movies hangout for a predominantly Jewish clientele who prompted racist slurs from us because all they ever wanted to order was a "vaffle vell done," and there were only five waffle irons to accommodate the rush of two hundred people.

After the vaffle people went home, kids lounged around and planned parties and went to them, so that because of Teresa you found yourself sitting at three in the morning with gay guys in love. English movie actors failing in Hollywood. Giddy girls, physically exhausted, emotionally serene. We passed joints around—and this was 1952, 3, 4. We listened to jazz. Once, late at night, Teresa, who wore Shalimar perfume and silken clothes with metal threads, said, "Laws doesn't know anything, do you, Laws?" And leaned forward and kissed me.

These two lives imposed on each other most in the summers, when I'd work five to two almost every night, party until five or six, sleep until seven, and haul out to a swimming class at City College that lasted from eight to ten in the morning five days a week. A good way, in theory, to get your phys ed requirement out of the way, but as we swam laps I'd often think I couldn't make it; I'd sink right to the bottom. And, of course, that was emblematic of my life. I was swimming pretty hard. After two years, we were going to graduate with our AA degrees.

I took a shine to a new fountain man named *Bill* Jones. My friend Susie, during a boring class, wrote in the margin of my notebook, "You love Bill/Use your Will!" Dick Jones, routinely snooping through my things, found this out and got pretty mad.

I began to think of an old friend from high school, Richard See (who had written in my yearbook, "If you have to have this to rember [*sic*] me by then there's no use me writing this. I will see you after you graduate. If I do not see you, then you should not want this to remember"). He'd been a college guy then. He had a car. Those buses and streetcars could get on your nerves.

Richard wore pirate shirts with full sleeves. He wore a Fu Manchu goatee. With a great show of ersatz irritation he'd drive

Jackie and me around in the afternoon as we ran errands. He'd heave great sighs and refer to himself as "Saint Joseph," because in his opinion Joseph was the most put-upon saint in the Bible, doing all the dirty work, hauling the Virgin Mary around on a mule, and never getting any sex or any credit.

When I'd been in high school, Richard had written me twenty-page letters, questioning the meaning of life and so on, but mostly filling up pages of lined yellow pads with lists of personal grievances: his mother was English-Irish, his father Eurasian, and he, Richard, had no sense of ever fitting in, anywhere. He'd been in love with his Chinese aunt, he told me, since she was in junior high and he was in high school, but since that was out of the question, he'd decided he'd make do with me. When I still lived with Jackie, Richard would come to call in the company of a few very cute Chinese guys. They'd stand out on the lawn until Jackie's mother said they couldn't come around any more: they were making her look bad in the neighborhood.

Richard was goofy. He was pretentious. His looks would come into style in twenty years, but right now he just looked darling-crazy. His loneliness—even when I was back in high school and he was a snooty college sophomore—was so rank and strong it came off him like an odor. In my life I'd never met anyone remotely resembling a soulmate, but Richard was my soulmate, because he was so lonely and freaky and sad. The trouble was, who wanted a soulmate if he was so damned *strange*? Being with Richard was like looking in a mirror. But I let him drive me on errands, and liked to hear him groan and complain.

Dick Jones got over his temper. But I was tired of him. Also I found out, by routinely snooping through *his* things, that he'd already been married and divorced. On the day of our break-up he tried to strangle me, but I have to say he didn't try very hard or I wouldn't be here today. I was able to call my father, who put his pants on over his pajamas, tore over to where we were, walked right past me where I stood gibbering with fright, and shook Mr. Jones's stunned hand. "I'm sorry we have to meet under circumstances like these, pardner," my dad said, and made small talk with Dick until all my belongings were stuffed in paper bags. Then Daddy, shaking, took me to a drive-in, bought me a burger, and told me I ought to look out for myself a little better.

A couple of weeks later, from the pay phone at Van de Kamp's, I called up Richard See's family. He was in the *army*, and had been for months. Richard had been my soulmate, my ace in the hole. From my point of view, he'd left without even saying good-bye.

A friend from City College named Marliss introduced me to some Communist-leaning students. I had a Hell date with a boy named Bill, who strummed protest songs at stoplights, jamming his guitar between his lap and his steering wheel. "One Christmas holy evening / They'll all be hanging!" (That would be referring to the Spanish fascists, of course.)

We graduated with our AA degrees. Marliss and Bill and I threw a graduation party for ourselves. My mother insisted on coming and I was so stupid I let her come. She brought Aunt Helen down for the occasion. They came in dead drunk and laughed themselves sick. Through their eyes I saw how Bill's socks flapped down around his ankles, how *bad* his revolutionary songs sounded, how Marliss was a cheap little waitress; how I was a cheap little waitress. How this whole enterprise was ludicrous beyond words.

For junior year, I would go to UCLA. My friend Joan from high school drove across town to UCLA every day and she'd recently gone to work at Van de Kamp's. She and Marliss knew each other. I finally found the perfect furnished room. It had a false window with venetian blinds; you opened the window and stepped into a shower. Marliss moved into the room beneath mine. The three of us began to talk about going to Europe for a year. We put up copies of the Paris Métro map on our walls and read *Tropic of Cancer*. Wynn gave me a copy of Norman Vincent Peale's *The Power of Positive Thinking*, with a silver dollar pasted in it, and the inscription: "With this dollar and prayer every day, I know you'll live your dream and next Christmas be in Paris."

—

The next year I *was* in Paris. But that was because a cunningly wired time bomb had gone off in my life. Richard See, in his army uniform, had come into town from Newfoundland. We slept together.

Richard took me to the screen porch of his parents' little house. He was sad, silly, resigned, full of stamina and imagination. You'd have thought he was going to the dentist; you'd have thought he was in a funhouse. Later in the night, I lay awake and watched him grind his teeth in his sleep. His skin was golden and glossy. You could say my heart went out to him, and more or less stayed there. Forty years later, I'm going to break down and say I was hopelessly in love.

A week or so after that my period was late. Reflexively, I adopted the hard-boiled stance I'd always taken with Dick Jones when my period was late: yes, you can marry me as a gesture of good faith. But if you *don't*, and there really is a kid inside this stomach of mine, you'll never see it—or me—again. Because if Richard had gotten his feelings hurt by life, I felt pretty strongly that life had insulted me, time and time again. I was enraged at all of them—everybody: my forever-bitching mother, my grotesque stepfather, my hardworking stepmother, even my happy-go-lucky dad. I was scandalized at Dick Jones and his concealed first marriage. And now just the thought that sensitive, alienated Richard See might let me down sent me into a fit.

The fifties were the days of the horrendous illegal abortion: you took the bus to Tijuana and came back on it, drenched in blood. My friend Teresa had suffered through it. (Her drummer had let her down in a big way.) My friend Susie had gone for an abortion, gotten up on a filthy table, got right back down again, had the baby, given it up for adoption. When I'd gone to a doctor for a diaphragm, he'd asked for a wedding ring (or license), and then told me that diaphragms caused cancer. Half the waitresses at Van de Kamp's were always taking quinine or castor oil to make their periods show up, or soaking in three-hour, boiling-hot baths, or all of these at once. And my period was late.

Richard thought about it. Just the idea that he would have to *think* about marrying me made me furious. And he was just as angry, trapped as much as I was. We were living our life in a stupid cliché. But through January and February of 1954 we made up our minds: we would get married and I would follow him to Newfoundland. Marliss and Joan would go to Paris alone. When Richard got out of the service, we'd join them in France instead of going home.

Until the day I left him five years later, Richard would never say he loved me. Two people can play emotional hardball, you know! He would study to be an anthropologist. He didn't, at that time, he said, believe in such a thing as love, except when it came to that Chinese aunt.

So why did we get married? Because, back in high school, the first day he drove me home from school, I said that my favorite movie star was Anna May Wong, and he said he'd played poker with that lovely lady only the week before. Or because his father, like his grandfather, had married a cute Caucasian girl, and here I came, fitting that tailormade description. Or because my period was a few days late. Or because his parents' bungalow was poorer than anything I'd lived in but filled with literally priceless artifacts. His family had culture and beauty and elegance. I'd be learning amazing stuff if I married Richard See.

Surely a powerful reason for Richard to get married was free, guaranteed sex, the bargaining chip for many women in those days. Newfoundland was the end of the earth. It gets lonely at the end of the earth. I could say I got married because UCLA was huge and cold. I had the sinking sense that my first two years in college added up to nothing. You could say I grabbed sweet Richard like a drowner grabs a raft. And drowning Richard grabbed me.

But very early on, when Richard was a college kid hanging around John Marshall High trying to pick up a date, he'd given me some throwaway information along with his family history. He'd already been arrested for drunk-in-auto. In fact, he would prove to be a riproaring, unending, absolutely awful and unpredictable drunk, following that strangest of all patterns—just a wonderful guy when he was sober, and a monster when he wasn't. A year or so into our marriage I'd wail to myself, or to anyone who would listen, "Why didn't I pay *attention* when he said he'd been arrested?"

I believe I was looking to explode. What a life I'd had! People had let me down! My fuse was burning right along and I needed someone to blow up at. Who better than a drunk, like my stepfather, who burned my baby pictures, or my mother, who took naps in her dinner plate and beat her children until her arms were tired?

So Richard and I got married at the Unitarian Church, where the FBI photographed all the "Communists" going in and out and we were exhorted, during the ceremony, never to cross a picket line. (A vow I've kept to this day.) My bridesmaids were Joan and Marliss.

Also at the banquet: My mother, Stella and Eddy See, my dad, Richard and me. Dad's still giving Mom the eye.

Richard's groomsmen were his uncle and close friend Cheun and another friend, Allan, both Chinese. Wynn turned up in a very low-cut satin suit: the guys were entranced. My mother showed, alone and bats in a badly cut muskrat stole. My father looked good. In the pictures, Richard and I look terrified and young.

The morning after our wedding night, Richard woke me—perhaps joking—with these words: "Get out of bed and make me some breakfast, lard ass!" We were in a honeymoon beach bungalow and I did, I made him some breakfast. I weighed 110 pounds at the time. Fury came down on me and didn't let up for five years.

This was the dynamic of drink that we followed. In Newfoundland, where Richard still had six months to stay in the army, in a one-road town by an angry dark sea, we rented a room in a houseful of illiterate, drunken, scurvy-and-TB ridden Irish folks named Kelly. In 1954, they thought we were still fighting the Germans. We kept warm with a wooden stove. We used an outhouse in back and kept a slop bucket in the bedroom. In the morning, I'd toss the contents of the bucket into the stream that ran in front of the

Kelly house. Richard would sneak off base to see me; I would sneak on base to see him—dressed as a Newfie, "an all-'round Newfoundlander," since army dependents weren't allowed.

We'd spend many nights at the enlisted men's bar. The music was Western: "I Gave My Wedding Dress A-Way" a big favorite. I danced and stayed up until I couldn't do it anymore and then took a cab home through wilderness and snow to our room in the Kelly house. Back at the base, Richard would be vomiting, flailing, carrying on.

When the commanding officer finally relented and Richard could legally come off base to see me, we would have his friends—young army guys—over for dinner. At our first "dinner party," Richard drank so much that he ended up in a ball, moaning in a corner, his hands covering his head as if he were fending off a beating. His friends left; I got Richard into bed (a mattress stuffed with old nylon stockings). I lay there in a helpless rage—because by this time I really *was* pregnant, and there wasn't a bathtub to take a hot bath in, and no quinine, and by God, I was married, this was *it*; I'd picked the guy and this was going to be my *life* (and my mother's words rang in my head: you've got to take *shit*, take *shit*, take *shit* in this world!).

The next morning Richard was still holding his head. "I think maybe I'll go in and see if I need glasses," he said wanly.

"Yeah, don't you think a hangover might be a better diagnosis?" I may or may have not said, as I hauled the pee bucket on out through the snow. But later that day a phone call came to the village and made its way through the farmhouses to ours—Richard was in the hospital with spinal meningitis. He sat up in bed with his horrible headache, imploring me and his friends to roll him some cold beer across the floor, since we weren't allowed to go in the room, and he wasn't allowed to drink. We did. We rolled them right on in.

A few weeks later he was up and around again, working as one of the world's least efficient clerk-typist while I hung out in the Kellys' kitchen watching with horror as they'd take a diaper off a tot called Baby Clayton, give the diaper a businesslike shake, and, without even rinsing it out, sling it over an indoor clothesline to dry. I watched as Clayton, in one of his foul diapers and nothing else, opened the kitchen door and marched out into a blizzard. "Aren't you going after him?" I asked, and his grandma, a sweet woman named Bride who felt sorry for me, would say, "Ah, nah. Clayton can take care of himself."

Richard and I went fishing in the bay and caught sculpin and lobster but we couldn't get water to boil on our dinky wooden stove. The lobsters would languidly swim in the warm water until we'd toss them back out. Miserable? We kept learning new definitions of the word. One morning as I moped in our room watching the sleet and snow swirl by, Bride Kelly knocked. "We're burying a baby, would you like to come along then?" They'd folded a newborn into a shoe box and a teenager slung it under his arm as we piled into a van and drove to the top of a cliff overlooking the sea. All the graves were laid out east-to-west, but young Clement Kelly, who'd been sent up earlier to dig the baby's grave, had dug it north-to-south. Bride Kelly lost her temper and screamed at the kid, who shifted his feet and looked away. Six or seven of us stood sheepishly as the sleet came down. Then they stuck the shoe box in the ground and piled up the dirt so that it looked like the grave went east-to-west.

The Kellys were sweet people. They were kind to us. They made sure we went to dances if there were any, and they told me I'd be close to God when I had my baby, and they scratched their scurvy and told tales of what it was like in the "San" when their TB flared up. At night, they left us to ourselves, and Richard drank.

When Richard drank he went out of control, his arms waving, knees buckling. He howled, he kicked, he cried. He was a handful, and his friends routinely pitched in to keep him vertical and OK. Once we spent a Sunday in the neighboring town of Placentia across the fjord from Freshwater, where we lived. The ferry back was an open dinghy and Richard, drunk, kept making expansive, would-be leaps into the icy black water. I sat, furious as usual, as his friends gamely tried to keep him in the boat. The ferryman who was rowing us finally lost patience. "Aahh, let him *go,* then, if he wants to so much!" His friends sat back. Richard quieted down.

As for the sex, it went this way: I was undecided about sex, but I loathed drunks, and when Richard wanted sex the most, he was drunk. This ongoing argument about sex gave us a way to structure our time. He said I was "frigid." (What a dated word!) I opined that

Richard and me on the Queen's Birthday, May 24, at a "garden party" in Freshwater, Newfoundland. It was sleeting.

he was a drunk. Also, if he wouldn't "love" me, I'd keep some of my compliments about his amorous abilities to myself.

But—what the hell? If we could just stick out six months in Newfoundland, we could get to go to Paris, where Richard would live the life of an artist and I could have a baby in a foreign land, away from my mother. So we lived our first married days in the town of Freshwater across the bay from Placentia and down the road from an army base so inefficiently run that they once misplaced a $250,000 bright-orange crane and never did find it. It's a good thing we weren't fighting the Germans, because they would have certainly won. The sun came out fourteen days in the six months we were there, and those had been the summer months.

We had our year in Paris. Richard was gravely depressed by life, but we had some fun. We lived in the same room with Joan and Marliss in another whores' hotel, on the Right Bank, very close to the Arc de Triomphe. A red-velvet curtain separated us from a sumptuous bathroom. Marliss was in love with a French jet air ace; Joan played the field, bringing home Siamese merchants with cowboys painted on their neckties, and Nigerians with tribal markings. Once Joan brought a guy back to the room, and while Richard and I feigned sleep, he tried his best to seduce her. He was American, so it was going to be a little harder than usual, because Joan felt that she had to draw the line somewhere. He got his nose down under her black turtleneck sweater, found that she was covered with an allergic rash, and his moans changed tone. Joan, Richard, and I laughed until we cried. The American left, sucker-punched.

Melancholy, but strangely organized, we drifted through winter days in Paris. Sometimes we went out to a museum, or to the Alliance Française. More often we stayed in the room playing 500 rummy. Marliss kept on being gaga about her French jet air ace. She brought a diaphragm over the border from Belgium, at great inconvenience and expense. It was corrugated and looked like a Goodyear tire. She spent whole evenings holding it up to a lightbulb checking for holes. She'd end up staying in Europe. Joan, a nice, well-brought-up Jewish girl, was desperately dodging her future. Her mother had platoons of Jewish doctors waiting out there somewhere for her, but Joan wouldn't have any of it. She looked for Central Americans on a spree, or Christian Arabs. Richard let his goatee grow again. He bought some paint, and did some paintings. But the art world of Paris was utterly closed to him and to all of us. We knew nothing about anything and were paralyzed about finding anything out. If we managed to buy pastries and not screw up, we walked home in a haze of joy.

Six nights a week we trooped out with various acquaintances to a restaurant six flights up in an almost deserted building. We ate with showgirls from the Lido. The restaurant's name was Melanie. The seventh night we went south from the Champs-Elysées to another, slightly more expensive place called Valentin. Joan and Richard always ordered the cheapest thing on the menu. Once Joan ordered calf's head, and that's what it was. Once Richard asked for peas and that's what he got.

I wasn't Penny Laws anymore; I was Carolyn See. I checked out books from the American library. I took long walks for the baby's sake. The baby didn't seem real to me yet. When Christmas came, Richard painted ornaments for a tiny tree, and then drank himself to sleep. When my birthday came, he didn't give me a present, and drank himself to sleep. Thank God for Joan and Marliss. Thank God for Paris, where everything seemed free and sweet, even if we couldn't understand it.

I had my baby in the American Hospital at Neuilly-sur-Seine, with the midwife shouting out, *"Poussez, Madame!"* The sun was shining in the room, and the baby, beautiful Lisa Lenine See (because Lenin used to study down the street from where we lived), gave me a stern, measuring look, and then went right to sleep. I was pleased and proud, but later that first night, when, again, I was looking at her and she was looking at me, I admit I cried. I knew the world we lived in was a sad place, and if Lisa was looking for good parents, she could have done a lot better.

When Lisa was six weeks old, Richard bought a 1926 Renault for about a hundred dollars. We went touring, with Lisa stashed as a handy piece of luggage in a blue canvas carryall called a *Bébé-Confort.* We drove down through Auxerre to Chalon-sur-Saône, to Avignon to La Ciotat, over the Italian border to San Remo, La Spezia, Firenze, Ravenna, Venice, and then over *that* border as far as Trieste and finally Rijeka. Then—desperate, regretful, and out of money—we turned around and came back. We were fleeing for our lives, as far away as we could go.

Poor Richard—in so far over his head he didn't know what had hit him—drove on the wrong side of the road into the town of Trieste drunk out of his mind on slivovitz as I blithered and wept. Lisa snoozed, oblivious, as he drove *down the stairs* of a picturesque castle and stopped just as the front wheels of the Renault hit the lapping waves of the Adriatic. The next morning the poor guy had to back up those circular stairs, without any of his drunken confidence, afflicted by a humbling hangover, prey to the scornful appraisal of the man who owned the ancient hotel-castle, and the injured martyrdom of Carolyn-the-mom, as I held the baby and sniffed back my tears.

Quel dommage.

And even then we drove the extra day into Yugoslavia like

hooked fish on a long, long line, and the town of Rijeka peacefully welcomed us, and everybody fussed over the baby, who was so beautiful, and the next morning the three of us sat outside the hotel, a family in spite of everything, kicking back on the terrace. Richard and I drank steaming coffee and chewed on fresh rolls, and felt the new day and loved it so much. It was as far as we could go. We'd run out of money and had to head home. Time to fake our way into the adult community.

—

They waited for us in hordes at the airport, ten thousand Chinese relatives and my wailing mother, who grabbed Lisa in a tearful tantrum. Then Richard's father, Eddy, wrestled the kid away. My shy mother-in-law opened her mouth and tried to finish a sentence. She always got the subject OK, batted five hundred with the predicate, and never made it to the direct object. Her husband finished her sentences for whoever cared to listen. Richard looked haunted, and I remembered one thing he'd said—when he was drunk—in Newfoundland: "I'd like for us to be a team."

But later that night, over at Richard's house with the smell of incense and furniture polish and fresh oranges, and bronze Buddhas everywhere, and Eddy peering at Lisa, making the first of many daily grandfatherly inspections, Richard looked around the spotless little kitchen where Eddy had removed the ceiling to expose the bare rafters; gazed at the old-fashioned stove up on high legs with the oven door open to reveal their silverware; surveyed the barrels of bulk soap powder and rice under the sink. I heard Richard sigh and say, "It's good to be home." It didn't sound right to me. It wasn't *my* home.

Over the next few days, I began to understand pretty thoroughly that if I wanted to go to school, be somebody, get to be treated like a human being, I hadn't made the best move by marrying into this family. Every time I saw Stella begin a sentence and then stop and look over to her husband to finish it, I wanted to cry, for her and for me. When I was with my in-laws I went to sleep. I still loved to be at my father's house with Wynn, but at my dad's house Richard had to go to sleep.

Our first day home, Richard suggested we live with his parents. I said no, and screeched for a while. Our second day home he said—I don't know how seriously—he didn't want to go back to college, he wanted to be a gardener in a convent. I said no, and screeched some more.

We found a first little house that rented for $35 a month. We really didn't have $35 a month. Richard went to school and got the G.I. Bill. I went to work at Van de Kamp's, waitressing once more. Wynn gave me some of her extra couches. The Sees laid some artifacts on us: a pigskin chest where we would store our family photographs, some Japanese funeral figures from Cheun and the rest of the folks. We found a cute little secondhand crib. After a few months, a friend of the Sees, a chubby Chinese guy named Albert Fong, said he owned a slum apartment downtown that we could manage—"the prestige apartment of the neighborhood." For no rent we'd have a roof over our heads.

The Sentous Apartments had thirty-six units, and was infested with rats and roaches. Richard went to UCLA graduate school three times a week, where he was a teaching assistant, and I went to the newly built Cal State LA over in East LA two days a week. Lisa put in some time at the Salvation Army nursery school.

Dear Mgr! I still have the bugs in bed! That was the note we found on our door the first day we moved into the Sentous Apartments. The people who lived there were more dreadful reminders of what could go wrong in life: a woman named Mrs. Morrow with an awful pair of false choppers, whose children never visited her because she had such a bad personality; a man who lived in one room with his three children and didn't pay the rent for a solid year; a woman, walleyed and obese, who pined for her husband in jail and stowed her used sanitary napkins under the bed—Richard and I got to clean them up when she left. A flock of Native Americans, who rented an apartment and sold all the furniture in it, paying us with a watch with no works or a ten-dollar bill soaked in blood.

Richard and I loved each other, I believe, but it was in the cards that we couldn't get along. I had too much ambition and he had none. He drank huge amounts and at that point I drank very little. We were bemused and bewildered by each other. We lived mostly off his parents. I'd been supporting myself for five years and was mortified to be handed cans of peaches or ski outfits from Richard's friends and relatives. When my dad held creditors at bay on the phone, Richard was amazed.

For two days a week I escaped from it, into a neutral world where you learned about semantics or philosophy, and hung out in the bare little Quonset huts of Cal State LA, a heaven where once again I found my friend Susie, and met La Monte Young, who would make a respectable run on becoming the father of avant-garde music in America, but then was just a perfumed little squirt who made the sweetest impression on me in semantics by lightly touching the bottom outline of my birthmark and saying, "I *love* that color. It's like pool chalk."

At least once a week we'd have dinner at a Chinese restaurant with Richard's parents. Eddy would be sure to order something he knew I didn't like. He was mean to me every chance he got, but I was Kate Daly's daughter, and I was mean to him every chance I got. I paid him no mind and gave him no respect. Eddy took me to lunch one time and lectured to me on the value of family, that the individual was nothing, family was all. I could barely be civil to him, because of the way he treated his wife.

At my father's, Wynn, who had never had kids, took care of Lisa on many weekends, went out and bought baby furniture, lavishing care upon her. They never gave us anything but a good time. Meanwhile, Lisa turned into a beautiful redheaded toddler who seemed to like the whole bunch of us.

Many years later, I was apologizing to Richard for something— my bad temper, or the breakup of the marriage—and I said that maybe it wouldn't have happened if we hadn't lived downtown, in the god-awful Sentous Apartments. "Oh, it wasn't so bad," he said, putting a good spin on a trying time. "It was just a way for us to live." And though the roaches fell into our salads and crawled over our toothbrushes, it had its diversions. There was a pay phone directly outside our dining room. One night when we had people over for dinner a man crawled around the booth pouring kerosene, planning to murder the man inside the booth making the call. But the man with the kerosene couldn't find a match.

A tenant got so angry at us for not defrosting the thirty-six refrigerators in the apartment by pulling a switch in the basement that he demolished his own refrigerator with an ice pick, letting loose a lot of Freon gas. We evicted him and he killed someone in a bar the very next week. A woman attempted suicide on the third floor. I opened the door one night to see another woman tenant, unrecognizable because a friend of hers had attacked her with his crutch, laying her forehead completely open so that the skin, pink and seeping, flapped down over her nose and mouth.

Richard studied hard during the week, he pulled his share of vile chores. But on the weekends he drank, and drank hard. I'd beg him to take me to listen to jazz—Warne Marsh was back in town—but he'd stay home and drink, and one of his army buddies who'd come to stay at the Sentous would escort me over to hear Warne—a beautiful sound.

By now, we were both in UCLA graduate school and I was a teaching assistant too, so we made a poor but honorable living. But if I felt marginally better, Richard felt marginally worse. He wasn't that crazy about graduate school. On weekends he drank whatever he could get his hands on, but mostly red wine. Red Mountain was his brand. It made his teeth loose, it made his arms break out in a rash that looked suspiciously like Newfoundland scurvy.

I lived my life on two tracks—toughing out nights in Chinese restaurants, or at my mother's watching the two of them get blotto, or at the Sentous, cleaning up after sleazebag tenants. But my secret and better life was at UCLA, where I took classes and taught. I'd finally fallen in with a wonderful bunch of buddies. Two of them would mean the world to me. Judith Wilson, a single mother, was making it on her own, working as a TA. Her baby slept in an easy chair. And Tom Sturak, a beautifully groomed Slovak-American who'd been in the Navy and swanned about in handsome Hong-Kong suits: he appeared one afternoon in my office doorway. I began to plot and scheme and wonder how I could get out of this cockroach life in the slums, and away from this comatose drunk I was married to. Could there be a way? Judith Wilson had left her husband; she seemed all right.

I'd already written a novel about the Sentous Apartments, about a tenant who "still had the bugs in bed." I'd put in Warne Marsh and his ratty little nightclub that had so much beauty. I'd picked a friend of the long-gone Dick Jones and imagined him into my book. My secret life had to have some purchase on the intolerable real life I was leading.

Meanwhile, my father underwent an explosion of his own: he began to feel strongly that he had to go down to Tampa, Florida, to go into the frozen shrimp business. He and Wynn said au revoir on amicable, even pious terms, but fifteen minutes after he got there, he found a sweet girl who was exactly my age, thirty-three years younger than he. Lynda was unloved, fatherless, and dying for a dad. I wouldn't want to speculate on what George was looking for. Wynn let Richard and me know that she wasn't exactly *perishing* for my dad's company, but later she gave me a piece of excellent motherly

Richard, Lisa, and me at a tourist attraction coming home from a visit to Victorville. It was hard, sometimes.

advice: "I speak of your father, and all my ex-husbands, with such affection that people think they're dead. I suggest you learn to do the same."

Because I was going to have an ex-husband soon. Tom Sturak and I had been carrying on an absurdly chaste romance. Richard, Tom, Judith, and a flock of our friends all took the PhD qualifying exams in June of 1959, Richard in anthropology, the rest of us in English. My first novel won second prize in the Samuel Goldwyn Creative Writing Contest, and pretty much made it OK for me to pass my exams and go on for the PhD. Tom passed, beautifully. Richard passed.

On a Saturday in late June, Richard and I went house-hunting in Venice, and found a great place at the beach. We could even afford it. I still hadn't made up my mind to leave. That night, at the beach, we visited some of his anthropologist friends. He fell over, he threw up, he waved his arms and legs, and when we went to walk down to the water, he crumpled in a rag-doll heap on the sidewalk. I stayed half a block behind, finalizing my plans.

A few nights later, just sobbing away, I told Richard I was leaving. He listened impassively and said, "You like this guy now, but he's new. What are you going to think of him in five years? What will he think of you?" Behind his goatee, the Richard I'd known in high school peered out, a scared little kid who used to play poker with Anna May Wong.

"If only you loved me," I wailed. But he wouldn't budge. He couldn't.

I tried to think of the summer in front of me. Tom was taking my daughter and me to Reno. The prize money from the Goldwyn Contest would pay for my divorce. Tom liked Lisa and she seemed to think he was OK. Tom had told me (in the mildest way) that he had a terrible temper. Tom was a runner. He wanted to spend time in Mexico. He had a daughter, Katharine, Lisa's age, who'd been taken from him in a treacherous custody fight. He wanted a family, he said. He wanted to take care of me. He wanted to live at the beach. He had all those Hong Kong suits. I had to get away from this family, away from this morose drunk.

And I'd be the morose drunk the next time.

Tom Sturak and I celebrate at the Foreign Club in Tijuana on our wedding night.

om Sturak had been hanging out in graduate school at UCLA, getting over a five-year first marriage and playing out a tempestuous love affair with a Latvian would-be American immigrant named Sylvia, who waited—with her family—to be allowed in from Tijuana to the USA. For years after this, when we'd go down to Tijuana to get the car upholstered, or buy penicillin or metham-phetamines, or check out the bullfights, or lay in a supply of rum or tequila, we'd see Sylvia. Whatever photography shop we passed in that dusty town, we'd see heavily hand-tinted pictures of his ex-girlfriend, rouged and with her blond hair glowing like lemons, smiling out of a gilded frame with that whipped-cream smile of the well-brought-up Mexican adolescent girl—so prized were Sylvia's looks south of the border.

But Tom had got tired waiting for Sylvia and spotted me. Tom seemed the very antithesis of Richard. Tom was clean-shaven, had decisive cheekbones, intense eyes. Tom refused to sleep with me until Richard and I had separated. (He could not do that, he said, to another man.) I fell madly in love with him. He was so beautiful, so funny! And so honest. Tom's grandparents had immigrated from Slovakia. His paternal grandmother worked as a charwoman in a Pittsburgh men's club, on the graveyard shift, in the kitchen, so that she could come home every morning, her bulky frame padded with a dozen half-eaten rare steaks. Her family ate well, no matter what.

Tom's aunts slept three in a double bed, head-to-toe-to-head. They were a rambunctious, giddy lot. They were the Sturak family and they couldn't remember any stories about home in Slovakia. The general feeling was that they hadn't *had* a home. The same grandma who "walked like 'lectric," she had so much energy, didn't have much use for her older son, John. When John came home after a night of carousing, he'd try the door to see if it was open, and if it wasn't, he'd stretch out on the porch of the ramshackle building on the steep hillside that overlooked the steel mills of Pittsburgh. He must have been dumb to do that more than once: when Grandma Sturak came out and found him in the early morning, she'd beat him soundly with a broom handle.

The Sturaks were fierce; you had to look sharp just to stay alive. When Tom was a little kid, his young mother took him home to visit the family. As Tom read a comic book, one of his cousins came up behind him with a hammer and knocked him out cold.

John Sturak, the strapping delinquent, took a liking to a pretty blond girl from downstairs. Mary Shack (who looked like Norma Shearer, everybody said so) was sixteen, worked in a bakery, and spent an entire week's salary on a hand-tinted photographic portrait. John, who would turn out to be a fabled miser, took Mary out on their first date. They were walking in the park, and Mary said she was thirsty. John took her to a public drinking fountain. (Later he would refuse to flush their toilet more than once a day, and never watered the backyard lawn, calling it "force-feeding.")

John would be going into the Navy. He might stay out of trouble in the service. The two married. John was twice her size, but Mary stood up for herself. She fielded her husband's brutality over the years with humor, distance, contempt, and sometimes with tears. They had the one beautiful boy, little Tommy, whom Mary would use as a buffer against her husband all her adult life—or until John died. One Christmas, when Tom and I drove down to spend the holiday with his folks, Mary opened the front door in tears: her brother had shot his wife to death on Christmas Eve. Nevertheless, when we went inside, the tree was up and sparkling, the presents wrapped, the turkey sizzling away in the kitchen. Mary sat on Tom's childhood bed, weeping. I perched on the other side, thinking dark thoughts. I'd betrayed Richard only to find myself in another domestic hell.

The door opened. Tom's father, pulpy, unevolved—a dead ringer for my own stepfather, if truth be told—peered in.

"Don't you think the turkey might be overcooking?" he asked.

In a hundredth of a second, his son was at him. It looked like he was trying to tear out his father's throat with his bare hands. Mary and I pried them apart. "I only *said* the turkey might be overcooked," John repeated, and backed cautiously out to the living room, where he settled himself back into his Lazy Boy and again became a part of the furniture.

Back in Pittsburgh, Tom had grown up with a puny cousin, Andy Warhola. Andy had been raised by a crazy mother who couldn't afford milk for the little kid and raised him on black bread and strong coffee—"Coffee-Nerves Warhola," the neighborhood kids would cruelly call him. When his mother went on errands, Tom's teenaged aunts—those rowdy girls who slept toe-to-head-to-toe in double beds—would baby-sit Coffee Nerves. They'd tie him to the bed with scarfs, where he'd scream until he couldn't scream anymore. The girls would put up their hair and leaf through movie magazines, all the while watching out the window to see if the old lady was coming home. When they saw her, they'd untie the kid, collect their money, and go home, while the scrawny little victim screamed. It made a good story and they told it a lot, and went on telling it even when "Coffee Nerves," who was Tom's age, grew up to be Andy Warhol, trying for the rest of his short life to forget his squalid beginnings.

So when my unevolved father-in-law—who would address twenty sentences to me during the ten years I'd be married to his son—opined to me that watering the lawn was simply force-feeding it, I'd feel curiously at home. Tom and I had been through a lot, and though some of it was different, a lot of it was the same. We felt the same light-headed relief when we drove home—from his father's, or my mother's. We'd place hypothetical bets: if we matched them in a boxing ring, who would win, his father or my mother? We both agreed it would be my mother, going away.

Tom hated bullies, because he had been so relentlessly bullied. When we first stopped by my mother's place after I left Richard, she asked Tom nastily, "What do your *parents* think about this state of affairs?" Tom got up, gave her a look of limitless contempt, and left the room. I'll love the guy for that courage until my dying day.

—

In the summer of 1959, Tom and I drove to Reno for a six-week divorce. We had a good time. We went to stock-car races and watched Steady-Eddy Monjar on the track. We went to triple features at the drive-in movies. I went for six weeks without watching anyone get drunk. But for the first time in my adult life, someone made fun of my birthmark to my face—and it was Tom. I was talking seriously to him about something and he got tired of listening. He puffed air into his right cheek, probably thinking he was mighty funny, but I went into the bathroom of our little bungalow and howled like a coyote for an hour.

Much worse, and far more unsettling, Lisa, who had always seemed to like Tom well enough, yearned for her dad. Her disposition, which had remained miraculously sunny for the three years she'd been alive, shrunk down and got sad. She was, as always, "well-behaved," but she didn't talk much. She was unhappy and I felt I'd caused it—although, to be fair, how could I have stayed with Richard much longer? But I thought of myself when I was three, and of how much I'd loved my dad. How could I have done this to her? Once, when Tom left the car during a triple feature at the drive-in, Lisa, sitting quietly in the back seat, screwed up her face and began to cry. "When are we going to go home? Aren't we *ever* going to go home?" When Tom came back to the car with hot dogs and lemonade, she shut right up, stifled her sobs, calmed herself with a great effort of will. Already, at the age of three, she had more control of herself than I had of my own life. *God.*

Now, in Reno, an acrimonious correspondence sprang up between Richard's parents and me. They were enraged at my leaving, saw me as a slut, and threatened to sue for custody of Lisa. I countered passionately and at length about what a good mother I was. None of us mentioned Richard's drinking. I didn't say: *Look!* I had to get out of that little apartment. I'm afraid of him. You didn't see him in Trieste, when he drove into town on the wrong side of the street. You didn't see how he drove down the stone steps of the medieval castle, stopping only when the front tires of the Renault rippled the surface of the Adriatic. We all could have drowned. You don't know that he throws up through his nose. I'm out of my depth here! I don't know what to do!

I bleated on about what a good mother I was and what a nice future Lisa would have with Tom, who was such a solid citizen. They countered with vague threats, but they were a mixed-race couple who had never gotten properly married themselves because of miscegenation laws. We ranted, used up paper, and never brought up the real issue: Richard had a drinking problem that was destroying his life. I found out later Richard had stood up to them on the question of Lisa, but the issue of his drinking remained unresolved.

—

Up in Reno, then in a pretty house in Manhattan Beach—where Tom went surfing and running—I saw a new kind of drinking. We drank at graduate student parties. But Tom got nicer when he drank! We went down to Mexico, and listened to wonderful mariachis. Tom wore his white linen suit. We avoided margaritas and drank tequila straight, in that sweet way which takes just a little coordination and somehow simulates a health drink. It tastes so fresh! It feels and seems so breezy! Down in the watery depths of the old Foreign Club in Tijuana, with its huge arrangements of either fresh or artificial flowers and an enormous, unused roulette wheel decorating the far wall, you ordered tequila—Siete Leguas, never José Cuervo—that came to you clear and almost yellow-green in perky little glasses.

They served you a dish of coarse salt and a saucer of sliced limes on the side. You sprinkled a generous pinch of salt on the soft flesh between your left thumb and forefinger, held the tequila in your left hand, licked up the salt, swallowed down a bracing oily mouthful, and then cut through those two tastes with a quick crunch to the lime that you held in your right hand. Then inhaled! Aah. By then the mariachis had strolled and sidled up alongside you, and Tom had been writing down his favorites on a napkin: *"El Niño Perdido"* (where a trumpet player gets "lost" in the restaurant) and *"Escaleras de la Carcel"* ("The Steps of the Jail," which Tom said marriage meant to him), or *"Los Barandales del Puente"* ("The Railings of the Bridge," which prompted in Tom an always-beautiful soliloquy about the imagination of the Mexican people, who were so poor in material wealth but blew it off by creating songs about nothing, and making the best drink in the entire world from the ubiquitous, lowly cactus). And then they'd play *"La Negra,"* the happiest song in the world, or the song in the world which most accurately gets the configuration of the *anticipation* of happiness, and they'd serve up another round of tequila and another saucer of bright-green limes, and Tom's face would glow with happiness and almost celestial contentment.

I could watch him then, seeing how the shimmering, underwater light of the Foreign Club would glance off his cheekbones, and how his blue eyes closed, listening to the music, and how his blond mustache looked so *good*. I was happy, in a beige linen dress, some carnelian beads that Tom had bought me, and I thought, *wow!*

But it wasn't always so great. Tom was an athlete. It took me fifteen minutes to run once around a track, and I couldn't see the point to it. I studied; Tom studied and ran. In Manhattan Beach, where we lived the first two years of our marriage, Tom surfed, ran, swam, and occasionally ranted. I kept house and studied. As with Richard, we both had teaching assistantships, enough money to call ourselves "nouveau poor."

A strange thing happened. I'd be sitting home in our little living room close to the beach, reading for maybe four hours before Lisa came home from school and Tom returned from working out—reading something tiresome like *The House by the Medlar Tree,* something terrific like *The Red and the Black.* But about two in the afternoon, I'd feel an overwhelming need to make a cheese sandwich and have a beer and then a beer and then a beer. I grew out of my beige dress within six months. Tom was disgusted with me.

Then the Russians shot down Francis Gary Powers in his U2. The Russian leader banged his shoe. I suddenly realized the repetitive whine I'd been hearing during the last year in Manhattan Beach wasn't *waves,* as I'd assumed, but mad scientists just down the road shooting off trial rockets. I went into terror, positive that World War III was going to start any minute. I worried that Tom was disgusted with me again. I worried that he'd gone from a scarily abusive home to a failed marriage, to a romance with a Latvian who spoke often of suicide, to a harmless-seeming graduate student who, as soon as they got married, began to pour in the beers, cry for no reason, and cringe like a whipped dog every time they ran a routine test at Rocketdyne!

But our will to make things normal and right was such that I ironed two hours a day, and Tom shoplifted so many filets mignons that we never worried about protein. He planted a vegetable garden so replete with turnips that if we wanted to we could still be eating turnips. We read Lisa a story every night, and made untold pans of "health cookies" full of wheat germ. And I (with a big glass of cold beer by my side) translated Italian after Lisa went to sleep.

Tom and I would often put Lisa in our Volkswagen and hit the road south. Eighty-five miles down the freeway, my father lived with

Lynda. They'd make us a great meal and Daddy would tell us his same silly stories, play on his ukulele, engage us all in a game of proverbs.

Then we'd head farther south to San Diego and check into Tom's house, where, while Tom's dad still lay out on his Lazy Boy like a big slug, we'd huddle in Tom's old room and make plans, which usually meant going to the Navy Base and buying up consumer goods at a discount price. Then a short stop by his aunt and uncle's—Tom always chatting about the metaphysical experience of running along Sunset Cliffs at *sunset,* or how much he preferred the *white* pavement of San Diego to the *black* pavement of Los Angeles. Then, on Saturday afternoon, we'd head south some more. We'd cross over the border and the minute it happened things always changed for the better.

The air itself would thicken up with the charcoal smoke from hundreds of open fires. We'd head for El Pulpo, a café for the gilded youth of T.J., where we'd feast on apricot nectar and the best taquitos of our lives. High school girls would come in, in groups of two or three, and eligible bachelors would linger at the counter. Tom told me about jalapeño peppers—that the seeds were the hottest part. We'd spend the afternoon on a shopping spree. We, who were poor in the States, could buy whole sets of cobalt-blue glasses, or bright-green glass plates, or trees of life that went ape crazy in their ceramic manifestations of the nature of the spiritual world. We'd hit the grocery stores to buy jalapeño mayonnaise and Mexican Nescafé, so much better than its American counterpart, and big big bags of *pan dulces* (you wandered through the bakery, picking up what you wanted with cumbersome tongs), and then to the liquor store, where you could get rum and tequila for about eighty cents a quart, and we'd buy a dozen bottles.

We'd drive up into some residential section of the city, park on a dirt road, pull out the back seat of the Volks and stash our liquor under it, along with a wonder drug we'd buy at the Bótica Sherr, something from Smith Klein and French for women who had difficult periods—pure Benzedrine with a relaxant for the smooth-muscle system.

Then it would be time for the bullfights, and a long, very interesting lecture from Tom on bullfighting. We saw so many fights! Good fights, one of them so good that the bull itself was allowed to live, and spend the rest of his life at honorable stud. Then back to the Foreign Club, where we'd drink tequila and listen to music until our ears rang with it, Lisa picking her own songs and loving the music. We'd spend the night at the Hotel Lee's, which cost two dollars and fifty cents, with sheets as old and soft as tissue paper. We'd wake up in the morning with a cold beer or two, maybe go to another bull-fight, maybe drive down to Ensenada, but finally get in the line to go back home again, putting something over on the customs men, sailing through with Lisa perched on hundreds of dollars of contraband in the car. Then we'd go to the Old Globe in San Diego, take in some Shakespeare, and drive on home.

Aah! The good life, or it should have been, except that I'd pulled Lisa out of one life and into another without telling her why, and Tom's first wife, Carman, had married a man in the Foreign Service, who, since he couldn't adopt Tom's daughter Katharine, settled for the next best thing, hopping from country to country, so that Tom was half wild with worry over his kid, writing her and writing her and never getting an answer. And I was going nuts. There's no other way to put it.

By early 1961, I was totally convinced that a nuclear war was going to occur. Tom and I decided to go and live in Mexico, down in Mazatlán. He argued, perfectly correctly, that being a thousand miles south of San Diego wasn't going to aid our health very much if the nuclear war everyone was promising by now actually did occur, but I didn't care. And on an earlier trip to visit his daughter Katharine, we'd come into Mazatlán around midnight on a moonlit evening. Tom saw half a dozen athletes running on the wide, deserted boulevard by the harbor. It looked like heaven on earth— the Pearl of the Pacific—to him. We both got fellowships, persuaded UCLA to send the checks to Mexico, packed up our books and— with two friends, Gerry Carson and Tom Mauch, in matching Volkswagens—headed south. As we drove through the California desert town of Indio on August 13, 1961, the news came over the radio: the Russians were building a wall straight through Berlin. *See?* I wanted to shriek at Tom. Am I the crazy one? *Am* I? But Tom was disgusted with my craven fear, and actually in pretty good spirits about going to live in Mexico. We crossed over, taking the highway across Baja, rode south past Caborca, where we spent the night in a roach-infested hole and a drunk Mexican danced in front of me saying, "Me Tarzan, you Jane!" Gerry Carson threw up after too much tequila, and invented an ironic name for four timid travelers and one little girl: *Los Extravagantes.* Some extravagantes!

We drove in simmering heat through the last customs check at Sonoyta, where Tom bribed officials with *Playboy* magazines and an electric fan. We stayed the night in Navajoa, waked to see the sun coming through the slats of our windowless hotel shack. Spent the night in Culiacán, where the Sonoran Desert had really (if temporarily) turned to green jungle and you crunched roaches three deep on your way to the hotel room, and by this time I was having serious second thoughts. Lisa, six years old, had given up talking. She curled into the little baggage slot of the old Volkswagen and only came out three times a day to order *huevos tibios* (barely poached eggs) and *una Coka,* since we knew the milk was unpasteurized. We kept telling her how much fun she was going to have—learning Spanish, going to Mexican school, but she wasn't buying it.

We got closer to Mazatlán, checked in at the Hotel Olas Altas—right on the beach, but old and cheesy and alive with flying roaches. The next morning, when Tom Mauch slung in drunk Gerry and drove his own black VW north along the *malecon* to catch the highway out of the city, we watched from our damp, salty balcony and waved. We were alone, and Tom looked chipper.

—

Mazatlán in the early sixties was boiling hot and far away. Outside of two other families we were the only Americans in the city. It was so hot that when you sat down to write a postcard the sweat from the back of your hand trickled down and obscured your message. Mazatlán—the Pearl of the Pacific—was a medium-sized town with a medium-sized harbor. You came down out of desert, turned off the Western Highway, drove through dense, alligator-infested jungle until you emerged in the city: a pretty place, bound on the south by its harbor, on the west by its mile-long strip of seedy hotels, on the north by a peninsula that dead-ended in clear water, and on the east by solid jungle.

We looked at places to live in the heart of the city, where sweat poured off us all and old ladies fanned themselves with limp, folded papers, saying *"Mucho calor."* We'd go back to the Olas Altas, sit on the veranda, and watch the sea splash up on a lot of rusted gear, leftovers from some marine project long forgotten.

Tom found us a house to the south of town, where the city slanted up into cliffs. There, next to a couple of mansions, stood three stucco

Katharine Sturak, Tom's daughter, and Lisa See. Two beautiful girls sweating it out in Mazatlán. *(Courtesy of Tom Sturak)*

cottages clustered at the top of a cliff overlooking the sea. Each house was painted a different color: yellow, blue, and ours was pink. You went into the living room, floored with flesh-colored tile. To the left was a kitchen and a laundry room. Then a bathroom, bedroom, and a wooden balcony for cooling off, having breakfast, checking out the dazzling ocean below. Between the houses and the ocean, growing out of the cliffs, hundreds of pine trees sang in the breeze.

We moved in, next to the other two American families in town; one older couple who'd worked for Wrigley in Belize, and a younger one, a millionaire guy who was trying to write a novel, with a nice wife from Wisconsin. George Gage, the millionaire, and Tom Sturak took to each other right away, assembling skin-diving gear, finding a "mole" that jutted straight out into the harbor, made of enormous rocks that sheltered perfect homes for moray eels. Virginia Gage took me marketing every morning at five, before the sun came up and the heat became unbearable. In September, Tom and I enrolled Lisa in Mazatlán's best private school, El Collegio del Pacífico, just at the bottom of our cliff.

After marketing, dropping Lisa off at school—she was too demoralized to tell us she needed school uniforms—the four grown-ups would repair to the mole. Virginia and I would bake in the sun—my hair bleached to almost white—then we'd come home for lunch. Lisa would go back to school, crying. She was sinking, and I didn't know what to do. Every afternoon, I'd drink a six-pack of Pacifico beer (eight cents a bottle) and read a novel for my doctoral dissertation. Tom would go back to swim and fish, and return, wild-eyed, with a dozen lobsters or a hundred-pound grouper, or lugging a stingray as big as a one-room apartment. Drunk as a frog, I'd watch him wrestle his catch through the kitchen door and into the laundry room, where he'd clean and cut it up. By that time I would have switched to rum and lemonade, a great drink.

I'd drink one rum drink after another, and cook fish, rice, and beans. The three of us lived on about a dollar a day. Two or three nights a week we'd go out to the rat-infested movies. Back at home, we'd turn on the lights and hundreds of flying roaches would flash and crack around us.

Lisa slept in the living room. Mosquitoes lived in the curtains, and at night they came out to bite her in droves. Our bedroom windows opened on to the balcony, the pine trees, and the sound of the ocean below. There was no screen and we didn't even think to ask for one. We kept the lights on, reading in bed, and every living insect came through the windows and landed on our bodies. Once, after the lights were off, when Tom and I were having disconsolate sex, I felt something in my hair as big as my hand and let out a shriek. Tom turned on the lights. It was an enormous iridescent praying mantis.

Thirteen hundred miles to the north, I knew they were still planning World War III, which by now drove Tom into an apoplectic frenzy. "You can get killed in a *car*," he'd scream at me, so loud that far off in the jungle the jaguars must have flinched. I'd pour myself another glass of Jerez, my nighttime drink.

At Christmas my mother and Rose came down for the holiday; of Mazatlán my mother said, "What's the big deal? It's just a beach where everyone speaks Spanish," and to Rose, as she sat reading the back of a Soupy Sales album: *"You make me sick!"* After my mother and Rose flew home, Tom and I drove back into town. I burst into tears.

Mazatlán. A neighbor, George Gage, and Tom Sturak, with one of their numerous fish.

Me in Mazatlán, working. Note empty glass.

"Oh, Tom," I wailed, "I feel so terrible I even miss my mother! That's how terrible I feel!"

—

So maybe I felt like the world was blowing up because I was blowing up. Maybe my alcoholic genes were just kicking in. Maybe what I'd done to Lisa made me too guilty to live. Maybe I wanted to be a writer, but knew for sure I couldn't. I looked at Tom gaining fame for running in every city track meet, labeled by the newspaper as "The Godchild of Uncle Sam," loved him, envied him, died of shame because I was so out of control. So I'd have six more rum drinks.

In spite of everything, Tom and I believed in love. Believed in it, experienced it, as laughing or longing or even yelling (because wasn't that an aspect of "passion")? But with all our running and traveling and "learning," our lust for scholarship, etc., etc., none of that meant shit. We were going to be thirty soon, but we could have been abandoned kids in playpens. We were trying as hard as we could to escape our pasts; we couldn't see the future. We were inventing ourselves, but we were both running out of ideas. Dreaming up the ideal life, but—not to be tiresome about it—running out of dreams.

Tom and I, with the best intentions, had created a holograph of the kinds of homes we'd come from. He had evolved into an exasperated bully, and I'd become—how easily and quickly—the drunken, hysterical bitch from hell. Lisa, poor Lisa, was either little lonely Penny, or little lonely Tom, depending on how you sliced it.

I knew the world was going to end, knew it, *knew* it. I was nuttier than a fruitcake, out of my mind. But by now it seemed to me that dying in LA was infinitely preferable to dying down here. I knew I had to go home. Tom seemed relieved. Poor Lisa just hung on for the ride.

Tom always had marvelous manners. When, earlier—along with a group of graduate students, visiting Tijuana—we'd stopped by a Mexican brothel, he shook hands with all the ladies and told them how beautiful they were. When, in a fluorescent-lit, windowless room, an earnest prostitute "inhaled" a cigarette in her vagina, blew out a smoke ring, and then—what a test of race and behavior!—handed it to a friend of ours to take a drag on, he drew back. Before she had time to be angry or hurt, Tom leaned forward, grabbed the cigarette from her, took a deep drag and exhaled a huge cloud of smoke with a happy smile. "Delicious!" he exclaimed, and made such a nice impression on the ladies that they all lined up to hug us as we left.

He loved *carnaval* and he loved music and he loved fishing and he loved races. He loved winning races but he loved losing too, because that gave him ample excuse to analyze the race in meticulous detail.

A lot of things made him laugh. He was capable of rough kindness and generosity.

He had a gut-level hatred of marriage, and so did I. But we both had an equal stubbornness: we would transcend what our parents had been and done. When we returned to LA in September of 1961 to go back to school and finish our degrees, I was sure the world would end; barring that, we were both pretty sure we'd stay married forever.

——

In October 1962, we visited my mother in Victorville. I once again opined the world would end soon. My mother sneered at me.

"You're a fool!" she slurred. "You're a coward." "I don't know," I said stubbornly. "I'm just sure something is going to happen." Tom sighed. How many times had he listened to this?

That Monday morning we drove "the back way" from Victorville down to LA. It was packed with convoys. Every truck from March and Edwards and every other base they had up in the desert was roaring along to somewhere else. Tom lost his temper: the whole *point* of the back way was to avoid traffic! He turned on the radio to hear what was happening, and of course it was the Cuban crisis. I went into terminal terror, but Tom got mad. We had to drive a little over a hundred miles in second and third gear and he knew what was going to happen to his Volks. By the time we'd got home, he'd thrown his camshaft.

On television, the news showed people buying four shopping carts of groceries at once. Helpful news commentators suggested that citizens should search out the manhole cover closest to them in the street, and be prepared to jump underground at a moment's notice. I found an intersection with a manhole cover and went out to look at it. The *idea* that we should pry that thing out of the street and live beneath the pavement when all of civilization as we knew it was being vaporized above our heads was so ludicrous that I went back inside, poured myself a beer and began to do the ironing. I watched Richard C. Hottelet at the United Nations totally freak out on our black-and-white TV, I watched Adlai Stevenson get totally betrayed on that same TV, I drank and lay down on our Naugahyde couch with a stomachache and lost five pounds in seven days.

That Saturday night we had people over for dinner. We played Mexican music and Ray Charles at top volume. Everybody got smashed out of their minds and nobody mentioned Cuba. The next morning I woke up with a hangover, and turned on the radio to see what our chances were for staying alive another day. John Steinbeck had just been awarded the Nobel Prize for Literature and someone had him on the phone, asking him how he felt.

"How do you *think* I feel?" he answered crabbily. "I'll get to enjoy it for about a *week,* if I'm lucky."

I gave Tom one of those *see?!* glances, because the nature of our relationship was that we'd be arguing up to and right through the Big Blast itself. But Tom declined to open his eyes. He had a hangover himself and was feeling pretty rocky.

In a couple of days it was over. Some Russian explosion wasn't going to get me off the hook. I had no choice but to get better. I began a strenuous diet, stopped drinking (temporarily), wrote five pages a day on my dissertation. We moved back down to the beach, turned thirty, tried to have a kid, gave many a dinner party and a great big party, where the pattern was: we'd eat as well and fancily as we could afford, listen to great music, drink all the wine we could possibly put down, then get up from the table, roll out the door, and go skinny-dipping in the cool passage that ran from Marina Del Rey out to the ocean. No moray eels here.

Tom in our Mazatlán living room looking seductive, along with our cat, Mary Ballerina See, who lived on a diet of tortillas and beans.

I believe that many people lived that way in the late fifties and early sixties. Marriage was an imperative from the last world war. Domesticity was an imperative. Drugs, as we know them now, weren't readily available to the common man or woman. If I have to be frank about how I got through my own late twenties and early thirties, I'd have to say alcohol, the beach, silly jokes, and the telephone. For Tom, I'd guess skin diving, the beach, silly jokes, alcohol, and running. For all our fancy talk and heated arguments about high things, great literature didn't even make the list.

———

Sometime in January of 1964, Tom and I lay propped up in bed, reading. We were still in Marina Del Rey, by the beach. Tom looked up from his book and said, "You know Mark Del Vecchio, down at the office?" (Tom worked part time now at the RAND Corporation while he finished his PhD, and so did a lot of our friends.)

"Yeah?"

"Mark's been house hunting, and he said he found a house the other day up in Topanga Canyon that only a crazy person would buy."

"Yeah?"

Tom distrusted property even more than marriage. He said it tied you down, made you a permanent member of the sell-out bourgeoisie. "Mark said there's this cabin at the top of a cliff. You can't even get there by road. You have to walk up a switchback path."

"Yeah?" I knew what he was getting at but I couldn't believe it.

"But they have a tramline you can haul things up on. And he says there's this old lady who goes out on the cliff every day, she holds on to the dirt like an octopus."

"Really?" One of my most irritating afternoons in Mazatlán had been when Tom had caught an octopus and told me to keep it in my handbag. By nature, an octopus doesn't want to stay in a handbag.

"So. You want to drive out next Sunday morning and see this place?"

"Sure."

We went back to our reading. The next Sunday we drove up Pacific Coast Highway and turned into Topanga Canyon. Tom began to rave. "This can't be right! This has to be wrong! He must have said *Tujunga* Canyon!"

He had a point. Parched brush receded straight up on either side. This was a two-lane highway to nowhere. There was nothing like a house even remotely in sight. But Monday evening Tom came home looking quizzical as he changed from his RAND clothes to his skin-diving gear. "Del Vecchio says it's Topanga Canyon. He says we didn't go far enough. He says we've got to go *up*."

The next Sunday, a sizzler, we drove again up Pacific Coast Highway, turned once more into the scorched canyon. It began to smell pretty good; arid, mentholated, medicinal, the air-equivalent of a margarita with plenty of salt and lemon. We passed a Quonset hut on our right (Fernwood Market), a post office and jerry-built building down to our left (Topanga Center), a sign pointing to the elementary school, and then Circle Trail. It went straight up, coiled in a tight circle, and if you didn't watch it you were down on Topanga again. But we knew to stop at the top of the circle and look for the trail. We trudged up the switchback, past eucalyptus and prickly pear. On the last triangle of steep cliff in front of the house, calendula and Martha Washington geraniums bloomed in crevices between hot rocks.

And there was a beautiful German lady in her eighties, with a tan, athletic body and long blond hair. She'd made dresses for Theda Bara and Mrs. Igor Stravinsky. Her friends, she said, had told her she had to sell. They were worried about her, they said, but she thought they just couldn't take the hike up the switchback path—and they were afraid of taking the tram. (I didn't blame her friends: the tram looked like the thing Humphrey Bogart used to haul out the gold in *The Treasure of the Sierra Madre*.)

The lady showed us the inside of the cabin. In places you could see air between the slats. "Rain comes in, in the winter," she said. "There's nothing you can do." She showed us the kerosene water heater, which you lit by pouring in a saucer of kerosene, making a spill out of newspaper, lighting the liquid, waiting forty-five minutes to let the water warm up. If the kerosene went out, you had to wait thirty minutes before trying again, or you could blow yourself to kingdom come.

Out on the splintery balcony there were two old-fashioned metal camp beds, piled with pillows bleached gray by the sun. You could sit down on a bed, hook your feet in the balcony, and your body balanced perfectly, haltered between gravity and light, brushed by breezes.

She took us out to the narrow backyard and there, on the other side of the house, was an equally steep cliff going down. If you had a party up here, you'd have to be careful. She took us along the bony ridge out to the side of the house, and showed us the outdoor shower, a shed with a tank on top. In it was a bleached-gray, two-legged wooden table with a cake of soap on it—it took up most of the shower. "My husband decided we needed a soapdish, and he sawed the kitchen table in two. Would you believe it? He never had a hammer in his hand before!"

All over this ridge, bamboo grew. Eucalyptus, three monster ones, shaded the patio. Big shimmering clumps of Scotch broom shouted how *yellow* they were. The lady pointed out all the different colors of ceanothus—California lilac—from silvery white to lavender to deepest purple. She never had trouble with snakes, she said. The best thing was to ignore them. When the toilet overflowed the best thing to do was let it run right through the patio to the back cliff and down the side. You could help it along with a hose. Putting in an actual pipe would be illegal. On the other side of the tram motor by the house where the tramline ended was a small flat patch of land, where you could plant asparagus or artichokes or tomatoes.

Tom wore a sappy smile that I'd never seen before, he couldn't get it off his face. When we went downstairs to check the cave-room that might be his study, he found a little postcard-sized sign in gothic script left by her late husband: *Arbeiten und nicht verzweifeln.* "Work hard and don't get depressed." Wasn't that *it*? Work hard and don't get depressed? We'd found our home. The price was twelve thousand dollars. We borrowed the tiny down payment from every friend we knew.

All our friends helped us move in over the course of a scorching day in July 1964. I remember someone taking the tram up about midnight, sitting in a rocking chair eating a hamburger, oblivious to the dangers involved. I remember, about one in the morning, sitting down at a dented table with more hamburgers and beer. There were about eight of us left. A chair that went with the table exploded under one of our friends. *"This is a stunt house,"* he roared, and opened another beer.

The next day Marina Bokelman, the current girlfriend of Richard, my first husband, telephoned. "He's broken up with me. I'm going to kill myself if you don't take me in," she announced, and we said sure, come on over. We were feeling a little daunted ourselves. When Tom had gone out running, birds swept down on his golden locks to grab good stuff for their nests. The lady had left five layers of rug on her floor, filled with pins and needles. She'd taken her hot plate, but left a hideous couch that her husband had sawed in half, horizontally, he who'd never had a hammer in his hand! Marina came up and we put her to work hammering in planks, unplugging the toilet to get the raw sewage to travel across the patio. Our second night there, Tom went out to buy groceries and didn't come back for six or seven hours, hopelessly lost in another whole canyon. Marina and I sat, utterly fatigued, and put away a six-pack of beer apiece. It sank right into us, like rain in the desert. Directly across from us was a sheer cliff, the other side of Topanga Canyon, nothing but a majestic wall of dirt and scrub but with as much living presence as a big sleeping dog. It was alive: you could imagine it getting up, stretching, ambling away.

Marina, in the next day or two, brought up some marijuana. She was intensely meticulous about it, sitting in the tiny kitchen working at the sawn-in-half table, separating seeds from leaves, rolling slim and perfect joints. Tom and I, coated with mud and sweat from working on the house, inhaled with all our might. Marina told us *A Hard Day's Night* was opening; we were exhausted but took outdoor showers and went down to Santa Monica, saw it, and saw it twelve more times in the next fifteen days. We began buying Beatles albums. If you turned the sound loud enough the whole house acted as a speaker. The circle of Circle Trail was actually an acoustic bowl.

Tom's mother came up and stayed for ten days. She slept on the balcony, outside, but her head was eleven inches from ours. Griped at having no sex for over a week, Tom and I sneaked down to the Volkswagen at the bottom of the tramline, jumped in the back seat, and conceived Clara.

The Stones came out, after the Beatles. We felt like we owned them. All those friends who'd helped us move felt like they had a stake in our place. Every Sunday afternoon we'd lay out a huge spread in the patio. Tom was still skin diving and we usually ate fish soup, drank quarts of white wine, and smoked until we were utterly placid. We couldn't believe our luck. Lisa went to school at Topanga Elementary. It was the kind of place where you loved, *loved* going to PTA meetings because everybody there was cool. When the principal suggested that some of the kids might want to be cutting their hair, the parents picketed.

Tom had Katharine, his daughter, who could finally spend summer months with us. Along with Katharine, Tom's mother always came, and the strings of affection tangled almost unbearably. One August day that first summer, the kids were baking out in the patio. Katharine came hotfooting inside, announcing that there was a snake! I looked outside the bathroom window and there it was, a rattler, coiled and fat and dangerous. I got Tom on the phone at the RAND Corporation. He had to come home and kill the snake. He asked for his mother and the next thing I knew she had his shotgun out and was fumbling with shells. "I don't know if I remember how to load it, dear . . ."

I grabbed the phone and screeched that I did the cooking and cleaning and the ironing, but that killing snakes was *man's work*! Twenty minutes later he was outside in the patio, fit to be tied, carrying a eucalyptus branch. Yes, he'd do what a man had to do, but if I couldn't take my place on this earth as a fullblown, genuine adult and learn to kill snakes myself, well there were a few things he had to say to me. At the top of his voice.

I stood in the bathroom, wedged between the old-fashioned tub and the rust-stained sink, my arms folded across a paint-speckled windowsill that dated back to 1917, and listened as Tom raved for another twenty minutes or so. Behind me, Tom's mother, Lisa, and Katharine sweated and listened. Eighteen inches away from Tom's muscled calf, the snake listened too. It hadn't moved in an hour. "Because if you can't do something as simple as *this*," Tom shouted, and took out the snake with one wonderful eucalyptus hit, "then you don't deserve to *live* in Topanga!"

Afterward, Tom was quite pleased; he cut off the snake's head and rattles, and hung the skin out to dry on the clothesline. We all ate snake that night. Later, during that same visit, Tom's mother drank a beer and another one, and then fell forward and cut herself badly. She begged us not to tell Tom, and we didn't.

Mary drank like this: nothing for days and days. Then something would bother or frighten her. She'd drink two beers in ten minutes, fall straight forward on her head and bleed. I drank white wine in copious quantities, and tequila. Tom drank on the weekends, and went skin diving. His life itched at him.

Lisa went to school and watched it all. She had developed quiet sweetness and a wonderful composure.

Work hard and don't get depressed! That's the trick to being an adult, right?

We worked hard. The day before Clara was born, a Sunday, I pulled weeds along the tram track. Tom went skin diving with a friend. When he came home I was steamed. Who was going to do the *work* around this place? He yelled so hard . . . and I yelled back at him—that I got premature contractions and had Clara a month early. The first morning she was home we had to burn a tick off her head. The first week she was home I read Betty Friedan's *The Feminine Mystique* and got a clue. By Clara's third week, Tom was in love with a girl, Jennifer, at the office—honest, straight-arrow Tom! (I wouldn't "find out" for three more years.) Lisa welcomed Clara and doted on her with what would become an almost saintly devotion.

All this mixed bag of stuff seemed OK, because of the Beatles, and the beautiful view in every possible direction from our little house. And every Sunday there were long, lazy daytime parties where we drank and smoked and ate like kings. Clara, as soon as she could walk, got into the black olives; she liked to put one on each finger, walk around with them, eat them, go off in a corner and throw them up, do the whole thing again.

Somebody always had grass and what a *production* it was! The transporting, the hiding, the sifting and rolling. The pitiful efforts to grow the stuff! The toilet-flushing! Because—in talk, at least—someone we knew was almost always getting busted by the cops, while somebody else was always locked in the bathroom, trying without success to flush two pounds of feathery dried leaves down a stubborn toilet.

My father decided that belonging to AA just meant that you didn't drink. He still went faithfully to AA meetings, but he and Lynda fell in with a raffish dope-smoking crowd, young artists and roustabouts. An artist named Robin, for instance, whose brother, always in the good search for new ways to get high, brewed up a tea from the wild nicotine that grew in his backyard, became paralyzed for three days, unable to move or talk, and lived to tell the tale. My dad always had great dope, and he too gave wonderful parties.

Some weekends, Tom and the kids and I would drive on down to the sweet house that Daddy and Lynda had bought for a down payment of a mere 250 dollars. They'd be puttering around in their kitchen getting ready for a party. There would always be chicken and potato salad and a huge jar of marinated vegetables that tasted great when you got stoned. There would be some kind of spiked punch in a big crock that Daddy had painted with sayings like WORK IS THE CURSE OF THE DRINKING CLASSES. (The spigot came out of a set of delicate, explicitly rendered labia.) Dad would roll a set of joints and concoct the punch. It involved soda and very cheap white wine by the gallon. Cribari.

Around four, folks would drift in, talking about art or the movies that they'd seen. Tom and my dad would lounge and tell jokes.

The wine punch would slide down and the joints would circulate and the Beatles wheeze on. I remember once, in the middle sixties, leaning against my dad's living-room wall, looking at a neighbor with a beard. He looked at me. I looked at him. He looked at me. I looked at him. Finally, one of us said, "Would you like to go out to the garage and play some darts?" The other one of us answered: "I don't believe so." I think that's as stoned on marijuana as I ever got.

My father, at that time, was in *his* middle sixties, and except for his house, didn't have a dime. He wrote a weekly column for a local newspaper. He ran a junk shop that he called an antique store. He hadn't written his great American novel, but he'd successfully escaped his tormented past. He was a man who—at most—would only break even in life, but every Saturday and Sunday he'd look that fact in the face, pare some vegetables to put in his secret marinade. He'd roll some joints, put on his party albums, get out one of his party shirts, survey his own backyard, as big as a postage stamp but a hundred times as pretty, and go for it.

Tom and I were young adults, with a total of three kids, his, mine, ours. We both had our PhDs. He worked at RAND and I taught extension classes to wealthy, very kind matrons. We had our crazy house—work hard and don't get depressed!

Tom had his girlfriend. And my own eyes might have been wandering a bit. But I was beginning to write little short stories, and we had our friends, our Sunday parties, and an unending supply of plain healthy marijuana.

One night we had a dinner party for six. One couple, anthropologists, old buddies from graduate school, had just come back from the Rif. The Bedouins had been very nice, but Roger had caught malaria and his wife, Terri, had had to sling him over a donkey—head hanging down on one side, feet on the other—and walk him for ten days out of that high, hostile desert. They were insanely glad to be home. Roger had written us long, wistful letters about cold beers when he was out there with his tribe, and tonight he drank about eighty-seven of them.

Our living room was long and narrow—23 by about 10 feet, the house cut in half lengthwise. We ate at one end, under a bright pink bookcase with one shelf taken out so it could hold our tree of life.

We must have eaten either fish soup or chicken-and-sausage stew. We listened to Ravi Shankar. Trees scratched at the windows and raccoons looked in. The place was lit by candles and it glowed. We were stoned out of our minds. When it came time for dessert, I brought out a board with cheese and fruit. Terri started to cry. "It's just so beautiful," she said. And it was.

Me, blissed out.

I heard about acid for the first time from Wynn, separated now from my dad. I'd pretty much written her off as totally cracked: she'd believed so passionately in Senator Joseph McCarthy, she'd plastered that kitchen with pink cabbage roses, she'd given me *The Power of Positive Thinking,* along with that silver dollar. My own mother made it a practice to say things that were horrible—but turned out at some level to be true. Wynn's approach to life was to make statements that were cryptic, oblique, and totally cracked. Then you found yourself in Paris.

So, at about the time that Wynn told me that Gerald Heard, the

English pundit-buddy of Aldous Huxley's, was "the second most intelligent man in the world," she also told me that Huxley was taking peyote and getting in closer touch with God.

Later, Wynn said that there were wonderful experiments going on at UCLA: *didn't we know about them?* They had another new drug that put you in direct touch with God. Gerald Heard had been to UCLA. Bill W. himself had gone on over "to see if he could recreate the same mystical experience that led him to create AA, and he could, Penny, he could."

I filed it in my mind under T for Totally Cracked.

I didn't know about Bill W., but I *knew* Wynn wasn't on a first-name basis with Aldous Huxley no matter how often she called him Aldous. And the God that Wynn kept referring to was that Norman Vincent Peale God, the One who would fix your carburetor if you asked him hard enough. If taking a pill or dropping a tab would get me an introduction to Wynn's God with those rimless spectacles and that smarmy smile, forget it.

Wynn told me about all the care they took down at UCLA with this new substance—that they had gray walls and gray carpets and gray blinds and gray tables so that when the "psychedelic" experiences came that introduced you to God, they came from your own mind and not from some picture on the wall. Sure, I thought. And the man who put those papers in the pumpkin you're always talking about was a treasonous Communist just like Harry Truman.

So we'd heard about these experiments for what seemed like years. Some distinguished gentleman or other was always dropping by UCLA and getting his brain fried in the name of science. (You never heard of women doing it.) What would become the counterculture seemed at first to mimic the culture: white guys made the drugs and took them. Later in the sixties, Tom would come home from the RAND Corporation with many dark stories about how some military assholes were using this great new compound to fry enemy minds.

When, as teaching assistants, we taught our own freshman comp classes at UCLA, half the papers we got were about getting high. We'd ask students to write about their rooms: they'd get stoned and write about their rooms. We'd ask them for their favorite recipe (perhaps to compile a starving-student cookbook): they'd advise us that if you baked oregano leaves you could get high off that, or let banana skins dry out enough, you could get high off that, or morning-glory seeds, or nasturtiums. One student earned Tom's particular wrath by writing that you could get high on three-quarters of a cup of nutmeg dissolved in a cup of warm water. "My God!" Tom raved, "you could get high on three-quarters of a cup of *dirt* dissolved in a cup of water, three-quarters of a cup of *anything!*"

Nevertheless, we always had something drying out in our Topanga oven; we were always grinding something into a powder and rolling it up and smoking it, so we were always feeling just a little bit stretched.

Marina Bokelman, who had helped us so much when we moved into Topanga, came back from an extended trip to the South, where she'd been gathering folk music. She rented a tiny house down by the beach in a swampy patch of land called Topanga Gulch.

The Gulch checked in at some line below sea level. You approached it from the Pacific Coast Highway and went down a long dirt slope to where about a dozen houses sank into the ground under big tangly capes of morning glory, anise, honeysuckle. For years this damp ground had been the place of the really great parties. Hundreds of UCLA students would come and mill about for forty-eight hours at a time. Gary Merrill, Bette Davis's husband, showed up once wearing nothing but a sombrero over his penis: He wanted to party, he sobbed, he wanted a good time.

When Marina settled into her little house, she'd shed a husband and a couple of boyfriends (including Richard), but she'd kept dozens of jars of herbs and ointments. There was always something simmering on the back of her stove, fresh herbs melting down in purified beeswax.

Marina Bokelman was the strange flower among our friends. She said that her feet were not formed to wear shoes, went without wearing them for five years or so. For five or six years she drank, and matched Richard See drink for drink. She developed a scurvylike rash on her arms and her teeth loosened up in her head as if she were six years old. Then she stopped drinking and that was it. Marina once came to a masquerade party dressed as a gypsy. She'd not only found an authentic eastern European pattern (with more than a dozen secret pockets for easy stealing), she'd dyed her face brown— not with makeup or fake suntan stuff, but with stain made from simmered walnut shells and skins: what the gypsies themselves used when they wanted to be darker than usual.

So when people started smoking pot she naturally always had the best stuff. Her shoebox was always with her—one end holding unseparated leaves, seeds, and twigs, another little plastic bag in the middle holding carefully collected seeds, and down at the other end, next to a couple of packages of Zig-Zags, leaves that had been sifted and caressed to the point that they were as smooth and soft as baby powder. And Marina didn't worry the way the rest of us did about police. She could slip the whole damn thing into one of her gypsy pockets.

She hated shampoo and brewed up her own. She hated toothpaste and sometimes she'd pull a toothbrush out of her pocket, roll it around in a pouch of goldenseal she kept dangling from her belt, and start brushing her teeth. She loved to gossip and spin theories. We talked once about a young friend of ours, who, at twenty-one, had dropped out of school and was getting into hard drugs. Marina sententiously announced, "Why, when I was her age . . .", realized what she was saying and finished up, "I'd gotten a divorce, clogged up my fallopian tubes, and was a confirmed alcoholic!"

So when peyote, mescaline, and acid came into our lives it was natural and seemly that it unfold down in the Gulch where Marina had already begun her life's work as a healer. She just didn't know it yet.

When Marina discovered acid, she figured that she might have happened on one of the greatest secrets of the universe. She was strict about it. If any of us were going to drop acid we would do it in her house, with our favorite things around to comfort us. None of us rushed into it. Even though we knew they were lies, part of us believed the stories of people looking into the sun until they were blind, or diving off skyscrapers. Tom said he had devils in his mind he didn't want to know about, and said if we *did* it, we shouldn't do it together. We had the children to think about. I asked Marina if it were true what some people had said, that the symptoms of acid were unbearable. She took her time about answering. "It depends what you mean, 'unbearable,'" she said. "What people may be saying is that this is 'unbearably beautiful,' or 'I'm unbearably happy.' There aren't words to describe it. And that's what they might find unbearable." Her words and Wynn's endorsement transected. I decided to do it.

I ended up down at Marina's one afternoon around four, jittery with nerves. I'd skipped lunch because some of the worry about peyote nausea had rubbed off on acid. I had some Thorazine with me, because that was supposed to be the way to bring you down from a bad trip. I'd be spending the night with Marina: she'd drive me home in the morning. The afternoon sun came in through green leaves, making lacy patterns on the wall. She smiled, gave me a piece of paper to chew, and then turned around to her desk to do some studying. She could be disconcerting sometimes. After about fifteen minutes, I felt a scrabbly feeling in my chest.

"That happens," she said. "Don't worry about it." The next thing I noticed was that the refrigerator—an old-fashioned one up on four spindly legs that she kept in the living room next to her desk—was alive. It had been watching me all along. It was sleepy, and it yawned. A wave of unbearable happiness washed over me.

The second most boring thing in the world after people bending your ear about dreams is people bending your ear about their acid trips. Nevertheless! I saw immediately that everything, not just the refrigerator, was alive. The chair I sat in was holding me up, with great consideration. The trees outside Marina's open door waved and said hello. The bedspread on the single bed next to the wooden wall stretched and wrinkled and said hi.

Marina, without saying anything, brought me a saucer of lavender and yellow baby chrysanthemums. Each petal on each chrysanthemum was a little open mouth, opening and closing and saying *hello!* Marina had sliced up a raw mushroom, I put a slice in my mouth. When Christ said: "This is my body, this is my blood," he didn't mean just bread and wine, he meant all, all, all of life was the same body, the same blood. The mushroom was pale and alive—it had the skin, the feel, of a perfect teenaged girl. The universe was one, and alive, and sentient—very smart and very funny.

I saw the walls breathing, shallowly and quietly. After a while— and I saw that time was an illusion, that we were spinning in eternity—Marina suggested that I might like to lie down. It was getting dark, and I did. Marina put on the Beatles: "Revolver" had just come out. And after straining and straining all through the fifties to hear the chord changes underneath the hectic flutterings of Lee Konitz, Warne Marsh, Charlie Parker, now, effortlessly—and with such joy!—I heard every single note, and the breaths of those sweet boys as they inhaled, and sang a line, inhaled and sang a line. I put out my hand to the wall, the breathing wood, and felt it was not solid, that nothing in the universe was solid.

If I can't feel that right now, it's because my senses are too dull. I can remember it, though, and I date that evening and night to the most important personal discovery in my own life: that I wasn't a desperately unhappy person faking cheer in an abominable world, I was part of a wide, free, joyous universe.

For the rest of the evening, I closed my eyes and listened. The world was asthmatic. It didn't just breathe, it snorted and wheezed and muttered and hummed. At one point, Marina lit a candle. That fire went back to the first fire any man ever made, and Marina's house was the first shelter, and Marina the first wisewoman. Around midnight, I felt like getting up and having some tea. Things were calming down. Except once I looked at my dear friend and saw her face two ways at once: full face and profile, and thought, Picasso, big deal! He only painted what he *saw*!

I went to sleep and woke with that extraordinary feeling, that sense that someone has sent your flesh out to the laundry and taken the opportunity to scrub down your bones until they're buffed to a gleaming shine. And everything everyone said was part of the Big Plan for a week or so, in the same way that in the last weeks of writing a novel the whole world decides to finish it up for you, so that waitresses, mechanics, the people in the booth next to you at the restaurant, all conspire to give you chunks of dialogue, so that all you have to do is take down the dictation ...

Until it's over, and you dull down again, but you still remember. And no matter how much you get stuck in grocery shopping or gassing up the car, you know that other world, the Big-Plan World, is still out there.

In October of 1966, Tom Sturak dropped acid with his best friend Jim Andrews and Jim's longtime girlfriend, Solveig. Tom still wasn't ready for us to do it together. There were devils in his head, he said, and I—remembering our hard days in Mazatlán—was inclined to agree with him. Tom was ordinarily taciturn and sometimes (from my point of view) given to tantrums, and, even worse, bouts of despair. Tom—*my* Tom, who'd offed that rattlesnake with a single *whack* of a eucalyptus branch—Tom laughed for two hours and a half, laughed so long and so hard and so loud and so sincerely that he pulled a muscle in his chest from laughing. Even after that he kept on smiling, and when he came home he wore a scrubbed, beaming look. Blissed out. All his fear had been for nothing. The devils he'd been scared of all his life—apparations that had turned up in his dad and his uncle—weren't there, in him. All he'd experienced was ecstasy.

The question then became, how do you take that ecstasy and match it to the rest of the world? It was a question that occupied us a lot. Marina seemed to have done it, but not really, her personal life was always about some stormy romance that didn't pan out.

Then, in the early spring of 1967, Rose, who was sixteen and still toughing it out in Victorville with our mother, called me, gasping and crying. "I can't take it anymore, I can't stay here any longer. Isn't there something you can do? Can't you get me out of here?" I thought of how my dad had helped me when I was the same age. I couldn't ask Rose to live with us, but my friend Judy found her a job as an au pair girl, and I enrolled her in high school, and she stayed at our house several nights a week. She slept out on that balcony where huge black spiders built their webs, and Tom, to amuse her, would take his trusty rifle and blow those spiders to smithereens, while Rose squealed. At least she was away from Mother, but what would become of her? What would the wide world do to her? I'd driven up to Victorville, packed her up, gotten her out, brought her to LA, but now I felt my imagination failing. I could barely help myself and my own children. How could I help Rose?

Lisa would be graduating from elementary school (where the world, in Topanga, was cool and groovy and endlessly forgiving) and going to be bused for an hour every day down to large schools in the San Fernando Valley, a part of the world (to our minds) unregenerately materialistic and square. Clara was only two, and had endless energy. At around three in the afternoon on an ordinary Wednesday, with Clara crabby and Tom due home from the RAND Corporation, and Rose calling from somewhere needing a ride, where was the ecstasy?

And it wasn't like we were the total acidheads who lived in the rest of the Canyon, the women who went naked under flimsy pieces of net (and made my father so happy when he visited), or the man dressed in white who sang mantras in the Topanga Center parking lot ("Oh, how beautiful is Topanga in the morning!") and the dogs around him heard that one long piping note and hit it right along with him, recreating the music of the universe—only the dogs and the man were sometimes pretty flat. It wasn't like we were the Canyon guy named Mo, a short guy with the biggest dick in Christendom, and all the Canyon housewives knew it, because when we carpooled kids home to the commune where he lived, there Mo would be, stark naked, fit and tan, with his genitalia hanging down to his knees, flipping absently at his dick, asking casually, "Does this hang you up? This doesn't hang you *up*, does it?"

Actually, it *did* hang us up. We were caught between worlds. Every night on the news we'd watch the awful reality of the Vietnam War. In one demonstration in front of the Century City Hotel, Tom and I stood in the first row of demonstrators while nervous soldiers pointed guns straight at us. Tom forgot what he knew about laughing and began to rant: "Go ahead asshole, *pussy*, pull the trigger!" I, wearing a JoAnn Lopez hippie dress and carrying a bouquet of homegrown marguerites, kept saying, "You don't want to do this," and, as was the custom of the day, stuck flowers in the guns, stem end first.

Meanwhile, Christmas was coming. That meant my mother and Rose together again in horrid acrimony, Tom's mother and father

Tom and me on our first day in Topanga Canyon. We've found our perfect home.

and aunt and uncle, my dad and Lynda, a few miscellaneous cousins, all the presents and the tree and the turkey—and driving around from place to place, since none of those people could actually stand to be in the same room together. My mother had been out of her mind with rage at Rose since she had left, and kept saying on the phone, "Is she on top?" (meaning "pot"). Several winter holidays compress in my mind, one at which we strove mightily to do the family thing. Sometimes it was close to what we dreamed of: a Thanksgiving in our cabin with about forty people, including giggling young Rose and my amiable dad, who rolled enormous joints and passed them down through the long dark room that was packed with laughing people, and Marina and I got hung up on making

My dad, loving the sixties, and his sixties, in Topanga. (He had another wife now, Lynda Laws.)

creamed onions that would be white on one side and brown on the other, the two of us spending the shady afternoon sautéing those silly vegetables in the darkest sherry we could find, *but only on one side!*

The gap between the true vision of what we knew life was, or could be, and the life we seemed to find ourselves in grew wider. We talked about how we could make our daily lives happier. One night, up in our pretty little house, I took it on myself to chaperone my friend Joan from junior high school on her first acid trip. Her marriage had gone badly. She'd been raising three kids alone as a single woman. I'd known her since the seventh grade; knew her as intelligent and cheerful, if a little reckless in her love life. Hell, I'd been to Paris with her when we were all in our twenties, and Richard See and I had observed jealously as she'd romanced half of France. So I thought: this will be a lead-pipe cinch. This will be swell.

But she said, "Don't you see it?" and began to shiver with terror. No Thorazine would help, no music would help. "No," she kept saying. "No, I have to see this. They want me to see this." I sat up all night with her while she lay on the couch and cried, spending the night with the Devil.

The next morning I took her to a flower nursery, teeming with beautiful flowers. Joan cried again, and the attendant asked her what was wrong. "All of these things," she told him, "all of these things that are so beautiful, they're all going to die."

Acid truth. The scrubbed kid in the seventh grade, the madcap in Paris who picked up Africans with tribal markings, had been a beautifully put together fiction. The weeping woman who saw horror was the truth.

We weren't acid freaks. Far from it. We fretted over every trip. Marina and I did it together one hot summer afternoon, and as the sun went down we saw how God turns off the lights. I threw some leftovers down the hill and Marina said, "That's it. Feed the hill and the hill will feed you." I believed it, I still believe it, and I wrote a novel off it. Marina, that day, striding into the chaparral, looked for a vision. "Aren't you afraid you'll find a snake?" I asked her, every word a syllable pounding with care. "I already have," she answered. "It didn't mean me any harm at all."

So it was inevitable that one afternoon Tom and I took Clara and Lisa off to a babysitter, that we cleaned up the house and went ahead and did it—took acid together. I believe we felt we'd each passed a kind of *Good Housekeeping* Seal of Approval. Our love was stronger than our bad temper. I was worried about a particular paperback book, that it wasn't put away, but soon its covers began to flutter and breathe and its paper contained all of knowledge, and *printing itself* was so beautiful, blah blah blah.

We went outdoors, the stiff sides of the Canyon holding us up, and looked far, far into the sky. There were some very big clouds up there and so we went back into the house, just to be on the safe side. Tom was so beautiful! He had that wonderful spun-gold hair and his athlete's body, and he'd begun to laugh again—not the lung-wrenching gulps of his first trip but constant delighted giggling. It got darker and we sat in candlelight holding hands. Tom had perfect white, even teeth and as he laughed the candlelight struck sparks off them that fell down to his chest.

We had a snack—marinated artichokes and mushrooms again— and realized that Triscuits, of all things in the sentient universe, were not alive. They'd been processed to death and Tom wouldn't touch them, but I figured, heck, they still tasted pretty good! We went back to the couch and then Tom turned to me, smiling. "Well," he said, in a friendly way, "I guess it's time to do it!" We kissed with true affection, and then we kissed some more, and then we got our clothes off. But it just wasn't going to happen. After a while we stopped trying and went back to listening to music.

A couple of days later we wondered out loud why we hadn't been able to make love. "I don't know," Tom said, a little ungallantly, "but that was about the closest to a bad trip *I've* ever had! No offense."

About a year later I "found out" about his other woman. I gave Tom an ultimatum. Her or me! He couldn't make up his mind. God, it felt awful! The naked man from the commune came up and showed me his dick again. Was this what my life was going to be like? But Mo gave me good advice: "You have a nice life. You've got your kids, your friends, your work, you've just lost one component." Wow, Mo, that's some component!

Marina came over and spent a few nights. She stayed up all night, working. No acid this time. People brought over casseroles. I went around like a madwoman asking rhetorical questions: "What was it? What happened? It's like I have a *mark* on my back!" (What pathetic Freudian displacement.) It was more like we both took a look at the "mark" on daily life. Tom must have thought, if I can only get out of this *past*! If I can only get rid of this unbecoming *present*! If I can only strip down like Mo, then I can feel the sweet breeze on my bare skin, I can have some ecstasy. (Not the drug, which wasn't even invented yet, but genuine *ecstasy*!)

Tom got his picture taken. His mother had been after him to get a haircut, so of course he'd let it grow to a wild frizzy patch of stuff that stuck out eight inches on every side of his head. He put on a JoAnn Lopez shirt with ribbons hanging off all over it, stuck his tongue out, and sent the photo to his mother. This is the truth, Ma! This is what I am. This is the acid truth!

I took a look around. I could barely drive a car. I couldn't write a check. I looked at my two scared kids. I got a phone call from a writer whose face had been deformed in World War II. "I heard about your separation," he said. "Why don't you go to Addis Ababa? The air is wonderful there in Addis. You won't find any fresher air on earth."

Eight months after Tom first left, Rose and I took acid together for one last time.

I was a wreck. I thought my life was finished. "Thirty-five years old and divorced *twice*" rang in my ears and in my soul. Rose had managed to graduate from high school, and still came up to the house all the time. She'd kept the job as an au pair girl. After she graduated, she left the little kids she was taking care of, got a job, found a place in a bungalow court, and with the help of a couple of girlfriends and my daughter Lisa, painted every last pastel inch of it, even using mascara brushes to get to those tiny corners no paint-brush can reach. When the apartment was finished, Rose took one look at it and decided that she couldn't live there, not alone. It was way too sad, and she was only eighteen. She dug up a boyfriend star-tling in his normalcy: Tony, who worked for the phone company, liked to sit on anybody's couch, including ours, with a six-pack and watch TV. Once, watching a travelogue about the Alps, he uttered the (to us) immortal remark: "Gosh! Who'd ever want to leave Switzerland?" Rose recognized his kindness; appreciated his apart-ment in Santa Monica Canyon only a few blocks from the beach, but she was bored out of her mind.

I'd been learning to write twelve-page pieces for magazines—and got them turned down half the time—but I was managing to make a living. I'd watch TV with my children, drinking sweet Cinzano, or—remembering Sylvia Plath—brandy and water. My first business trip

Katharine Sturak visiting with her half sister, Clara, in Topanga. Little hippie chicklets.

to New York was coming up, and I'd gone out and bought a brown linen pantsuit that I thought was the absolute coolest, and perhaps a ticket to a newer, better life.

Tom came over, as he did once a week, to fix a "healthy" dinner for Lisa and Clara. He paused in his task of grating beets and beet tops together, and braising up a nice batch of kidneys and lamb hearts, to go to the bathroom. Along the way he paused to snoop in my closet. He came out the door holding up my precious new brown linen suit, swinging from its hanger. "All right!" he raved, *"Who is he? Why does he keep his clothes in here?"* I was depressed. I knew that dressing for success would be forever beyond me.

That night, on the balcony with Rose, the inside of the house seemed unbearably inviting. The brown-paneled walls made a sweet enclosure. Through the window just behind us, above the table, a big crazy oil painting of Tom Sturak shone in the lamplight. It had been painted by Joan, the tormented woman who'd seen Evil when she dropped acid right in that room, but when she'd done the picture she'd been in a better mood. She'd taken grousing Tom and laid him out on the couch, perched a toy helmet of Clara's on his head, piled up Clara's toys around him, and begun to paint. She'd caught him, his blond brows scrunched down over his eyes, his blond mustache safely covering up his lips, his eyelids safely scrunched closed. But she'd caught the ridiculousness of this position too. All those defenses, but for what? Couldn't he break down and open up his *eyes*, for crying out loud?

Rose and I lounged on the metal cot older than the century, covered with mattresses and those pillows bleached cleaner and cleaner by the sun. Around us the Canyon turned deeper and deeper black. You could hear it (the cats, coyotes, squirrels, rats, voles, rabbits, raccoons, skunks, snakes, shrews) but you couldn't see a thing except the stars in the sky.

We took the drug and in fifteen minutes felt that scrabbling in our

Tom, posing with his portrait by Joan Weber.

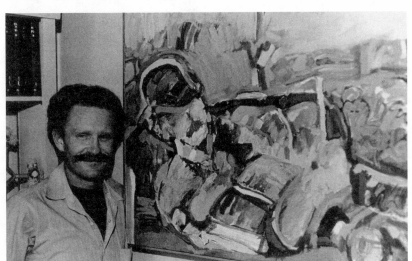

chests. The sky, with those bright stars, got really busy. Whenever a plane flew over, looking like some marvelous Oriental caravan, carrying blue and green and red lights in its underbelly, and leaving ribbons of that color behind it, it would *push* the stars out of the way. They'd whirl back to their original position, some of them swirling in a circle like certain kinds of breakfast pastry. (It came as another dopey revelation—how Van Gogh had seen the sky, where bakers down through the ages had gotten their ideas.)

"Penny?" Rose asked, "Have you had many men?" (Because in my family I was still Penny, and would be forever.)

It had been my worry since I'd lost my virginity that anything more than one man a year would mark me forever, to myself, as a slut. I went a little above my self-imposed average before I got married to Richard, and way below after I got married. Since Tom had left, and it looked like I was soon going to be thirty-five with two divorces under my belt, who knew what would happen? I felt gloomy about the question.

I pondered for an eternity, did some sixth-grade math, and came up with a provisional answer. "Eight."

She thought it over, her baby face changing in the starlight. "Oh, kid! Oh, I'm sorry! You haven't had any fun at all, have you? Gee, what'd you do when you were young? I've had fifty-three and I'm only eighteen!" The universe, curious and intelligent as always, buzzed along. *Issat so? Issat so!* Stars whirled around.

I tried to explain to Rose that when I fell in love, or felt like doing it, "it" didn't last very long for me. And besides, it seemed to me that some of the men I'd been with had been assholes (although cute).

"Tom wasn't an asshole," Rose offered loyally.

"I don't know, Rose. I don't know."

"Take a look," she urged. "See what you think." She turned me around to look through the window. There was *that guy*! Covered with toys, the Devil's own liar. Was he a good man or a bad man?

I watched as his face moved from loving to treacherous to deceitful to spiteful to sad to lonely to loving to childlike. If only my heart didn't hurt so much! If only I didn't have this pesky broken heart! And I realized that acid can't tell you what you don't already know.

"Beats me," I mumbled, and Rose and I lay back to watch the stars. The stuff was strong, stronger than anything I'd ever had. It came to me with embarrassment that while this night was a big, big deal to me, this was what Rose did a couple of times a week. I asked her, and she allowed as how that was true.

Amazing.

My little sister. And God only knew what my little girls would grow up to be doing.

But a thousand years later she stirred and asked me another question: "Penny? Are you strong?"

I thought about that one. About the furnished rooms. About my mother. About my dad. About the kids. About my friends.

"Yes," I said.

"I'm not," Rose answered. "I don't think I am."

By dawn it had worn off. I spent the day doing chores. We put on the TV and there was interminably boring Ed Sullivan. He waved his arms, and on the black-and-white set his arms flashed red and blue and green and sparks came out of his hands. Heavens, I thought. Even Ed Sullivan. That was the end of acid for me. I had to become a responsible mother.

But that year stayed like a silver wire in all our minds.

I have another memory from that time, visiting Rose when she was still working as an au pair girl. The house, which could have been attractive, was pretty foul. Rose didn't know any more about taking care of kids than she knew how to train fleas. There were toys all over the floor and dirty dishes all over the furniture and the kids smelled like a sump.

She talked about her life in Victorville, and down here in LA. She talked about some of the drugs she'd done, because they'd been all over the place up there. She'd had all the pot she could possibly smoke, and meth, and Benzedrine, and she'd shot acid into her foot. "I felt it climbing up my body and it hit my heart, right *here.* There are things I don't remember now, but I can't remember what they are. I'm not what I was, Penny. I'm not what I was."

It was hot as hell inside that cracker-box house. The kids were sniffling and prowling. Rose sat in a skimpy shift. Her face was pale and sweaty.

Tom used to have a fairly standard rant-and-rave about the nature of the world. There is no absolute meaning, he'd boom along, driving like mad in the car. Dostoyevsky knew it all along! If God does not exist, then all things are possible. I never listened to it very much (one of our ongoing troubles, obviously). I put it down to generic male grumpiness, the kind of thing that made Tom go crazy every time they inaugurated daylight saving time.

But watching Rose, or hearing her later on the balcony, or wondering why America changed from grass and acid in the sixties to speed and heroin in the seventies, and cocaine and crack cocaine in the eighties and nineties, it occurs to me that Dostoyevsky (and Tom Sturak) had their emphasis wrong. If God does exist, that's when all things are possible. You can see smart stars and hear the humming earth. You can see your life *down as far as you can see.* And if you care to look, you see the abyss.

Rose wasn't strong.

She'd seen it all along.

Lisa, Clara, and me. Our passport picture now
that Tom had gone. Someone said we could be a
rock group—Rapunzel and the Split Ends.

or years, since I met them both in 1958, Tom Sturak and his best
friend Jim Andrews had been ragging on women. So that while there
was nothing Tom and Jim loved to do better than crank up the
Mexican music and polish off a bottle of tequila and laugh, there was
another side that Jim's wife, Dot, and I, sometimes saw. Late at night
at dinner parties Jim loved to get out his bullfight cape and practice
his *verónicas,* his *media-verónicas,* in front of his house. "Where have
all the dreams gone?" he asked Tom, periodically. Jim drank a lot,
and worried about his health. He had noticeable swellings in his
armpits.

Tom had been going to write a novel, but after Clara was born he more or less gave up on it. "Wives and children have killed more artists than the cholera," he liked to say.

Tom had divorced his first wife, of course, but Jim kept his, and one morning in 1967, as Jim was enumerating Dot's faults to Dot— her inability to dream, to aspire (which closely corresponded to Tom's kidding-on-the-square complaints about me: when I gardened, I always looked down at the *dirt,* never up at the *sky*)—Dot suggested that since Jim didn't like her, and since she wasn't about to change, he probably ought to get out. He got out, but he was flabbergasted.

This left the door open for him to follow his dreams, though, and he was happy. There was Solveig, his own Latvian girlfriend from Tijuana, up in America now, working on a landing gear for some rocket. I was understandably griped because Tom's Sylvia still kept calling our house at midnight, drunk as a hedgehog and twice as disoriented, asking where all those *dreams* had gone! But Solveig was a nice woman, and since she'd been Jim's great love for over ten years, he decided to marry her in the winter of 1968. The wedding would be at our house. There would be at least a hundred guests and roast suckling pig. We would tape *"Escaleras de la Carcel"* instead of the wedding march, and the wedding party would drink golden gin fizzes before the ceremony.

Solveig didn't have a family. Most of her family had been massacred in World War II; her father had hanged himself and she'd discovered him, so I was the hostess for this event. I became obsessed. We would have my father's marinated vegetables, and every dip known to man. We would have enough tequila to float a battleship. (For weeks ahead the boys made Tijuana runs, smuggling cases of booze over the border.) We would have the best music—Ray

Charles and Otis Redding and Janis Joplin and all the mariachi music we could pull together. Tom commissioned a green ribbon shirt from JoAnn Lopez and I ordered a flowered pink chiffon dress. "He's the stem," she suggested poetically, "and you're the blossom."

The wedding day dawned bright and clear. The pig, when I picked it up, laid out with a very small apple in its mouth, looked frail and sick. I'd forgotten it would be just a baby. But there were mountains of other food, beer from FedCo, all that tequila, gin for the fizzes, and our two big connections, Marina Bokelman and my dad, were bringing up mountains of grass.

So everything was going to be OK. The judge huffed up the switchback path, took a look at all of us in our hippie finery and said, "If I'd known, I'd have worn my *robe*." Someone switched on "*Escaleras de la Carcel*." In the sweet morning breeze they got married. We drank the golden gin fizzes, which made us a little bit sick. Then, as I drove Clara over to the baby-sitter's where she would spend the rest of the day and night, I got a traffic ticket. That's all right, I thought. That means nothing else can go wrong.

By the time I got back to the house the reception had started. The house acted as always like a boom box: it shuddered with sound. People got drunk too fast and there were a lot of people we didn't know. Office workers! Everything seemed slack and sad. Daddy stood in his usual place in the kitchen rolling joints and passing them out to disappear in the party. It was his duty by now. But the dope soaked up the conversation. I cursed the damn suckling pig. There wasn't enough food.

As the sun went down, I tried to get Tom to dance, but he wouldn't. A light mist fell and he sat in the living room, not looking out to the patio where the party was, but out on the other side, into the abyss of the canyon. I felt a wave of tired resentment. I'd worked so hard on this thing! And it was turning out to be a dud. By ten that night it was pretty much over. Lynda and Lisa and I worked putting leftovers away, Daddy hung around the kitchen making uneasy jokes. In the patio, Tom put furniture back the way it usually was.

I was on the stairs when I heard one of the last leaving guests say to Tom, "So how is Jennifer doing in school? Studying hard?"

And Tom said, "She's got exams right now, three courses, she's stressed." Jennifer, Tom's editorial assistant at RAND, whom he had mentioned every minute for two weeks after Clara had been born three years before, and then never mentioned again. *Jennifer?* And I got to have a true Jamesian epiphany.

On the porch I asked him, "Tom, are you sleeping with Jennifer?" The patio light caught his deep-set eyes. "Yes. Yes I am." He swayed from everything he'd drunk and smoked, and took a stack of dirty dishes into the kitchen.

A lie! It had all been a lie! The last five years and everything he'd said and our wonderful parties and the feeling that life was getting better—all that was a lie. I took a bottle of tequila and thrashed out into the field by our house. In the black night I screamed like a bat. "You fool!" I screamed. "You fool! How could you have done it?" It seemed to me that he must have been out of his mind to throw away a life and a family and a place and a direction. I rolled around in the wet ryegrass and sobbed. Over there in the house Tom and Lisa and my dad and his wife, Lynda, waited it out. It wasn't until years later that I figured a good part of those screams were retroactive and directed at my dad. *You fool!* How could you have done it? Thrown away a life, a family, a place, and a direction? Sure, Daddy, you said you "had to leave or go mad." I *get* it! I understand it. But what about me? You jumped ship, you bastard.

The next morning, when I came into my house covered with foxtails and leaves, poor Lynda was washing mountains of dishes from the party. Daddy looked like he wanted to kill himself. Lisa was out of sight, holed up downstairs. Tom and I went to pick up Clara from the baby-sitter. We parked and Tom talked. He still loved me. We drove Clara home and resumed our lives. Because he certainly wasn't going to see that *Jennifer* again.

Sometime during the six weeks after that, Rose's boyfriend Tony, who worked so hard for the phone company from midnight to eight in the morning, got off work early, right around three. He was pleased. He'd get a chance to sleep, and the next day he and Rose could go to the beach.

But when he got home, instead of finding Rose asleep, he discovered her wide-awake out in the kitchen, washing a sweater in the sink. It was funny, because she was wearing a sweater, and that was all she wore.

"What are you doing up so late?"

But Rose couldn't answer. Her teeth chattered so much she couldn't talk.

Tony looked at Rose for a minute or two and then began to search the house, looking behind the couch and under the bed until he finally opened the closet that had a naked man standing in it. Tony ignored the naked man and went back to get Rose. He punched her and punched her again and then pushed her down and banged her head against the floor so many times that the naked man began to get concerned. "Don't you think you might want to let up on her a little?" he asked, as he slipped into his jeans, grabbed his T-shirt, and made his way to the door.

And one night, three weeks after Jim had married Solveig and I'd found out about Jennifer, an hour-long monologue, Tom more-or-less changed and launched into The Limitations of Monogamy.

He jawed on for about fifteen minutes without, perhaps, noticing what he was saying and he'd just about gotten to the part about Wives and Children Killing Art when I hauled off and slugged him. I'd never done a thing like that before, but I was filled, for that one moment, with pure joy. One punch, to knock out about a decade of what were getting to be really tiresome lectures.

It was a language old Tom understood. He'd fought a dozen bouts in college, winning all except the last. Tom flew along the length of the couch, then laughed, then said something about getting it out of my system. He had a few knocks he wanted to get out of his system too. But it was never a question of "wife-beating." We duked it out fair and square—for the next three weeks.

The kids heard all this, of course, and took cover.

Six weeks after Jim's wedding, Tom decided he had to go down to Ensenada to go skin diving. Because life wasn't worth living if I didn't trust him. From the kitchen I watched Tom Sturak, brown, blond, high-strung, hosing down his wet suit, peering down into his snorkle, sharpening the spears on his speargun. Then came the weekend and he drove away. I had lunch at the Polo Lounge with an editor from Little, Brown, who told me I ought to be writing books. Either that information or tainted shrimp kept me throwing up all night.

The next day, Sunday, Tom was due home in the late afternoon. Clara came down with one of those classic kid fevers where I had to put her in a basin of cold water and alcohol to keep her from going into convulsions. (Or so Dr. Spock said.) About eight at night my trust dried up. I called the person Tom had gone fishing with and got his daughter.

"I just want to know if your dad is back yet."

"What?"

"I'd like to know if your dad is back yet, or if Tom is over there."

The little girl got fed up. "Oh Dad, you take this, will you? I can't remember what it was I was supposed to say."

Later on this Sunday night, after I'd looked up Jennifer's address in the phone book, I was down in Venice Beach, waiting for the happy couple. Clara was home, teeth chattering with fever, getting dunked in ice water every fifteen minutes by her harried sister. What a world. Tom had betrayed me and now I betrayed Clara and Lisa, leaving them to fend for themselves while I chose to play out a part in a hackneyed soap opera.

I'd never laid eyes on poor Jennifer. What got me is that all her luggage matched. Cream-colored Naugahyde, including one of those girlie-pieces in the shape of a hatbox that they advertised in the pages of *Seventeen*. She saw me and burst out crying. Tom started laughing. Jennifer's little house was bare and immaculate. It had African violets on the windowsills and one of Tom's shirts, blue with a white pinstripe, perfectly ironed and hanging from a doorknob. I'd wondered where that shirt was! Tom said, "I really love you both, you know."

He offered me an envelope of time; he sent me home first. I could have picked up the girls and left, but I was too scared. I stayed and the next hideous six months began: Tom and I fought over this little twenty-three-foot cabin, eleven and a half feet for him, the same for me. I refused to take alimony: how could I take money from such a slime? He happily agreed.

He'd said that no one with a PhD could write. But by sending off twenty pages about the carnaval in Mazatlán to a newspaper, and getting paid for it, I'd stolen Mazatlán, and stolen his dream of writing. If there were a gun around the house—except for that rifle it took fifteen minutes to load—he'd kill me. If there were a gun around the house, I'd kill him. He lived with Jennifer, and called me twenty times a day.

Insanely, we went to Europe for six weeks, because we'd already bought the tickets. Jennifer stayed home with a broken heart. Tom won a big race in Germany. We traveled to the far end of Slovakia, arriving late at night. Tom banged on the door. "I'm here to run the marathon!" he yelled. "Are you *crazy?*" someone yelled back. "Don't you know the Russians have invaded? There isn't going to *be* any marathon!" Tom was revolted. What kind of world was this, that war came before a marathon? Each night we'd decide if we were sleeping together or not. That determined the kind of hotel accommodations we got.

Then we were home and I was alone with Lisa and Clara in our house. I had actually thrown Tom out, put what was left of his clothes in two paper bags and told him to leave. I fed the kids lentils and instant hot cereal and black-eyed peas and Italian sausage and polenta. I loved polenta because you could look in the refrigerator and see it any time. Tom, by now out of the house and into a place of his own, was paying a hundred a month in child support. And I was making some money, writing for *TV Guide* and *Holiday* and *New West*. Each check, when it came, was enchanted money. There was never enough, but what there was belonged to me and the kids.

Lisa and Clara were having a hard time, I knew it, but it was rowdy, different from the tomb-hard times I remembered. I picked up a part-time job testifying in pornography trials. I went out with the defense lawyer. He had a nice disposition and looked like Sidney Greenstreet. The kids developed a tolerant exasperation that would last them eight years. Sometimes it wasn't that tolerant. But listen! The boat was sinking! Most mornings I woke up and wondered: will this be the day I go on welfare? But it never was the day.

I went out with an ex-priest who wore red gabardine slacks. Tom ran up the hill to check him out and ran down again without saying hello. I went out with a Pentagon colonel, who said he was going to bring lunch—which to me was wine and cheese, but to him was Coke and Twinkies. I never forgave him. We needed protein over at this house! I went out with (or had up to lunch) the brother of a famous celebrity who told me that his chief erotic thrill in life was exposing himself. I couldn't remember anymore what it was to be a regular person.

My friend Joan was, of course, divorced, with three children. My friend Judy had dumped her husband, left him and the kids to run off with a lawyer who promptly dumped her to run off with an eighteen-year-old who liked to drape her naked body in the American flag.

During this period I got an assignment to do a profile for *TV Guide* on Walter Huston, the old guy from *The Treasure of the Sierra Madre*. He told me that if you put all the Jews and niggers and Communists on one boat and then sank that boat, this would be a better world. When he disappeared into his trailer on the set a camera-boom operator told me that, yes, the guy was always like that. As I left, the old actor came up to me. "Sister, there's just one thing I don't want you to say."

I waited, my heart sinking. "Don't mention that I've got emphysema!"

The camera-boom operator called me a few times and then asked me out. The night after my last acid trip we went to an excellent French restaurant, where I had my first decent meal in months.

When he wasn't eating, Harvard Gordon talked all the time. When he wasn't eating and talking he was listening, in restaurants, or around the house. Everything struck him funny. He treated my girls with brusque cheerfulness, and they decided they liked him. We went through an Indian-food phase, all of us together, eating so much Indian food that our sweat smelled like curry. We went through a water-pistol phase, secreting water pistols around the house, soaking ourselves and soaking the furniture, screaming, roaring. One Sunday afternoon when Lisa, Clara, and I sat on our soaked couch, exhausted, Harvard came around the corner with the garden hose, turned on full blast.

Once, when I was worrying about money, he wrote me a $1,000 check, which I tore up, but never forgot the gesture. He gave me bracelets and a velvet cloak, and night after night after night, the four of us went out for dinner except when the two of us went out to dinner or Harvard cooked.

Harvard Gordon and me in the seventies. "Eat, drink, and be merry" would be the best way to describe Harvard.

Harvard was chunky—how could he not be, with all that eating? He wore dumpy khakis and tweeds, and a golf hat. His preferred mode of speech was the crazed monologue—usually about kinky sex at whatever set he was working on. He loved dumb stories, about how he used to surf in Hawaii, swim out with his buddies, tread water, and look into hotel windows where honeymooners, convinced there was nothing out the window except the sea, would outdo each other showing off in acrobatic sexual acts. Harvard and his surfing pals would laugh so hard they almost drowned. Or they would climb trees in Hawaiian parks, watch American sailors making out with their girlfriends, and laugh so hard they'd fall out of the trees.

Harvard would get a yearning for Armenian food, and for weeks at a time we'd have nothing around the house but basturma and lamogen—Armenian pizza and cured beef—and all the red wine you could pour down. He yearned to see Paris, and took me to find the perfect meal. I got so homesick for Lisa and Clara, I cried. The next year he took me *and* Lisa. We got so homesick for Clara we cried.

When Tom wasn't juggling his romantic life, he'd run up the path and circle the house and run down again, just checking. He'd still phone me ten times a day to remind me of my character flaws, one time calling me up to say, "Yeah? What do *you* want?" before he got flustered and hung up.

"You're always *doing*, you're never *being!*" he raved at me once during this period. "Why don't you do what Jackie Kennedy did, just *be!*" And another time, "You think you're the sun and I'm the moon, and you want to burn me to death, make me a *wasteland!*" And while Harvard and I stuck to good red wine, Tom came to one of Clara's birthday parties wearing a butterfly appliquéd directly to the crotch of his jeans and opined that "mescaline was a great teacher."

The second Christmas after Tom left, our family decided to rent a vacation chalet in Big Bear—a lake in the mountains that divide the suburbs of Los Angeles from the Mojave Desert. Leaving home for the holidays was a custom we'd follow for years. The first Christmas after Tom left, when he'd come up to be with us in Topanga Canyon, had been too heartbreaking.

For this one, Tom would be with us for Christmas Eve afternoon, then peel on out to pursue his social life. He was two-timing his girlfriend, and he kept me up-to-date on every deception. But the rest of us would be there. The "family" included my mother, Rose and Tony (he forgave her after the sweater incident), Lisa, Clara, Harvard in his golf hat, and me.

We put up the tree. Mother picked a bedroom and unpacked. We ate a buffet of cold things. Mother began to hit the Hill and Hill Blend. Harvard and I built a fire and we turned on the Christmas-tree lights. It was Christmas, for God's sake! We—Lisa, Clara, Rose, me—crowded into the little rustic kitchen, cleaning up. Rose was beginning to freak. She was scared to death of Mother. I put out some milk and cookies on the kitchen table. Clara was so little that her chin just hit the rim. She wore a pink trundle bundle, a little sleeping bag she could walk around in. Mother appeared in the door, as threatening as an armored car.

Rose began to shake. "Are you putting out those cookies for Santa Claus?" she asked me brightly.

Mother blinked in the light, then snarled, *"There isn't any Santa Claus!"*

"There is too, there is, there is!" Rose and I said, as Clara began to sob and Lisa sneered. Mother turned around, moved blindly to the door of one of the two bedrooms and disappeared, shutting the door behind her.

What was there to do?

Rose and Lisa began to giggle, nervously. Out in the living room, Tony opened up a daybed; Rose snuggled beside him. Lisa (who had been sewing and getting ready for this holiday for months) calmed Clara down. We hung up stockings. Harvard waited until Clara was asleep, her thumb in her mouth, her head on somebody's lap, and then began a series of pointless, lighthearted stories about blow jobs on different sets in Hollywood. Rose and Tony rolled some joints.

Then the door from the hall of the bedroom wing opened. A draught of freezing cold air blew in on us. We stopped talking. Dead silence. *What's going on? Is she coming in or going out? Or what?*

Flapping and snapping, a sheet floated out far into the living room, hung there, dropped slowly to the floor.

We stared into the dark doorway. *Snap!* Another sheet twanged out from the doorway, hung like a ghost in the middle of the room, then slipped down in collapse.

There were two twin beds to each bedroom, so eight sheets would zing out and into our decorated Christmas Eve. The assembled group included a child of four, a beautiful young girl of fourteen, a newly single mother in her middle thirties, her sister, who would be twenty on her next birthday, and two gentlemen friends, one a man who worked for the phone company (and took night classes in anthropology), the other the son of an Armenian doctor, a Stanford graduate who'd decided to spend his adult life surfing, traveling, and checking out the fine restaurants of the world. The lakeside chalet they were in was made for family holidays.

—

Those sheets flew out (carrying with them Kate Daly's heartfelt reminder that "you've got to take *shit!* Take *shit!* Take *shit!*") The gentlemen must have reflected upon the circumstances that brought them to this place. The adult sisters and the adolescent silently got their defenses in order for whatever would happen next. The toddler, with God's help, snoozed through it all. But I want to take a time out. Time Out! I want to look at it all again.

—

What's the pact here? What are the explanations, the expectations? The people in this living room are all pretty nice. They haven't committed any crimes. Even the woman who is slinging the sheets has worked hard for most of her life, nursed her dying mother, withstood divorce and widowhood, and has a devoted circle of friends. Somewhere out there, maybe even in the vacation chalet next door, families unself-consciously gather around a piano and sing carols. Grandmothers dandle children on their knees. Women gather in back bedrooms and gossip. Men kick back and watch sports events, or they sit at the kitchen table sorting out flies and lines, getting ready to rise at dawn, to go out and fish on the lake. In some houses in America (not just in situation comedies, not just in television commercials) people are reasonably happy.

Where is the division here? It doesn't have to do with a belief in God. As Irish Catholics, we were always ending up at a midnight mass. Our earlier Christmas stories have to do with poor Uncle Bob deliberately disregarding instructions for everybody taking communion to go up the center aisle and return by the side aisles. Drunk and terribly dignified, he goes up the side aisle and returns by the center aisle, while Aunt Helen sobs and my mother commiserates in a voice that can be heard by all.

Or Tom Sturak sits in at midnight mass in Victorville, where an Eastern European priest is telling a Christmas story: in an elementary school in Bucharest a Communist teacher is making his sixth graders stand up one by one and renounce the Lord Jesus Christ.

(Why he would *do* that instead of tackling beginning algebra is a real question, and Tom, who's had too much to drink, loudly addresses the question: "Why would anyone *do* that?") But one student won't renounce the Lord. He just doesn't feel like it. The Communist teacher taunts the kid. "If you believe in the Lord so much, why don't you ask him to come in the door right now?" Of course, in sails Jesus. "And that teacher," the Eastern European priest intones in barely understandable English, "is in an *insane asylum* today!" Tom Sturak calls out, "My God! Wouldn't you be too?" The congregation titters, my mother sobs, my aunt commiserates, and the mass goes on. So, no. It isn't religion that separates us from the happy few out there.

Is it politics? In my own lifetime the American middle class has taken some awful knocks. America is destroying itself. More specifically, America's middle and working classes are destroying themselves, with a little help from—could it be those Republicans over at the golf course?

We came from England and Ireland—mother countries. But mothers don't always have the best interests of their children at heart. Britain's Poor Laws weren't designed to help the poor, but to keep them under control. Thomas Carlyle had a plan for them: he wanted to harass them to death. Some people will do anything to keep up their country-club membership.

Karl Marx opined that "Religion is the opium of the people." Could he have overlooked the obvious: *Opium* is the opium of the people? *Alcohol* is the opium of the people? You can't engineer a revolution with a hangover. You're lucky to keep down a breakfast, lucky to get the laundry done, lucky to show up for work.

If I were a Republican on a golf course, I'd want a working class that was efficient but subdued, hardworking but depressed. I'd want them to have a low energy level. If my country was involved in a series of Asian wars during the twentieth century, I'd remember the curse and the cash crop of Asia, and I'm not talking about rice.

My sister Rose, a few years further into this story, will get turned on to heroin, not in a low dive in Europe, but at a joyful end-of-the-Vietnam-War party on the north shore of Oahu. "All the boys were coming home, and their duffle bags were stuffed with the very best Asian heroin!"

Couldn't the working class just say no to heroin, gin, Hill and Hill Blend? Maybe. But let's consider the woman snapping sheets out into the living room of the rented vacation chalet on the shore of Big Bear Lake. Or the unknown grandfather tipping forward to die in the snowdrift. Or that grandmother going into the bathroom late at night, pushing the barrel of a gun into her mouth. Let's consider the deceived wife, rolling around in weeds clutching a tequila bottle, screaming *you fool! you fool!* If that stuff is what you think of as *life,* how can you give up drugs and drink? If Uncle Bob doesn't set himself on fire on Thanksgiving, how do we know it's Thanksgiving?

I hope that some day a scholar will do a study—not just a biography—of the Kennedy family. They had enough money for the yachts and the house and the universities and the country clubs. But they couldn't shake the other stuff! The womanizing, the brutal dad, the forever-weeping mom, the son who said "She was never there for me, never!" And the other brother got killed in a hotel kitchen and another brother got drunk and drowned a secretary. (And the guys on the golf links breathed a collective sigh of relief.) Because who knows what the working class might do if it really got some education and money and power? It's already hard enough to get good steady help.

So, yes. I think that drugs and alcohol in America have a political base. They keep the underclass under.

Mother has snapped out another couple of sheets. I'm going to suggest two more aspects to this . . . *thing* that envelops America. Alcoholics and drug addicts are depressed. Now, in the last decade of the twentieth century, we're just beginning to understand depression (although my mother, even before her divorce, would spend whole days in her back bedroom sobbing, tugging at her hair, convinced that her head was in a vise). My father, in the last five years of his life, said that flowers grew everywhere but in his yard. Tom Sturak spent hours lamenting that he was "too little and too late." Richard See was convinced that he was "only smart enough to know how dumb he was." Many times, especially in the set of months after the sheet-Christmas, I had to think: what's the use? What's the point? What difference does any of it make?

Scientists say rather primly that "alcohol is a depressant." They measure blood levels and God knows what all, but—forgive me—

Tom Sturak before acid.   **Tom Sturak after.**

might they not be putting the cart before the horse? Alcoholics are *depressed.* And maybe that's why they drink alcohol? Why they snort cocaine? Why they smoke dope? Why they shoot heroin?

And what if *this* happens? What if depressives clan together in a series of genetic secret handshakes, so that depressed men meet depressed women and they breed depressed children and so on, in perpetuity?

Depressives think they're smarter than their compatriots. That's why they struggle with scholarly papers on Hemingway, while their happy classmates take engineering classes and don't even worry about the atom bomb. They pay off their mortgages, invest wisely, coach Little League teams, sing in the choir, and look around for good country clubs. (And maybe a few of them once in a while do slide off into the abyss, hit the rehab clinic, perish from AIDS.)

Drugs and drink deaden the disappointments of American life. In some countries—let's say the Netherlands—a house painter never entertains the thought of a lovely home, money in the bank, a thriving career, a chance at transcendent love—the whole American kit and caboodle. If he has a few beers, he just has a few beers. In *America* (I see the fifth and sixth sheets snapping now, and I remember there are only eight sheets back there, two to each bed, two beds to a room) the people in trailer parks drink, the kids in the slums do crack cocaine, the wannabe rock musicians shoot heroin, the sobbing wife cracks open the Southern Comfort, the mail-order merchant hides his scotch in a desk drawer. *Because there was supposed to be more to it than this.* There really was.

Can it be that the system is totally rigged? That when they repealed Prohibition, they did it for tax purposes? That California's biggest cash crop, marijuana, is there for a reason? That kids are killing each other in unspeakable slums so that the guys on the golf course don't have to be bothered? Has America become the old country again, and all in a few hundred years? Is the American Dream, to put it bluntly, nothing more than a sham and a crock? Oh, no no no no no. That can't be right! And so the merchant opens up his scotch, the hippie shuts her eyes and holds out her arm for a hit, the divorced novelist rummages through the cupboards for the Cinzano, and the camera-boom operator puts another case of twenty-year-old burgundy into a temperature-controlled bin. The disappointed woman in the bedroom wing of the Big Bear chalet takes a hard slug of Hill and Hill Blend straight from the bottle, makes a terrible face, and strips down the last twin bed in the icy bedroom. She bundles one sheet under her left arm and tucks up the other in her right. She knows how to snap a sheet, she's been doing it forever! She snaps first one and then the other, taking time to note the sheep-looks on her family's sheep-faces. There's nothing she can say to them about the tragedy of her life, and so she snaps the sheets.

—

The next morning I wake up on a bare mattress with blankets piled inefficiently around me. It's freezing in this room. I try to remember where I am and where the others are. Lisa took one bedroom and kept Clara with her. Rose defiantly kept on sleeping in Tony's bed out in the living room, since she thought that's what sent Mom into her fit. Mother took one twin bed in here and I took a bed in this room with her. With *her*.

My head is splitting. We put away some brandy last night after the wine ran out. Christmas morning, my second Christmas since Tom left me. I'm sleeping in a bed without sheets next to my mother. I know Rose is leaving the country soon, she can't stand her life the way it is now. I think of Lisa, who asked for only one thing after the divorce, a sewing machine. She's had her head bent over a sewing machine since the week Tom left—working, working. I think of Clara, all child-bluster and bitten fingernails. She started biting them when Tom and I took that stupid trip to Europe. How could we have done any of this?

I think of the future and I don't see anything. I don't see anything at all. Then . . . I begin to get an awful feeling at the small of my back. I hear . . . tap tap tap! My mother's nails drumming on a hard surface. With a feeling of dread I turn over to face her bed.

She's sitting straight up on the mattress ticking, fully dressed in polyester slacks, clean blouse, Orlon cardigan sweater. Her face is bright; she's ready to talk.

"Do you know that man you brought up here? *He sleeps with his hat on!*"

After this holiday episode, I begin to lose heart. It's so hard, so hard to keep things going. It takes me forever to write out the bills— I never learned how to do it before. I have terrible times with editors: one of them locks me in an office until I get a 1,500-word piece right. Lisa learns to drive. Her dad gets her a car. She begins wearing turbans and staying out late. I take Clara in for a new school wardrobe and unerringly pick up a bunch of stuff in polyester: the poor kid has to go to school in pink polyester.

But Tom perceives that things might be getting better for me—or at least that's what *I* perceive—because he cranks up his case against me. Maybe it's because the actual legal divorce is finally going through. He calls me more often than when we were married. I look out of the kitchen window and see him pacing the patio at all hours: "This is *my* house, *my* house!"

I go so far as to put a spell on the house, scattering ashes and praying: "If anyone lives at this house except me and my children, may they get sick and die an awful death!"

Talking (screaming) to Tom on the telephone about which of us is going to pay the property taxes this one last year before the divorce comes through, or why he stole certain Mexican records when he knew I was out of the house, I feel myself beginning to lose it. We begin calling each other to hang up on each other. Sometimes we don't even say anything at all, just call, hang up. We've got to get every last insult in before the papers are signed.

"You live every day as if it's the first day of your life!" Tom says.

"I do *not*," I reply, stung to the core. "I live every day as if it's the *last* day of my life."

"It's the same thing," he replies grumpily. But he picks up on this theme a week or so later. My magazine pieces are beginning to come out and Tom says: "*Sidney* says you write every sentence as if it's your very last sentence."

Sidney? Sidney's the guy who pretended he was going spearfishing with Tom, and he's got the fucking *nerve* to comment on my prose style? Nevertheless, I ponder, and try to tone the prose style down. (And to get over it about Sidney, since my friend Judy went off to join her lover—who got dumped by the naked girl in the American flag—on the Island of Yap, and I've been covering for her for two weeks now, saying, to the man who *thinks* he lives with her, and that she's visiting me, "Oh, she just stepped out." Yeah, stepped out of this house, down the switchback path, and eight thousand miles across the Pacific Ocean.)

The glass of Cinzano sticks to my hand so steadily that when I have pictures taken for the jacket of my first novel, it's there in the picture.

I get so strung out that I scream at Tom on the phone, "All right! You can have everything, you weasely little scum, you black-hearted lying bastard! You can have EVERYTHING! You can have the Mexican records, TAKE THEM ALL! You can have all the first editions, you BOOK SNOB! And all the good pictures, TAKE THEM, TAKE THEM! But there's one thing you can never have, never, never, NEVER! You can't have MY GOOD OPINION!" (But Tom takes no more than his fair share of stuff.)

I drive the kids down to Cardiff, where my father lives with Lynda and my brand-new half brother—thirty-five years younger than I am—Brother Bob. He's a big baby, calm and placid. I complain to my father, I cry. But my father has gone through some changes. Maybe it's because he finally has a son. Maybe it's because my howling reminds him way too much of my mother. Whatever it is, he seems unmoved by my grieving.

Wynn, his AA wife, is finally dying. The cancer has caught up with her. Wynn's mother has called my dad, asking for money to pay the hospital bills. He's told her no, and is having Lynda answer the phone now. There's no way he's going to pony up, and no way he's going to talk to her. Lynda doesn't venture an opinion. But I hit the ceiling. "She was your *wife*." He looks at me, uncomprehending as a steer. *"She was your wife."* I can't help it, I just don't get it. I'm astonished at how these guys can be married, death-do-us-part, and it's all a total lie, they're scot-free, they've been lying from the beginning: they help you out the way cats help mice.

I call Wynn up, to say good-bye. She mentions God, her Old Friend, and how she's not worried about death. But she doesn't sound as confident as before. The last thing she says to me is, "I always loved you, Penny."

Rose by this time has dumped the steady Tony. She's taken up with a Hungarian named Ferenç and has been conning my mother for enough money to leave the country. I get a postcard from Rose. She's left without telling me. She has a way of sneaking out. She sounds happy and says she's living with Ferenç in a tree.

Now Clara and I live pretty much alone in our little house. Lisa spends most of her time with her boyfriend. Tom has taken up with a new woman. He hasn't dumped Jennifer yet, but it's coming. The new woman soaks up a lot of his time; he doesn't call ten times a day anymore. Sometimes he goes weeks without calling. I've been so tough on Harvard that I go weeks without hearing from him. Clara, who's five by now, doesn't sleep downstairs but upstairs in the double bed with me. When she goes to sleep, the silence is some goddamn silence. I've never heard anything like it.

My first novel has come out and sunk like a stone. I don't know what happened. I thought it was pretty good.

I don't even feel like going out anymore with those weird divorce-fish at the bottom of the sea. Besides, I know by now I can't be trusted more than anybody else.

When Clara leaves for school in the morning, I'm alone. I cry the day away, just like my mother. One afternoon in 1969, after five or six hours of this, I pick up the phone and call the Suicide Prevention Clinic. I tell them I can't stand it.

"Are you holding a weapon?" the voice asks urgently. "Have you taken any pills?"

It's as if someone has pulled a commonsense lever in my chest. Well, *no*! I'm only saying I can't stand it! I'm *certainly* not going kill myself this afternoon! (And I'm reminded of my mother, who used to threaten suicide so often when I was a kid that when I grew up I'd tease her about it, saying that if I had a nickel for every suicide threat she'd made, and invested it wisely, we'd all be millionaires.)

The voice, just a little vexed, refers me to a woman psychologist. I get the first six meetings free.

I hang up and call the woman to make the appointment. No one in our family or in our circle of friends has done anything remotely like this before. This is far stranger than going to Europe or going to college or dropping acid or even writing a novel.

Our whole heritage, as far back as I can remember, and including everything I've heard about, has been about suffering. That's been a *given,* like a stain on your suit, a birthmark on your cheek. What I think—and I can hardly formulate the thought, since I'm winding down from a daylong crying jag, and a domestic explosion that's lasted for years or maybe a century, and gone through all our family—is: what if we could manage a way to try to sneak out from under all this? What if we could all manage to sneak out?

PART II

Mother and Rose.

After Tony beat Rose up so badly, she began to take a look at her options. The carefree sex life she'd told me about on our acid trip wasn't exactly as easygoing as she'd portrayed. When she was still an au pair girl she'd been screwing some guy on the couch and felt so incredibly sad about everything that her vagina had actually done that thing people joked about: it had clamped down on the poor guy. It was terribly painful and terribly embarrassing.

Her boyfriend Tony bored her to tears. He was good and kind, but his idea was: go to work. Go to the movies. Take a class, hear a lecture, buy a few beers, smoke some dope, zone out in front of the

TV, sleep, surf, be peaceful. It worked, off and on, but it wasn't going to work forever. Then, one night, a girlfriend came over to visit, and brought a friend with her. Ferenç Balaz. "I could see he was interested in me. He was funny and smart and different. He was exactly my age, born in 1950. We were both twenty-one. He was Hungarian, his father had been a Freedom Fighter, and he and his mother were refugees, living in Basel, Switzerland. He'd come over to America with this chick. I think he saw a meal ticket. Her father was a studio musician. Ferenç wanted a music career. He played the guitar and he was good.

"But the girl was *so dumb*! She kept bringing him around. By that time I'd inherited the little money that was still left to me from my dad's trust fund. So Ferenç just ramrodded into my life. We took off in my Volks and drove north. Then we stopped in Big Sur and we were sitting in a meadow by a river and he was smoking hash right out in the open. He never got it that what you could do in Europe you couldn't do over here! So up comes a ranger and a great big dog and busted him. So already they wanted to deport him! But, as I remember, we bailed out, cash. We bailed out.

"And not too much longer after that, we took our first trip to Europe. Ferenç figured it was time to go back to where he knew what he was doing. He regretted losing his family ties. He kept waiting for me to pull rabbits out of the hat, but I didn't have any. What we did do, though, was go all the way on up to Northern California where your friend Marina was living by then, remember? We slept out in back of her tent in sleeping bags and we bought ten thousand hits of acid for ten cents apiece. Blotter acid on those clear sheets of paper? We just put them inside a book and put the book in a suitcase. We sold the acid in Basel for six dollars a hit."

Rose and Ferenç stayed with his mother in a fourteenth-century building that had been completely renovated. This was Switzerland, middle-class land of poor old Tony's dreams, but Rose was living there with shifty Ferenç. "It wasn't scroungy Europe," Rose would say. "There was no poverty. Everything ran. Everything worked. But we didn't stay long that first visit. We stayed through the winter. I got every virus there was. And we didn't do many drugs then. Just an occasional pipe of hash." When I ask her what Ferenç was like in those days, she says, "I would say he treated me the way Tom treated you. Like I was an idiot. Of course, he spoke five languages and I only spoke one. So to him I *was* an idiot! So we lived in this good place, you could cross the street and be in Germany—I had a German dentist—and you could take the train to Paris to buy clothes. But I didn't know the language. I didn't know Swiss-German. I felt very isolated over there. I was very sad. I was very lonely."

They came back to LA, smuggling in reverse, purchasing quantities of hash and opium for almost nothing, returning in the summer of 1972, when they settled in with me for approximately one week. Divorced by then, teaching sedately at a Catholic college, I was now infatuated with an entertainment lawyer who was on his own sixties quest of going back to nature in Bolinas, California (and trying to find a woman who would put up with his mean-spirited ways). He had already worked his way through two of my women friends—Joan and Judy—and had settled, like a sweet leech, on me.

That's why it took me about a week to notice that when before Rose and Ferenç had moved into our little cabin the phone had rung maybe ten times a day, now it rang about two hundred times a day, with desperate, harassed voices saying into the phone: "Melrose and

Vermont, northwest corner in two hours," or "Sheraton Hotel, the lobby, nine tonight." I was too busy to notice that two professional drug dealers had moved into my house.

I couldn't stand Ferenç. He looked as if he hadn't had a bath since childhood—though in fact he hogged the bathroom and repeatedly used up all our hot water. He also hogged the television set, always finding terrible shows like *Let's Make a Deal* and then sneering, "Isn't that America in a nutshell? *Let's make a deal!*" But that didn't mean he ever stopped watching *Let's Make a Deal.*

Finally, I told Rose that they had to move out—and they couldn't use the phone for their dope deals. To tell the truth, I was scandalized at what they were doing, and what she had become. Rose and Ferenç did move out—to the patio. They came in to take showers, and they sat restfully in the patio all day, except for when they went out to sell drugs.

The killer question was: what had happened to my sister Rose? In my eyes, she'd gone from the sweet, horridly put-upon victim of my mother, the scapegoat of a desert town, a funny girl, a real sister who could ask me: "Penny, are you strong?" to a fairly scary criminal. Or if she wasn't, she certainly hung out with a criminal, and he had a bad personality besides. When I tried to talk to her about it, she just glanced away like a bad female in a Raymond Chandler novel.

One day on the patio they were joined by a pale, tiny, petrified Swiss teenager named Tom-Tom. I was at the end of my rope by then. My ex-husband Tom was yelling that he, in fact, *owned* half of the patio, and my sordid relatives had to vacate the premises at once. The entertainment lawyer, whom my daughters detested, had invited the three of us to spend a long weekend in Bolinas, at his lovely farmhouse with two private lakes. (But he'd already begun to tell me, in a series of circuitous conversations, that he felt my daughters were sadly lacking. I'd been a bad mother to them, and it would actually be to their advantage if I packed them off to their respective fathers for the rest of their/our lives. Then he and I could live in Bolinas forever.)

I knew there were grave things wrong with this logic, but as I'd try to pin this elusive emissary of the Devil down, Ferenç would sashay through the house wrapped in nothing but a skimpy towel, brandishing a bar of soap, on his way to his third shower of the day.

The momentous weekend in the meadows of Bolinas was coming up. Lisa and Clara might even have been looking forward to it. But here were these three reprehensible hard druggies on the patio, and Screaming Tom having a tantrum about his property rights.

I told Rose I was going away for two days and that she was absolutely not allowed in the house. I locked the upstairs and the downstairs, gave the key to a neighbor, and told Tom what I had done. For once we were in agreement, since stealing seemed to be Ferenç's second hobby after dealing dope.

The next day, a Saturday, in the middle of the morning in Bolinas paradise, where the girls and I had been fed a squash casserole in the shape of a mandala, escorted back to check out the two exquisitely beautiful private lakes, and refreshed with cinnamon rolls and wonderful coffee, the phone rang. The lawyer answered it, and handed it to Lisa. His face registered prissy distaste that any *teenager* should receive a phone call within the confines of his very own farmhouse.

Lisa's face looked suddenly intent. "What are you saying, Rose? What packets? What nineteen packets? Nineteen packets of *opium*? No, I did *not* take any nineteen packets of opium!"

I grabbed the phone and heard a hysterical Rose accuse my daughter Lisa of stealing nineteen packets of opium and planning to sell them for enormous profit—perhaps even now, up in Bolinas.

The entertainment lawyer, with his look of prissy superiority, hung back. He was Jewish and very rich, and he *knew* he was looking at white trash. Rose insisted, sounding crazy, saying, "Because if she didn't, who did? They were at the bottom of her chest of drawers. Down there, in her own room, where she sleeps."

All this made for a good deal of discussion, Lisa denying, Clara crying, the attorney sneering, and me trying with a pitiful lack of success to be a grown-up. But I was angry now. Marijuana, sure. Everybody did it. Acid, yes! It was the key to the Divine. Mescaline, sure. We were just out of the sixties, after all. But *nineteen packets of opium?* That was dark, fetid, low, criminal. And they'd been hiding it in my daughter's room.

We decided there was nothing we could do about Rose and her sidekicks. We would wait until we came home on Sunday night. We spent the afternoon swimming and watching hawks float across the perfect blue sky, listening to Van Morrison, picking apples and nasturtiums. It was heaven, all right.

Except that on Sunday morning my screaming ex-husband called, and he didn't even need to use a telephone, you could have heard him without one, straight from LA. He was incoherent with rage. I couldn't get his tirade clear, but it had to do with Rose and "his" half of the house. I listened to his voice and watched Lisa, distancing herself from it all, Clara looking forlorn and pale, and the attorney looking prissier than ever. I was deeply, deeply into my own ongoing persona of the hardworking woman-alone-with-two-children (except that, of course, here I was, picking flowers with a man who hated children).

I agreed to meet Tom with the kids that night as soon as we got off the plane in LA, at the China Palace—a low-priced haven for harried divorcées and all their children. A safe place, because Tom sounded violent. But that night, as we ate dried sautéed string beans and moo-shoo pork, even as Tom told the story, he began to laugh. He'd gone up at dawn that Sunday morning to check on "his half of the house"—all eleven and a half feet of it—and peering through a window into the living room, found the remains of a landmark party. Beer cans, liquor bottles, chairs turned over, and a few unconscious people passed out cold. Livid with rage, he went downstairs, and found, sleeping in Lisa's bed, the very tiny Tom-Tom, just in from Basel. (*He* was the owner of the nineteen packets of opium: they were his grubstake for a new life in America.) Tom began to roar at this intruder but soon realized that the little kid couldn't understand a word. "So I was reduced," Tom said, grinning in spite of himself, "to yelling, '*Aus! Aus! It's my house!*'" Tom-Tom, terrified, put the pillow over his head and prayed in Swiss-German that the foreign monster would go away.

Fuming, Tom ran down our switchback path to check with our neighbors in the Canyon. They confirmed that, yes, there had been a landmark party, and yes, a young woman had gotten the key to the house by saying she was my maid. As mad as only Tom Sturak could get, he ran back up the switchback path. About halfway up, next to a sappy homemade "statue," a papier-mâché and plaster-of-Paris construct of a guy hitchhiking up the long and tiring trail, Tom encountered Rose, naked under a flowered wrapper, taking a morning stroll, sipping coffee. In his own words, he unleashed a tirade. "I gave it everything I had," he said now, in the China Palace, "and she wasn't even scared. She started yelling right back at me! She called me a *cocksucker*! You could hear it all over the Canyon!"

Tom had thrown them all out. Poor Tom-Tom was so terrified and traumatized by the whole thing that he took the next plane home to Switzerland.

Talk about mixed emotions. Rose had stood up to Tom. What reckless courage! You had to admire it. Except that she'd lied to me, she'd broken into my house, she'd dealt dope out of the house, she'd stashed it there. She had done, in effect, all of the kinds of things that my mother had accused her of. I was furious that Rose had put my job and my children and me in jeopardy, but what made me maddest of all was that somehow she had maneuvered me into a position of agreeing with my mother.

I cut Rose off. She couldn't come to my house anymore and jeopardize my life. Through all this, she didn't seem to understand that she'd done anything wrong. I knew as long as she stayed with Ferenç she'd be like this. The thought of heroin also crossed my mind. Because the feeling was, then, that if you did heroin, you'd gone over. You were a different kind of person. There wasn't any coming back. Of course, from Rose's point of view, I was the third person in our family—after our mother and Aunt Helen—to betray her.

That was in the early summer of 1972. During the next eighteen or twenty-one years—depending on how I count—I only saw her six times. The first five times crowded into the first two or three years. I visited her once at Sybil Brand Jail. I met her once for breakfast at Nate 'n' Al's, a Beverly Hills deli mainly for television comedy writers. My mother was with me. We got there early and went to the women's room. It was small in there. Another woman looked up from applying her lipstick and said, "Hello, Mother." Of course, Mother didn't recognize her. I saw Rose again at Nate 'n' Al's with a new boyfriend, Michael, who asked me wistfully, "Do you yell as much as Rose does?" (But Rose looked beautiful and well-dressed and composed and had a new Vidal Sassoon haircut. I, on the other hand, was beginning to fray.) I saw her again in Beverly Hills, with Michael, at the Swiss Café. The maître d' told me never to bring those people in again. "Don't worry," I said with feeling, "I won't." The last time I saw Rose was at Loyola Marymount University, where I worked as a nervous assistant professor of English. She'd come to visit, she said, but she was clearly frantic. Nuns and priests strolled past my office as she told me she had a terrible case of genital herpes, could barely walk, and desperately needed twenty-five dollars. I wrote her the check and told her I was too busy for lunch. Rose left, crying.

That would be the last time I'd see her until I caught up with her two decades later in a rehab in East Oakland, smiling and looking unbearably sweet, and then in her own apartment. But we wouldn't really spend time together until the summer of 1993—on the quiet island of Alameda, in an apartment next to a lagoon, where mother ducks quacked at long strings of ducklings—when we started getting to know each other again. Eighteen to twenty-one years, and for at least fifteen of those we didn't have clue one about Rose and about her life. She was lost; she was gone.

———

After getting tossed out of the Topanga house, Rose and Ferenç found a place in Silverlake. A week or so later, Ferenç got arrested for smoking a joint out on the street with some friends and went to jail. He promptly got raped and Rose called me in an attempt to get me to put up my house for his bail. I told her she was living in a dream world.

"Well, when he got out he knew there was going to be trouble, so on June 18, 1972, we drove on out to the Calabasas courthouse to get married, to keep him from being deported. It was just my friend Kathy Rosalez, his friend Larry, and me. I knew this had the makings of an adventure. This was getting to be a wild story!

"Then the rest of that summer I must have snapped out of it. I worked at Alice's Restaurant in Westwood. I made seventy, eighty dollars a night and that's *after* I tipped the busboys. We had to wear long scarves and dresses, the whole hippie deal. I saved all that money and told Ferenç that we had to go to Hawaii. I was sick of LA. That would be the fall of '72. The minute we landed Ferenç went into this depression on me. I guess he felt he was another three thousand miles away from where he wanted to be. But he got over it pretty quick. All he needed was his guitar and people welcomed him anywhere. We got out of Waikiki right away and went to the north shore of Oahu. We stayed there through Christmas, until the money ran out. Then, it was either go home or *try to stay there*! I was up for trying to stay there.

"We wanted to see Kauai. And that was the high point of my life. We stayed at Taylor's Camp. And then, you know, the island is round. There's an eleven-mile stretch where the road ends. We hiked into it. I was crying because I was so exhausted. But when you got there it was the most beautiful place in the world. It was paradise. We put our little tent into a cave. We took our showers under a waterfall. We'd take hikes to places nobody had ever been. You know those hippies, they said the next valley over was the Valley of the Lost Tribe—fair-haired people who had lived there long ago and then just disappeared. You had to swim out and around a cliff to get there, and we thought we were their descendants. We didn't have any acid, but we got high on mushrooms that grew on cow piles. The minute you got there people would say 'get up early in the morning and try the mushrooms that grow on the cow piles.' So you'd get them at dawn and clean them under the waterfall. They tasted *horrible* but a couple of hours later you were in another world and it was much better than acid, because it was natural.

"You had to bring all your provisions in from Taylor's Camp, but all you really needed was rice and beans, because there was fish and fruit and everything you needed. But then, in March, when the rains came, it was going to be too dangerous to hike the trail. So we hiked out from Kalalau back to Taylor's Camp. That was just flat beach, but it had fresh running water. There were a lot of people from New York there, living on food stamps. And all these elaborate tree houses. But I don't know, *you can't stay forever on the beach!* There were times I'd be at the beach and I'd think—there's nothing here between me and Alaska. And the Stones were coming to Oahu, so we went back over. Now come the life-changing events! Here is where history comes in.

"When Ferenç and I decided to go back to Oahu in the spring of 1973, Nixon was bringing the troops home. The troops are *all over* Oahu. They are *happy!* And they're all bringing their heroin back. So, at a welcome-home party out on the North Shore, that's the very first time I fixed it. *Everybody* was doing it. It was as common as passing a joint around. We were living at the North Shore at the time, and we had a very nice place. I was pretty happy in my life. But you know? I just stuck out my arm and closed my eyes and somebody stuck the needle in. I wouldn't have to stick a needle in my own arm for over two years.

"I still talk about that moment, that first time. I LOVED IT! Other people say they got sick their first time, but that's probably because they use dirty Mexican stuff. This was pure Asian. It was like the missing link for me. I thought: for the first time, I'm a whole human being. Walking on the beach, starting to come down, I already wanted more. My sponsor says he's been doing some work, some research, and he feels the genetic . . . *thing* that makes you an alcoholic is the same thing, the same genetic thing that makes you love heroin. Like, later, I'd choose being sick rather than do something like morphine. I just couldn't see it. I wanted the *heroin!*"

In the spring of 1973, Rose and Ferenç made it back to LA. Rose went to work as a waitress again, while Ferenç began to panic. "By this time, he was more in love with me than I was with him. And around this time we met Frank. Frank could always get heroin and Ferenç was off and running. It was different stuff, Mexican, and I'd always throw up. We'd do it once or twice a week, always with Frank. The hearings were coming up, and more and more I'm thinking, *I do not want to go back to Europe!* We had to spend days down at the INS. It was terrible. Finally, they gave him an ultimatum: leave by August or go to jail.

"So he called his mom and she came through. She sent us two one-way tickets to Frankfurt. We're both twenty-three by that time. Ferenç could never come back to the United States because he had two felony counts of possession. *But guess who didn't want to leave with him?!* The night before we were supposed to leave I said I was going out to the liquor store to get some cigarettes. Then I went over and hid with the girl who lived next door to Frank and his mom. I *knew* Ferenç would have to be on the plane the next day. He had no other choice. So I hid, and waited until the plane had already taken off before I went back to the house. It was probably the most exciting thing, as far as what a woman goes through, as anything I've ever done. So I stayed in our house and once in a while got high with Frank.

"But you know what Ferenç's mother did? She sent me another ticket. And I was already sleeping with Frank! It wasn't easy. I did *not* want to go." And still Rose can't or won't say why it is that she finally went, except for a throw-away sentence—"You're never poor or hungry in Switzerland."

It took a couple of months, but in the fall of 1973 Rose landed in Frankfurt to be reunited with her husband. He was waiting for her at the airport. "I was crying so hard when I got off the plane. But one of the first things he said was, 'Don't worry, honey, don't worry. I'll go out and get some stuff and you'll feel better about it tonight.' And that was that. That was that."

Rose had mixed feelings about Switzerland. It was clean, heroin was cheap—"ten dollars a night for both of us, just what you'd spend for a good bottle of wine"—and she got to furnish their own apartment, all from scratch. Rose's mother-in-law, a fabric merchant, took her to Paris to pick up more good clothes. Ferenç got up early and—just as a devoted husband brings coffee to his wife in the morning—he would cook up some stuff, go over to the still-sleeping or drowsy Rose, ask her to stick out her arm, and then go off to work.

"But I never liked Switzerland. Especially Basel. It's such a *drug* town! It's such a company town!

"There's only one industry there, the drug industry. Ciba-Geigy, and Hoffman La Roche, who invented Valium, and Sandoz—that's where they discovered LSD. So they *live* off drugs. But everybody in Basel gets up at exactly the same time and goes off to do pretty much the same work and they come home at pretty much the same time, and then they do their little laundry and they eat and go to bed. But I'm going to say, Ferenç had this *amazing* job at Hoffman La Roche. You know those little brochures you find in doctors' offices, advertising a particular kind of medicine? Well, Ferenç would go off to work, perfectly loaded on heroin. And they'd hand him a stack of magazines. His job was to look through the magazines for pictures of people who might need a Valium. You know, like a tired mother with children pulling at her skirt? Or a man with a briefcase who's just missed his train? Then Ferenç would give all these pictures to the Hoffman art department and they'd show up in doctor's brochures with the caption 'If you have a patient who looks something like this, chances are, he or she needs a Valium.' *I* even worked, believe it or not, giving little tours of Hoffman. Because all kinds of people would come through, but the common language was English. That was, like, February of '74. And we used and used and used and used.

"But, God, I hated the routine. I was raised in California, for Christ's sake, where you had 7-Elevens! In Basel, if you wanted milk, and if the stores were closed, you were out of luck. In the apartment they even told us what days and hours to do our laundry. I was— like, I'm from California! I'm gonna do my laundry whenever I want! This is a free country! But Switzerland wasn't a free country. So they thought I was the belligerent American chick. And even though I was loaded I couldn't get used to it."

Once, Ferenç and Rose were busted: "They came in, the po-lice, at five or six in the morning. I just didn't expect it! They have two jails there in the city, the jail for real offenses, and the interrogation jail. They put us into the interrogation jail, without our ever having been charged. It turned out they could keep us there as long as they liked. It was like with the laundry and the 7-Elevens. I was, like, 'I'm an American citizen! You have to have me up in front of a judge within seventy-two hours! You can't just keep me here. Call the American Consulate! If I don't see a judge within seventy-two hours, you have to let me go!'

"But they just laughed at me. They spoke to me in German and turned around and shut the door. It was my actual first time in jail and it was like a good hotel. I had a room of my own, but I had no one to talk to. In America it's horrible, but at least you have people to talk to. I stayed there around five or seven days. They didn't want us, they wanted our connection, and they weren't going to let us out until they got him. They wouldn't let us get to a phone to warn him. We were all waiting until Pépé got back from Amsterdam. As soon as they caught him they let the rest of us little mice go. You know, they *say* Switzerland is a democracy, but this whole experience made me glad I was an American.

"So then, our life went on. We worked. His mother would take me to Paris and buy me more clothes." When I ask her where, Rose shrugs and says, "God, I don't know. I was loaded all the time." Then she fills me in about her mother-in-law, whom she never calls by name. "His mother had been in a concentration camp. She'd gotten a disease in her eye, and she really couldn't see out of it. She'd get checks from the Nazis all the time. Her brother threw himself in front of a garbage truck when he was still in the camp and committed suicide, he got so depressed. She got compensation for that, too. But her business partner was German, I don't know how she could stand it . . ."

Not only that, her husband had been killed in the Hungarian uprising against Russian occupation, and now here she was in Basel with a son who was a dope fiend, who cut out pictures from magazines for a living, and his space-cadet young wife who couldn't or wouldn't do her laundry on time, who couldn't speak the language, who was loaded out of her mind, and who was sinking deeper, faster, and further into a serious depression: "I remember being sick for the first time, when we couldn't get any stuff. It was, OK, we won't do it again! But as soon as we got some, of course we *did* do it again. I was very very very lonely. There was nobody to talk to. It was *so* sad and lonely. Then, in March or April of '74, his mother got the idea to put us both in the detox. It was spring, and beautiful in the Swiss countryside. Ferenç had to go to all these counseling sessions but I didn't understand the language so I didn't have to. I'd go outside in the hills and relax with a book.

"And the Swiss detox, that was my first experience of methadone. I liked it. It gave me back . . . my self-confidence and energy. You remember that old TV commercial where a man is just standing there and somebody throws a baseball at him but it doesn't hit him because he's got his COLGATE SHIELD? It's like an invisible suit of armor. You can drink, but not too much, something like eggnog at Christmas. It's like having all the benefits of the heroin experience without being loaded. The Germans originally invented it, did you know that? During World War II, when all the morphine was going, gone, and Hitler said, 'Can't you guys come up with some sort of a synthetic?' So methadone came from that war.

"Even now, they give methadone to terminally ill patients. They start with five milligrams. A block dosage of forty milligrams, what you give a dope fiend, is eight times what you give to a terminally ill person. What methadone does, it fills up all your chemical receptors, so you don't want anything else. And if you *did* take anything else, it would probably kill your liver. So with methadone, you don't ever get sick. And we stayed there at the detox about six weeks. And the Swiss health insurance *paid the rent on our apartment* for when we were gone. Can you imagine?

"In Switzerland, it's so easy. Drugs are right *there* for you. In America you have to do crimes and go to terrible jails. If I'd been in America then—I'm not sure!—I'm not sure I would have gotten to where I did. But in Switzerland, at that time, it didn't really sink in what I'd done to myself. So after the hospital, we stayed clean for a while. I worked in a hotel restaurant, but they put me in back with the wine and the espresso, where I didn't get any tips. And I had to work a split shift. I was *so* tired! I worked very hard and got very depressed. Then . . . I got a little kitten. And we'd go out for jaunts in the countryside. We tried to have a family life . . .

"But we started in *again*. Actually, it wasn't too bad of a habit. But it was there. His mother came up with the suggestion that maybe if we separated for a while, things might get better. She had two propositions: I could go to the States, or they'd send me on a holiday to Spain or Portugal. Of course, I said I'd take the ticket to LA. It wasn't so *bad* in Switzerland, I guess. We went skiing. Or, really what happened, he made me go and for three days I tried. And we went down to Lake Lugano. And we'd *always* be going to Amsterdam for drugs. But the Swiss were starting to ask me questions, like, how long are you going to stay? I'd made it up to green-card status, but there was no way I was going to stay. My love for Ferenç had just worn off.

"The day after I came back was the day Nixon resigned. I went to stay with Kathy Rosalez at first. I was a little bit sick, a little bit shaky, but not much. But right away I went back again, to Frank. You know that classic phrase, *a man turns you out to drugs?* Frank taught me all that. All the thievery and the petty scams and the low, low life that we lived! The famous shoplift-refund scam—you could make hundreds! At Robinson's, The Broadway, Robinson's Beverly Hills.

"You dress up as nice as you can, then you go out to shop. You go in and pick up a real expensive sweater. You don't even leave the store! You just walk up to the counter in another department and get the refund—you don't need receipts. Robinson's had no cash limit. I was better at it, and did more of it, than Frank did. We had a little place on—what was it? Orange?—in West Hollywood. And I kept it up until they put me in for six months in the County Jail.

"After I got out, I got a job at the LA Tennis Club. I worked in the bar-snack club thing. I worked there for quite a while before they caught on to me. Because everything I didn't write *down*, I could take home the cash for. I was bagging all the cash. It took months for them to realize that they did better business on the days I wasn't there. They never said anything. They just laid me off." While Rose did all this, Frank, a young Latino kid, painted houses, moved in furniture, worked on cars.

In certain insurance claims, investigators construct a fault tree and trace it back. You can—*I* can—always pin some of this on my mother; she's tough enough. But what about the soldiers who swarmed over Oahu, all of them so happy to be going home, all of them with duffle bags jammed with heroin? You can't blame *them*, you can't blame Nixon for bringing them home. You might have to take a look at Kennedy, at Johnson, for sending troops over in the first place. At a recent writers' conference, I met a pilot who'd been in Vietnam and who was there to learn how to write down his adventures. He'd flown all through the war, he said, not against the North, but flying *South* in huge cargo planes, shipping opium for the United States government. He was depressed about his life and was trying to find a way to put it into words.

If not fault, what about remorse? I ask Rose a little more about those nineteen missing packets of opium, not whether she's sorry or not, just asking. It's only a footnote to her. But she's proud, I think, of having stayed away from all of us—not stealing from us through that twenty years. She feels guilt about our mother. She feels as if she abandoned our mom. But she says: "Nothing on earth, not all the money in the world, in the *universe*, could make me ask her over for, say, Thanksgiving. I just couldn't do it."

"I did it for years," I say.

Rose looks at me sadly. "There should have been a medium ground between what you did and what I did," she says.

—

Rose admires something she calls "the Berkeley Gestalt. There's a whole feeling up here," she says, "that with a little education and some hard work, and the willingness to take some risks, that you can make something of yourself. Right now, in 1994, you see it happening again. Somebody across the bay is importing heroin again, the good Asian stuff. They're bringing it straight over from China, and right now, this month at least, it's cheaper than crack. College kids are falling for it again, they think it's cool. It's like you think—pot didn't ruin my life, acid didn't ruin my life, why should *heroin* ruin my life? And there are some people who can try it once, or twice, and then forget it. But there's a lot of people like me—you go, *ah! ah! I'm human.* That's the transplant that I needed."

I ask her to tell me some more about the seventies. What happened after she got fired from the LA Tennis Club?

"Spring and summer of 1975, Frank and I were trying desperately to use every day. We had a little apartment. A studio. One room, kitchen, bathroom sort of thing. After the Tennis Club I got a horrible job working at a Denny's type place. I'd work a split shift, then go home and wait for my connection to wake up. (Because, you know, the mornings, and just waking up, are horrible for junkies. Something happens to your body while you sleep. You're always sick when you wake up.) So I couldn't stand that job. I went and got myself fired and on unemployment. Back then, in California, you got an automatic fifty-two weeks of unemployment.

"And that brings me to my one claim to fame with a movie star! I was on unemployment at the end of '75. People who were desperate would go down to pick it up as early as seven o'clock on Monday morning, and you'd wait around until the doors opened. Frank was always very good at seeing movie stars. You remember how much I always loved that movie *The Lords of Flatbush?* It was like *American Graffiti,* only better, more real. It had Perry King and Henry Winkler and the guy everyone forgets, and Sylvester Stallone in his very first role as Stanley. I *loved* him in that. So one morning Frank says, 'Look! There's Stanley!' He was parked outside the unemployment office at seven in the morning. He had to be as desperate as we were.

"Now Frank's mother had gone shopping one day and come back with a black silk jacket somebody had brought back from Vietnam. It was real pretty, real feminine. It had an embroidered dragon on it and in back it said DANANG. So every Monday morning, while we were waiting, I got my nerve up and said, 'Hi, Stanley!' and he would say, 'Hi, Danang!' And we did that for weeks. This would be either while we were waiting for unemployment to open or for the check-cashing place right across the street to open.

"Finally one day I asked him, 'Whatcha doing? Making more movies?' And he said, 'No, I'm writing now.' So he must have been writing *Rocky* right then. But he wasn't buffed at all. In fact he looked a little overweight. One day I asked him, 'Whatever happened to Perry King?' And he screamed at me, 'Why do all the girls ask about Perry King? He's not even *Italian!*' I just found it so funny that he was screaming at a little junkie in a parking lot.

"It was then I got into the shoplift-refund really badly. I think I told you, Robinson's was the best, I'd hit both stores. Because by Tuesday all the unemployment money would be gone. We were both hooked like dogs. I got caught. But they just looked at me and said go away, you're on two years' probation. Then, about November, I got caught again. It's funny! I got caught stealing a hardcover copy of *Prince of the City* because I wanted to read it. The judge gave me six months in jail. *That was kind of steep!* I walked in court with the public defender, I'd already pled guilty. The PD said, 'The judge is talking substantial jail time.' I didn't find out until later what that meant. *Some jail time* is, like, sixty to ninety days. *Substantial* time is usually six months. And *significant jail time* means the pen. The judge was up for reelection. Nowadays, they just give you a ticket for shoplifting, like a parking ticket!

"I was sick as a dog in jail. I was kicking a pretty large habit. I went in January of 1976 and I was going to get out in June. That's when you came and visited me in jail."

Rose's uncle, the successful lawyer, had phoned me. He said that Rose had been caught with a raft of very expensive sweaters and was selling them to support her drug habit, and maybe—since she was my sister—I might want to go and visit her.

I went down to Sybil Brand Jail to visit Rose. They took my purse and frisked me. I couldn't believe the oppressive heat, or the thick plastic "glass" between us. I almost couldn't recognize the chubby little lady who lolled on a stool on the other side of the plastic. Fat packed itself on her young body. Her eyes were duller than a dog's, but she said she had the best job in the jail. Her hair was in big curlers. She sure didn't seem glad to see me. I left there feeling scalded. About fifteen years later, though, when I met Sybil Brand at a party in Beverly Hills, I was able to chat: "Oh, my sister did time in your jail. She loved it!"

Now Rose says, "Jail was not a horrible experience. There was this one really pretty, feminine guard. She got me a job in the officers' dining room. It really *was* the cushiest job in the jail. You got to serve the officers and you got to eat officer food. You got your little dresses and your pantsuits. You had the run of the jail. I made *some* enemies with the white girls. A few of them didn't like me, but I always got along with Latinas. That was the whole part of my life. Until I got into the drug program, I was raised as a Mexican woman—by Frank and Michael and their moms.

"I asked the judge for modification of my sentence. He just laughed at me. There was only one other way you could get out and that was sheriff's parole. Five out of fifty people got it. That's when I called up my uncle again. He sent some attorney over. *He* said it was outrageous. Nobody did six months for second shoplifting! When it came time for my sheriff's hearing, Mr. Attorney never even showed up. I walked in there *alone*. I was just as remorseful as I could be. And they let me out! From one second to the next, I was free. I found out later that my uncle had talked to the judge.

"I got a ride out of jail and went straight over to Frank's house. Then I headed for unemployment and picked up thirteen checks that had been waiting for me. In *minutes,* Frank was there, waiting to help me spend my money. That was May 1976. I had all these stringent rules with the parole, so I got a job at Grand Photo Litho, but I hardly worked any hours. I still wanted to use. I wanted to get high.

"Now I'm going to say that Frank and I had a lot of fun. Kind of like *Panic in Needle Park,* the beginning part. Frank reminded me of Al Pacino. His life had never been anything, so he didn't expect anything. His mom, she was a saint. She had nine or seven kids. She named one of them after Damon Runyon. She wasn't your typical East LA mom. She was a good little hustler, boy! She was *so nice to me*! Frank and I went back and forth for years. He always wanted kids. He would have been a good father.

"Two things happened that summer. I got another job, delivery driving for Phototype House. I got to deliver the posters for Barbra Streisand and Kris Kristofferson in *A Star Is Born.* I drove a Datsun B2-10. A Mexican woman ploughed into me, and that was my famous car accident! The accident that will live in history! I got fired! Then I got a laywer. They started sending me checks once a week. I had a hundred a week income. Then Frank's number came up at a methadone clinic. He'd been on a lot of waiting lists and always said no when the time came. But this time he said OK. It was in West LA, right across from the Design Center.

"At that time methadone was totally free. They got Frank on it and then they gave me the hustle. They never really asked me, they *told* me. At that time you had to have been an addict for at least two years. Now they've taken it down to only one year. What I'm going to say now is: you shouldn't sell your body, mind, whatever, to the country, the city, the state. You don't realize that you're selling your *body*. And now they get these little kids started. You're talking the government as pusher. Starting people on drugs free of charge and then raising the price, and if you can't come up with the price, they cut you off, as mean as any pusher.

"They say heroin is strong but methadone is a million times worse. What it is, you drink a little bit of stuff and you're feeling no pain. You don't feel *anything*, the pain or the joys. You think you're living a regular life. You can settle down and have kids. Two weeks after Frank, I was on, too. That was October 1976.

"I have to say that it certainly did take me out of the role of being the one to burglarize their house. I was no longer a 'criminal.' So if people are worried about their car jackings and their crime, methadone is the thing. You can work with it. The Dead are on methadone, for instance. But somebody's making a lot of money on this! The clinics are franchised like a McDonald's. It costs a center fifty dollars *tops* for a month of methadone. In California now, it costs the client $285.00 a month. And some people will fall a little back into crime to make those fees. At these centers, there's no *service* involved! They see you for maybe three seconds a day. So who's making all this money? It must be the government that's making this money. I know, you think, some junkie's got a two-hundred-dollar-a-day habit, he's lucky to be paying ten dollars a day, but that's not the point.

"On methadone maintenance they tell you not even to think of detoxing for at least two years. Frank and I found an apartment of our own. I went to work in the domestic service industry. Frank went to work fixing German cars. (Linda Ronstadt came in.) But without heroin, I realized Frank and I didn't have a fucking thing in common. I mean, he *did* know movies, he *did* know books . . . but I just got bored. Frank would go to the clinic around seven, before he went to work, and I didn't go in until about nine. And there was this extremely good-looking guy down there. . . . Well, I don't have to tell you! You met Michael at Nate 'n' Al's. You must remember him . . . don't you?"

Yes, I remember Michael, small, dark-haired, and a hopeless druggie. Yes, I remember meeting them at Nate 'n' Al's, and Rose tried to borrow another twenty-five from me. Then she went off for her Vidal Sassoon haircut, and I went back to work.

Rose fills me in on Michael, the love of her life. Latino, like Frank, slender, good-looking, and, improbably, third-generation Californian, a young man of what was once a good family. His maternal grandmother had grown up in the prosperous LA suburb of San Marino, "playing tennis with the white girls." But his mother, Sylvia, had been wild, and run off with a zoot-suiter during the forties. Sylvia, spurning the hard-won privilege of her parents, settled down to what seemed to be the far more glamorous life of a crook.

Her husband hung around long enough to give her a couple of

louts named Louie and Keith, who would grow up badly. Then the husband waltzed off because he couldn't stand the kids and his wife's loose life. He waltzed back eight years later to sire Michael. Then it was *adiós,* Dad.

Young Michael grew up neglected, repulsed by his mom's generous habits with strangers, noticing that his older brothers were dealing wholesale heroin by the time they were fifteen and sixteen. When Michael was eight, cops wearing bullet-proof vests raided his house with smoke bombs. Both his brothers were busted, jailed, and (when they came of age) sent to the Pen.

That left wild Sylvia and little Michael. But he could always visit his Grandma Elena, who spent her time doing charity work, domestic chores, and in prayer, ironing his pillow slips with her own hands, sprinkling baby powder between the sheets before he got into bed.

When Michael was about ten, he was able to persuade his mother to move, with just him, Michael, up to Northern California. "Because he knew, from visiting his grandmother, that people didn't have to live the way he and his mother did. On the other hand, his grandmother spoiled him rotten. He learned that the whole purpose of women is to be *beyond reproach,* and to make men happy, comfortable, and satisfied. I'm going to say that he was deeply religious, but the Devil won out.

"When he was thirteen, it got to be the time that the brothers were getting out of the Pen. They followed Michael and his mom up to Northern California like a bad disease. Keith and Louie got jobs working in foundries. Once you get out of the Pen, you have a seven-year tail. You can't do anything. You can't afford to do anything. So they were the first ones in their family to fall into the methadone program. And Louie turned into a redneck. He had an

RV and a five-bedroom house and five kids. You just couldn't *see* the criminal heroin addict anymore. Keith had a white wife and he bought her a home but he didn't change that much.

"But Michael was having a pretty good time. If you're a kid who knows the ropes, you can do real good up here. Michael said it was like Disneyland. He went to school, he had friends. But somewhere along the line, when he was fifteen or sixteen, the government just let *all* the heroin in here. Berkeley was the big stop-off for it. *Even though he knew* what had happened to his brothers, by the time he was sixteen, he was hooked. By the time he was seventeen he was fighting charges of seven armed robberies. He got taught what little boys should never learn.

"So it was Christmas of '76, down in LA. Michael had come down to be with the rest of his family, his Grandma Elena. He was down at West Hollywood Maintenance, and that's where I saw him. One day I was on my way to the neurologist in Beverly Hills, and I was walking to the bus. He said, 'Can I give you a ride?' We got there early because a car is faster than a bus, naturally, and we went for coffee at Nate 'n' Al's. Michael told me he was a working musician. He played for a band called Innovations, mostly jazz rock. He'd be playing a jazz club down in San Diego, and then fly up to LA to get his dose. I was impressed by that. I thought he was out of my league.

"We carried on a big affair! Poor Frank'd be at work and Michael and I would be at the house fucking our brains out all day. It took a long time for me to get up the nerve to bail out. But Michael and I had so much more in common than Frank and I did. On the other hand, Michael was always getting in so much trouble for such little things! He was driving home one night and he had a mortar and pestle in the back of the car, like, what his mother used for grinding spices? He got arrested for carrying a lethal weapon. And another time he bought a hot stereo. Just these dumb little things! But I didn't care, I was in love.

"By this time Frank had wised up. He put a cheap padlock on the door, which we broke. We took my clothes and my cat. Off we went to San Marino and moved in with his grandparents. The old man was a trip! And Grandma Elena was a large Mexican lady. She prayed in her wheelchair all day with her rosary. But . . . Sylvia! Michael's mom! She reminded me of our mother in a lot of ways. She thought she could have had a great life without her kids. She went on and on and on.

"Meanwhile, Michael's band fell apart. They got busted on two or three of the dumbest cases you'd ever dream of. Michael hated LA! But LA probation wouldn't let him go back to Berkeley. His whole dream of being a musician fell apart. He'd get a gig in Hong Kong and he couldn't go because of his probation. He couldn't go anywhere. Finally, after a year, in June 1978, he talked the probation people into letting him come up north, and he wanted me with him. I was worried. Like, he's going to take me up north where I've never been and don't know anyone. But he considered himself an artist, and his dream had fallen apart. He'd keep saying, *what have I done to my life?* He was still in his early twenties—I was twenty-eight. He kept telling me, 'Look. If I'm going to be poor, if I'm going to have this fucked-up life, I'm going to do it up north. Because you can be poor in the Bay Area and still look good.'

"It's true. We lived much better up here on the same amount of money. Things happen better for you—it's *easier* in the Bay Area. We stayed with his brother Keith for six weeks, and then we got our own place in El Cerrito. It's a real quiet, pretty little town. We had a nice house in back of another house with a beautiful garden. Life was so easygoing. And I finally got off *my* probation.

"This is by now the late seventies. Punk rock was starting to come in. Michael was in Eddy Money's first band. Michael was the rhythm guitarist. (But he got *fired* because Eddy Money said *I don't want any mother-fuckin' hippies in my band!*) But Michael was getting back in the music scene. Life was starting to be really fun. He was even going to work for the Tubes, but the Tubes didn't hire him.

"One day I befriended a girl named Delia. She was beautiful, Swedish-looking, and she had these almond eyes. She had a beautiful little baby boy who was so darling it looked like she got him out of a Cracker Jacks box. And she had a big grumpy old man named George. He was the biggest methamphetamine manufacturer in the Bay Area! They really took to me and Michael. Michael would say to me, 'Can't you see, they're buying our friendship?' I didn't see what he meant, because George looked just like the kind of people we ought to know. George wanted to start building a recording studio. He had all this cash from meth and he had to do *something* with it! They'd take us off to the city on excursions. They bought Michael a guitar. Michael was like, *He's the Prince of Darkness!*

"George and Delia moved to Orinda. You've got to have some money to do that. They leased this *big* old home. They had more money than *I'd* ever seen. So I began to say to Michael, '*Why can't we be rich like them too?*' Oooh, Michael resented me saying that! But George could spend two or three hundred dollars on chemicals and turn it into hundreds and hundreds of thousands of dollars' worth of meth. I really admired George, because he was a self-made man. He was just a high school grad. He taught himself everything he knew. He went down to the library and he read books and he talked to people and he did the work and he bought the equipment and set up the labs and he figured it out! So he'd come a long way.

"But Michael would say to me, 'Don't you know it's poison? It's so poisonous you have to wear gloves and suits and masks in the lab while you're making it! And then you make hundreds and hundreds of thousands of dollars because some poor schmuck is putting it in his veins. A *lot* of poor schmucks! And it's poison.' But I bugged him and bugged him and bugged him. I wanted to have some money, because we were still living in this little, little house, and we were still getting around on foot. I would say to Michael, 'If George can do it, we can do it!'

"George would *give* you four pounds of speed; he had so much of it, just as a present, to see if you could build up a clientele. If you got rid of it, then he could see he'd gotten a little worker. The thing about speed or PCP, or even acid, is you don't have to *get* them. You can *make* them. You don't have to worry about finding your product or shipping it, or getting it through customs. You have to remember there's only a finite amount of marijuana in the world. There's only a finite amount of hash. There are only so many opium poppies in the world! But there's an infinite amount of chemicals. You can make a tiny, tiny investment and make a huge, huge, huge amount of money. But there's a disadvantage to it. The labs are physically dangerous because they could always blow up. The fumes are dangerous—they're poison. And you have to keep the temperature of the lab constant—if you don't, *that* could blow you up. And it carries a sentence of fifteen to life. (Except that when George finally did get busted, he only did three years, and he's back on the street now, making a whole lot of money.) So that's why I nagged Michael to do it. Because it was *so much money!*

"Michael firmly believed in Karma. He firmly believed that if you were getting rich off little kids putting poison in their veins . . . that something bad would happen. And it did happen. All the people we worked with were finally busted. But the real bad guys all went to prison for five minutes and now they're out doing it again. They're all stinking rich."

I ask Rose what the chances are for a woman alone to succeed in the meth business.

"A woman alone could *never do it.* You'd be shot and killed in two minutes. And in fact, you can't really be *awake* and do it. You can't think about what you're doing, little kids putting that stuff in their veins. We never even *tried* it! The drugs we made we never used. We stayed on methadone. And PCP, oh my God! You could never try that. That's just like death.

"So! In November of 1980, we finally moved into a condo in Piedmont. It wasn't cheap. All of a sudden, our life had changed. All of a sudden we had one or two cars, and a condo with a pool. We just had a lot of fun! The famous George was still building that recording studio he'd been working on. Just like with the meth, he taught *himself* how to do it. You know, I hate him more than anyone in my life, he treats women like shit, but I respect him too, for what he's been able to do with his life.

"Michael, by this time, was really fulfilled. All he had to do for business was make a couple of phone calls a week. He worked with George to finish the sound studio, he bought a mixing board that once belonged to the Beatles. And *then!* MTV hit the scene. I thought, *Oh! OK! That's what I want to do!* Then Michael started buying video equipment. I worked on *Jenny 456719* and one other real dumb little tape. During that time, I edited tapes of a lot of bands. Editing tape—that seems to be something that women are able to do. Either that, or that's what they let you do. Anyway, during 1981, '82, '83, '84, that was our life. We hung around with musicians and went to clubs and edited tapes. We lived in Piedmont. Michael had a Grand Prix—it was like driving around in your living room—and I had a Datsun 280Z and I was happy.

"Then, in October of 1983, a series of events occurred. I finally got that settlement from the car crash I was in. Forty thousand dollars just came in one day. And right around the same time we met some more people, another couple, Max and Sasha. They had a lot more class than George and Delia. Sasha was always running off to London like a regular drug dealer's wife. In fact, she's out of the business now. She's down in LA selling stocks and bonds. But she loved to travel. And *he* never did any work because he had all his little monkeys to do his work for him. Max was sort of white trash, but he was another one of those guys who came from the Berkeley drug mentality—that you could make something of yourself if you really wanted to. He taught himself everything, and he could make everything. They had a pretty good lifestyle—they had the fine wines and dinners and Porsches and Lamborghinis. They had a little boy too. Boy, they really *spent money.*

"But Max wasn't very nice to Sasha. You know how I told you you're always sick when you're using? Well, Max wouldn't let Sasha touch any stuff until he woke up and that would be real late in the day, so she'd be sick and she had to get up with the kid. So she began to drink and he hated that. He said he hated to see a drunk woman. In fact, Sasha took me to my first AA meeting back in 1984. She was all the time deciding to get out, to get away from him and his methamphetamines, to be shut of all that stuff. Because he was mean to her.

"Around 1984, Max had this big disaster happen to him. He had one main lab, right there in the middle of Berkeley, in the basement of a little house. The guy who managed it was this little gay guy from New York, The Squirrel. As far as anyone knew, The Squirrel had taken some money from his contacts in New York and hadn't paid them off in product. So these characters from New York came out here and put a gun to The Squirrel's head and cleaned the place out. They took *everything*. They took the finished meth and all the chemicals and all the cash and everything. Now, you have to have these big machines to manufacture meth, to make the liquid into a solid. And here in town they're always bolted to the walls, not because of thievery but because of earthquakes. So these guys cleaned out the place, the cash, the product, and they unbolted the famous machine and took it along.

"So ... Max was beside himself. He needed money to start all over again. Nobody was willing to cough up money for the machine. So, who did he come to? Us. We had part of the forty thousand I'd gotten from my settlement, and it cost about twenty-five thousand for the machine. I handed it over to Max, I invested in his business. And we wouldn't get anything in return for about three or four months. Max made fun of us later—'Yeah, like Michael's teeth were chattering when Rose handed over the cash!' "

I ask Rose why she and Michael didn't just go into business for themselves if they had that kind of capital, and she gives me a pitying look. "Because we didn't have the *formula*! You can't do anything if you don't know the *formula*! But we became one-third partners with Max. For our initial investment of twenty-five thousand, our very first payment was eighty thousand. For two years we had plenty of money coming in. It was the funnest time of my life."

Rose had two abortions in the early eighties. Michael didn't want any babies and he was annoyed the first time with Rose for getting pregnant. She waited a long while, hoping he'd change his mind, but he was clear he didn't want the kid. "When I went into the clinic, I was getting to be three months pregnant. When I went in, I was crying, crying, crying. But he just didn't want a baby. He would have been twenty-six then, I was thirty-one. But the second time I just *rushed* down there. I went down there by myself. We were branching into a lifestyle now where I saw it the way he did. We couldn't have any kids."

There was more trouble in the early days of 1984. A rich Iranian drug dealer was gunned down in his van, leaving behind a beautiful widow and a fortune in drugs. Michael immediately moved in on this beauty, partly to "protect" her, partly as a financial venture. Repeatedly, Michael reassured Rose that he was only using this woman, that their affair meant nothing. Rose, still in the condo in Piedmont, decided to hang in there, to tough it out, to see if she could keep Michael. She had heard that the beautiful Iranian had a terrible temper and banked on that to drive Michael away to return him to Rose. The affair lasted from September 1984 to the end of that year. Rose remembers the next six months as the happiest days of her life.

"Michael was sweeter and nicer to me from December to June 1985 than he'd ever been. He had me out looking for a house. He had me out there with actual real estate people, which was difficult, because we didn't have jobs. Even if you have a fifty thousand down payment, they want to know whether or not you have a job. Before, we could have said we were working for the recording studio, but now it was closed.

"On June 9 of '85 we were going out to dinner with a friend of ours named Sally, a customer. She would make us maybe twenty thousand a month. So we were going to go over to San Francisco and have a crab soufflé with her. Michael had stayed up late the night before, and we went to bed, but around four or five in the morning he jumped up and said, *what was that?* Then he got up again around six, which wasn't like him. He'd said, *did you hear the pounding on the door?* And when he couldn't go back to sleep he got up and gave the cat a bath and blow-dry. Then he decided to go downstairs and work on his 1964 Grand Prix, which was like a collector's item. That's what he did that day. He had a few visitors, one guy who came over with some cocaine. But Michael said he didn't feel like cocaine, why didn't they go out and see if they could find some *stuff?* Because he felt like some stuff. Michael's friend always blamed himself after that, because he said no, he didn't feel like it, he'd rather do the cocaine, and drove away.

"By that time it was five or six in the afternoon. Michael said why don't you take a bath before we go out to dinner? He said he was going to go down to the 7-Eleven, then he was going to lie down for a while and read. He came home with the *Rolling Stone* with David Letterman on the cover. He came into the bathroom, I was just letting the bath water out and getting up to turn on the shower. The radio was playing—do you know that song, "Two Birds of Paradise" by the Pretenders? Ordinarily Michael hated that kind of music, but he looked over at me and said, ' "Two Birds of Paradise." That's *us,* baby.' Then he walked out and shut the door.

"After a while I came out of the bathroom. He's not in the apartment. But we'd been together for eight and a half years, I wasn't going to get worried about something like that. I just thought, well, he'll be back. I started getting dressed and just lollygaggin' around. I put on a little red miniskirt. I was thin and cute then. And I started working on my makeup. Then the doorbell rang. I looked through that little hole in the door and saw three cops. *I thought it was Michael's worst nightmare come true! OK, we're busted!* I scurried around with nothing but my skirt on, just ran around like a chicken with my head cut off, because we had four ounces of PCP in the freezer, and eleven thousand in cash in the dirty-clothes hamper, and several handguns, only one of which was legal. I literally ran around in circles! I finally hid some Zig-Zags which were out there on one of the end tables, and I put on a blouse and went to the door.

"They said, 'Does someone named Michael live here?' I could see a commotion from where I was standing in the door of the condo. Something was happening down by the pool.

"The three of them came in without asking. They said, 'Michael's had an accident.' I looked out and I could see somebody there, a body. But Michael was Latino, and the legs I saw were so white! I said, no, that can't be Michael. Then I saw the stripe on the side of his trunks.

"I said, 'Is he breathing?'

"They said, 'Not at this time, ma'am.'

"This is why I'll never ever say a word against the Oakland Police Department. Because I just went nuts, screaming and crying. Finally a policeman had me pinned up against the wall, not hurting me, just holding me. I was screaming, *he can't be dead!*

"And they said, you have to get ready because we're all going to go to the hospital.

"I went over to my side of the bed to pick up my rosary, and they saw one of the guns. One of them asked, 'Whose is that?' And I said, 'That's mine.'

"As we went down past the pool, there was this nice little guy who'd dived in to save Michael. I asked, 'How long had he been down there?'

"Jack said, 'Thirty minutes.'

"It started to hit me. During his youth Michael had been through a couple of heroin overdoses and a real bad car crash. I'd always

thought he was invincible. I never thought he would die. And I knew
he wasn't loaded that afternoon. But he was dead.

"They put me up front in the ambulance, while they took us to
Merritt Peralta Hospital. Michael looked so calm, like I'd seen him
a million times, like he'd caught good nod, perfectly at ease. I began
to think—he got to go out young and beautiful, with no disease. The
lucky son of a bitch. *Boy,* did he get off easy! They took him into a
room at the hospital and kept on working on him. But . . . do you
remember that movie, *Jason and the Argonauts?* Remember when
Jason was sailing around and he had a goddess for a figurehead on
his boat? And sometimes when Jason would get into trouble, the
goddess would open her eyes and talk to him, and then turn back
into a figurehead again? Well, I prayed so hard to the Virgin Mary,
let him live, let him live. I don't know whether you could say I got a
vision. But it was like this lady with a big face came and said,
'There's nothing more I can do for you. It's over. You need to take
care of yourself now.'

"They came out and said, 'Michael didn't make it.'

"And I said, 'I know.'

"Then all of a sudden *reality* said, you have four ounces of PCP in
your freezer. You have eleven thousand in cash in your dirty-clothes
hamper. You have handguns all over the house. I tried to phone
Max, the big dealer, but all the times I'd ever called him, I couldn't
remember his number now. I ended up calling a kid I didn't even
know very well, who lived over in San Francisco. That kid was there
at the hospital, *boom.*

"It was going to turn out that the only drugs they were going to
find in Michael's body were methadone and Valium. And one of the
neighbors said he'd seen him with a beer. There was no foul play, no
bumps on the head, nothing like that. But the pool *was* unheated, and

when it's cold like that you're not supposed to stay in more than eighteen minutes. No one will ever really know what happened.

"So, the kid and I went back to the apartment. We collected all the drugs in the house and put them in garbage bags with garbage on top of them and put them in the trunk of Michael's Grand Prix and parked it on a side street. I got all the cash out of the house and put it in my purse. Then I realized I had to call Michael's family. But there was no *way* I could do it. I just couldn't *call* his mother! So I called the hospital back and talked to the doctor and he did it. His brothers were thirty-seven and thirty-eight by then, both back at home, living with their mother and their grandma. Louie answered the phone—it was late at night by that time—and he went into where his mom, Sylvia, was reading.

"He said, 'Hey, Mom! I got a dead brother!'

"By Tuesday I knew I had to call Sylvia. They were all up here the next day, Wednesday afternoon. Sylvia brought a *hundred* Valium with her. I was the one who had to arrange for the funeral, of course. All they did was send flowers, and even their checks for the *flowers* bounced. I paid extra money so that the Monsignor would come back from his vacation early. I couldn't bring myself to look at the body, but I did put photos of me and of him, and tickets to concerts where we'd had a good time, and some guitar picks—I put all that in the casket. George and Delia didn't come to the funeral, Max and Sasha didn't come. None of the dope-dealer people came. But the poor guy who pulled him out of the pool came.

"Sylvia and Michael's brothers stayed around, Louie and Keith stayed for weeks. I didn't mind.

"Nine days after Michael died, the famous George and Delia were busted, up in their Orinda home. There were so many cops from so many agencies that they went out and bought special jackets so they'd know each other during the bust and not shoot somebody who was on their side by mistake. They got 'em all right. It was front-page *Chronicle* news. It had been Michael's worst nightmare that something like this would happen to us!

"Delia got out of jail right away, but George had trouble making bail. They were five thousand short to get him out. Michael had been dead a month. I gave them the five thousand. I knew it was what Michael would have done. After that, they were around the house a lot, but they didn't help out any. I'd had the eleven thousand in cash and about thirty thousand in different bank accounts, and I just saw the money dwindling. One morning about six weeks after Michael died I saw Louie hanging around outside. He said, 'Why don't we go out for some coffee?' I said OK, but then I saw he was just driving around, and *I got it.* I said, *Take me home right now!* But by the time we got home Keith had stolen my 280Z, the beautiful one! My own car! Later on, Sylvia told me they just wanted some of Michael's money, and they thought I was keeping all of it. I said, *Why didn't you ask?*

"I started using heroin again, to get off methadone. Michael meant methadone to me, and it was the end of an era. I was smoking heroin instead of shooting, it was very expensive. *Don't ask me what I was thinking!*

"We're into 1986 now, I guess. I started bouncing checks. I had OK jewelry and OK clothes and I still had the Grand Prix. I'd go into a Safeway and buy some food, and cash an extra fifty. I'd do that twice a day. After the money ran out I just wrote checks to get cash. I was finally picked up outside a Lucky's in Walnut Creek. I told them it was all a big mistake. I went to jail, stayed for three days, and got out.

"I thought the check thing was over, but it wasn't.

"I lost the apartment and I got a job as an au pair girl back in Orinda, working for two hotshot lawyers. Their house was on two levels and my room was down and outside, by the pool. I was only paid six hundred dollars a month. That woman worked me like a dog. She left at seven in the morning and didn't come back until seven at night. She had a list of things I had to do that wouldn't quit. Those poor little kids had every minute of their lives mapped out. I started using but only on the weekends. She got it right that I was having a performance problem that had to do with drugs, but it was the drugs that got me *through* it. I worked real well when I was loaded. When I wasn't, I could hardly do a thing. They said I had to leave.

"Max said, 'I've got some stuff for you to do.' He was facing a horrible federal case and he had to be extra extra careful. He rented this really nice hotel room in the Berkeley House. My job was to live in it. Once or twice a week a person would drop thirty thousand off with me. My job was to sit in the room. Now, we're into 1987, and then he just abruptly told me, 'I don't need this room any more!' But I understood what he'd been doing. He was looking after me the way Michael would have liked. And Max was the one who told me, 'You've got to get yourself together.' He rented me a room in Fruitvale, the Mexican district of Oakland. It wasn't so bad.

"I had really started getting my own little life then. I was *mostly* clean . . ."

About this time, since I'm taking notes, I have the clear and conscious thought that I'm so glad I decided not to use a tape recorder. I'm so glad my glasses are on. So glad I'm focused straight down on the pages of my notes. *Boy,* I don't want to think of my sister, thirty-six, all alone, flat broke, living in a furnished room in a place called Fruitvale. We're sitting again on this balcony in Alameda, the sun is shining, the lagoon beneath us is pristine, and the mother ducks have hustled their ducklings in for an afternoon nap somewhere in peaceful green reeds. Safety! Stability. We have it now, but for how long?

"*Very rarely* was I able to get high. I didn't have the money or the opportunity. About that time I met a couple called Sharon and Mel. Sharon had a real good job at Easter Seal bingo games. They have these things called pull tabs and, you know, people pull them. Mostly old folks played, and if they'd win they'd tip you.

"Sharon said, 'Why not come and live with me?' I stayed there until the summer of '87. I started using again and I got busted in Concord. I wasn't sweating my court date. I was still living at Sharon's, so my court date was like a preliminary hearing. But then somebody said to me, could you just have a seat there by the bailiff? Time went by and went by. Finally I found out what it was. They had *refiled* those charges on the checks I'd cashed right after Michael died. They'd had a year to do it. 'You have forty-two felony counts of check-bouncing in Walnut Creek.' That's what they told me when I got in front of this lady judge. My bail was something like thirty-five thousand dollars. I stayed in jail for weeks. I called Sharon and she had sympathy for me but she certainly wasn't going to bail me out of jail. Then another judge put me out on my own recognizance. She said, 'OK, Miss Daly, I'm going to let you out, but if you're not back for your next court date, you can kiss your ass good-bye.'

"Sharon had turned on me. I went back to the room in the Fruitvale district, but I was only there a couple of days. I needed a permanent address and a job. I was going up and down the street looking for work, and I met the famous Mr. Al Rodriguez.

"We ended up having an affair. He was married, maybe forty-eight. I was thirty-seven by then. He had four kids—the youngest was sixteen. Of course, Al said that his wife—the usual spiel, you know?—that he and his wife didn't make love anymore. And that his wife was a ballbuster. He eventually rented a little house for me. It was going to be his play house, and I was going to be his mistress there. He made sure I made my court dates. That's what was happening all the way into winter. The case was getting ready to settle but it wasn't looking good. I just saw jail, you know? I just saw jail.

"About November I was coming up for sentencing. I panicked, and I didn't go. Then, on New Year's Day of 1988, we'd been drinking all night and we were into drinking all day. We were at the house Al rented for me with some Mexican guys. I drew the short straw, and they sent me to Safeway for more tortillas and brandy. That was 4:00 P.M. New Year's Day, 1988. The brakes on the car were shot. This guy pulled in front of me, I swerved, hit a parked car, and hit my head on the steering wheel. I actually tried to get out of the car to run. The police came and arrested me for drunk driving. And I didn't get out of jail until *June*.

"I was in Contra Costa jail, it's a rich county and it has a nice jail. It has a cable TV, and room for only two women at a time. It has a kind of nice living-room place, a weight machine, two little patios. I got a job in the laundry. It wasn't *too* bad. Al would come and visit me.

"In June of 1988, Al picked me up from jail and took me back to the house. It was like he had the ability to take me out of my life and put me in another whole one. A lot of crazy Mexicans came in and out of that house, but I didn't mind, I was out of jail. I got a job as a hotel maid at the Apple Inn. It was horribly hard work. Then, about August or September of '88, Al and I had a fight. I was all alone in that house, so lonely. Al wouldn't even come and see me. I'd be drinking but I wasn't using. I drank brandy and Southern Comfort.

"So, Sylvia and her son Louie came up to see me. I couldn't drink by that time. More than two drinks and I'd get real sick. They said, *'God!* Don't you think you should come back down to LA with us?' I did *not* want to go. But I was sick, so I did. I was on probation in two counties, so I called up and told them where I was. The first place said, oh forget it. The second place said if you don't get your ass up here, you can consider yourself *absconding.* I thought, oh, well.

"So, on a Monday morning in LA some people and I were sitting on the lawn drinking beer. The cops came by to get us to go away. But I didn't move. I waited for them to come up to me. I said, my name is Rose Daly and if you don't find any warrants for me down here, look statewide.

"They took me to the county jail. I wasn't even under arrest. On the third night they came and started to let me out because Berkeley had declined to follow up on the warrants. But Contra Costa county had a *no bail* hold on me, like I was a murderer or something. They *flew* me back, just me and one officer. And they didn't put cuffs on me. They had this whole other contraption, a big metal brace that goes on your leg to keep it stiff so you can't run away. It has three or four leather straps on it, and every strap has a separate lock and key. It digs into your flesh. It's so painful. I had to go through the metal detector at the airport and the officer had to hold up his badge and say he was a policeman and I was an escaped felon. It was horrible.

"Up north, I went to court pretty quickly in front of a lady judge who they call the Black Widow. She gave me ninety days for *absconding.* This time I applied for work furlough in a halfway house. I was the landscaper out there. I met this nice white girl. She kept telling me to call Al again, to try and make up. I was scared to, but she said, just try.

"He was excited to hear from me. His first words to me were, 'When are you getting out?' He was still in the same house, and in the summer of '89, we actually had a while of living together. We had the funnest time! We did things together I had never done in my whole life. He took me fishing, he took me to the State Fair. He took me to Lake Tahoe. I'd never been in a casino before. He took me to the races.

"But then, toward the end of the summer, he went off on a vacation with his wife. I enrolled in computer school, but I got lonely and depressed and I started using. My grades in that school went down. And one night Al came over and he just *caught* me. He hadn't known I was using again. There was a whole lot of fighting. He left me there. I was so lonely. I started back with the old shoplift-refund deal. I got dressed up one day and went out to Neiman-Marcus in Walnut Creek. A customer saw me and they busted me for shoplifting again. I talked them into citing me out. Then the Oakland earthquake happened and the house sustained a lot of damage.

"I realized that the end of the house was the end of that whole thing. The end of me and Al. The end of the end. I was facing another shoplifting charge which—with the first five or six other ones—probably meant that this time I was going to the Penitentiary. I put my name on the waiting list of every kind of rehab, hoping my name would come up on one of them before I had to go back to court. New Bridge called first. It was either the Pen or them. When the day came up, it was December 6, 1989. Al came and picked me up and drove me over there. He was real sad, but he said, 'I think you're doing the right thing.'"

When I ask Rose what would be her favorite thing to do in this life, what would be her first choice if she had it to do over again, she says, "I wish Michael would be alive again, and we were back in business. I know I'm not supposed to say that, but that's what I wish."

PART III

... They could never be parted because their love was rooted in common things. ... All the time their salvation was lying round them—the past sanctifying the present; the present, with wild heart-throb, declaring that there would after all be a future, with laughter and the voices of children.

—E. M. Forster, *Howards End*

John Espey. A class act.

*D*uring the week of Thanksgiving 1974, I drove down to Cardiff to see my dad a couple of days early. I popped open a beer and relaxed back in a chair—my father's places to live always had this incredibly soothing capacity: the same books that I remembered as a kid, the same Botsford watercolors that shimmered with visions of easy living. And—thanks to Lynda—a cleanliness that seemed effortless and left room for the little notes and pictures my five-year-old half brother Bob brought home from school.

Daddy's new profession—writing funny, hard-core pornography—had paid off for him. He was supporting his family now, and underneath his careful bravado, his painstakingly laid-down barrage of jokes, he seemed happy. I thought that what I was going to say would cheer him up: "I've met this man, Daddy. He's wonderful. He's twenty years older than I am. He reminds me of you. He supervised my doctoral dissertation at UCLA. He was a Rhodes Scholar! I want to, you know, stay with him forever. Because I really love him!" And I thought by now I might even deserve him, since I'd spent six years in therapy, learning how to be sane.

Daddy looked over at me with some chagrin. "Penny," he said, "you mean you're hanging it up?"

"Well, yes," I said. "We both seem to want the same things. We want to travel. And we want to do some real work. And the kids like him OK."

I didn't get it. I'd thought my father would approve. But then—like some bizarre medicine you soak up through your skin—I got it. For years, I'd been living *his* dream life. He'd (on a night in his bachelor apartment, after he'd left my mother, and couldn't stay sitting up on his Murphy bed because he was too damn drunk) made the decision to go straight, to sober up, to stay married even if he had to give it two more shots. Any of those infidelities he hinted about were, after all, only hints. It could be that my high-living, womanizing dad was a respectable citizen, and I'd been the substance-abusing ding-a-ling, the person he'd always wanted to be. In my mother's words, "just like my father."

A day or two later, when John Espey came down for Thanksgiving, it was Godzilla meeting the undersea monster all over again. Daddy and Lynda and I smoked dope, John and Lynda and I drank vodka. The two old guys glared at each other across a social abyss. They could both be very funny, but they weren't going to be funny tonight. John pulled out his semibogus English accent. Daddy quoted

Plato, Aristotle, Plotinus. Lynda and I looked blearily at each other. Of all the misfits I'd ever been associated with, Daddy picked this upstanding man not to like.

It was the part about getting down to work that offended my father most. It had always been our unspoken but laid-down, absolute law that if you suffered too much you didn't have to work. George Laws might have been a real novelist if his mother hadn't exploded her head, if his brother hadn't rotted away from typhoid, if his sister Nell hadn't died, if a bullet wasn't lodged beneath his own collarbone. But what if working just meant writing a thousand words a day, five days a week, for the rest of your life? To go to work, or even talk about it, was low betrayal.

John and I went home, feeling strange.

John Espey had been married thirty-five years, had been faithful to his wife, was a widower now, but he drank like the proverbial fish. The son of Presbyterian missionaries in Shanghai at the beginning of the century, his upbringing had given him perfect manners, a very kind heart, and an absolute disinterest in God. In any social gathering he always honed in on the oldest, saddest, most unattractive person and devoted himself to him or her for the rest of the night. (I hated to consider that this was why he might be here, now, with me.) He was a terrible dancer, because his zealot father had told him dancing often led to the creation of illegitimate children. John's main rebellion against his rigid upbringing had been to drink, and to make up stories about the mission that were so forcefully clamped together by good humor that no one, not even the most pious Protestant, could object to them.

It didn't take a genius to notice that every sparkling little story told by John concealed a painful sore. There was a story about John and his then-wife going up to Ridgecrest to give his sister moral support at a Mormon wedding reception, because John's nephew was marrying into that religion. The two families distrusted each other—Mormons sitting uncomfortably in a tasteful house full of Chinese antiques, with nothing but pink lemonade to open uncommunicative throats. But John carried a quart of hundred-proof Stolichnaya in the trunk of his car. He excused himself, went out, "hid" on the street side of the car, and drank down two long pulls of vodka made scalding hot by the sun. "After that there wasn't a problem. I talked to everybody, and they talked to me."

When John's wife was dying, he told of stopping at a bar near the hospital before his daily visit to her for three or four martinis and stopping afterward for another few, until he finally got picked up by a policeman, who asked him to recite the alphabet. John haughtily insisted on reciting it *backward,* and ended up in the drunk tank. If you looked at the whole narrative closely, there wasn't much that was charming about a professor of English languishing alone in a San Fernando Valley jail while his wife lay dying a few more off-ramps down the line.

And John's stories of visiting his mother as she lay dying and he sipped on glasses of "milk" that were one half hundred-proof vodka, revving up his manic good humor to hurtle her wheelchair down gruesome hospital halls, since that was the only kind of movement she'd ever be likely to make again—that was a good story, but you didn't want to have to think about it.

John Espey had called me (a year and a day after his wife had died). He wanted to come up for lunch. He arrived with two grocery bags of mementos and scrapbooks—postcards I'd sent him from Mazatlán years before, a pictorial history of a mountain-climbing expedition he'd gone on with his brother-in-law (to prove he was still physically fit), one bottle of vodka and another of tequila. He looked terrified. He spoke in riddles: "Is it opening day in the Japanese kindergarten?" (That was the caption of one of the postcards I'd sent him long ago.)

I'd had lots of strange men up for lunch in the old Topanga cabin over the years: that Pentagon colonel who brought the funny lunch, the brother of the television producer who talked about exposing himself. But this was weirder yet, because each of us knew it could be serious. And because of differences in our accents, social class, and ignorance of each other's backgrounds we understood about one word in three that we said to each other.

"It's a question of parity," John said at one point about consideration between the sexes. I heard "parody." "He's a Coffin from Maine," he told me. I'd never heard of a coffin from Maine. We both drank a lot of wine. I had to look at all those climbing photos. I asked him what he wanted out of the rest of his life. It was a beautiful Topanga afternoon, green trees clicking against windows on three out of four sides around us. He was sixty-one; I was forty.

"I want to travel before I die," he said, "and I want to get back to my writing." At the very time he spoke—despite those hearty backpacking photos—Mr. Espey had walking pneumonia and was about 70 percent convinced he was going to keel over and die. (For the first weeks of our courtship I thought it was my animal magnetism that made his temperature go up every time we embraced.) If he hadn't thought he was going to die, he might not have made those heedless remarks about starting to write again.

John had two grown daughters, Alice and Susan, and a grandson, Jordan. When Susan had gone back to school so that she could support her son, John had stayed home with his grandson. John—

because of the length of his wife's illness, maybe—seemed divorced from the world. He thought you needed a tuxedo to go down to the dress circle of the Music Center. On the other hand, he knew medieval Italian. At one of the first university luncheons we went to together, I made the mistake of saying to an elderly matron seated next to me that my mother was Irish. "Irish!" the matron echoed, "the Irish are the servant class!"

Well, fuck you, lady.

I played to my own strong suit in those first days. John felt that we should be together, and be faithful. "Oh, I don't think I could ever be faithful to anyone again," I said meanly. "I just don't think I'd want to tie myself down like that."

Does it ever matter how two people get together? Does anybody

John Espey said that this picture of me, upset with pigs in our front yard in Mazatlán, made him consider that there might be a second woman in his life.

ever care except the two people? What kept John and me together, especially during the first two or three years, was John's relentless goodness, and the fact that we both loved to drink.

When Clara, nine years old and used to the idea of boyfriends who came and went, realized John had it in his mind to stay, she spat in his bottle of Coca-Cola. He smiled, chugalugged the Coke, and then chased it with about four fingers of Stoly. When he and I took my mother to a white Protestant resort that was over her head socially—and mine too—we stuck her in bed and headed for the bar, where we struck up an acquaintance with a brain surgeon and his wife. "There will always be brain tumors, so we'll never have to worry about recessions," the wife said brightly. "Thank God for that!" And martinis, thank God for them.

Clara told John straight out: "I'm jealous of you!" He retaliated by picking up Clara and her classmates from school every day, taking them to drama lessons in the Topanga Community House, along with sacks full of nuts and cookies and raisins, because Canyon kids were always hungry.

John got up every morning and made me coffee. He told silly stories. We drank a lot of vodka, and many of our memories are simpleminded and one-dimensional: sitting at bars down at Warner Hot Springs, or up in San Francisco, or out on a stony beach in Hawaii, or up in Oregon, or Washington, or over in Nevada or Colorado, drinking martinis in a happy haze. We liked each other; we loved each other. We didn't have all that much in common, but, maybe again, we did.

Because it only looked as if John had come from a stable, happy home. (And he fostered this impression, with his graceful narratives.) In reality, he and his sister had been the only two American kids in the Shanghai Presbyterian Mission compound. His father was plagued with religious melancholia. (John himself had weathered two bouts of clinical depression.) John and his sister had been sent upcountry to a boarding school in Kuling, and such was his loneliness that he sometimes stole one of his mother's cat's-eye necklaces to wear when he was at school, under his collar . . .

He was too tall for China. And he was too thin. And he suffered from asthma. He was too smart for the lot of them—those missionaries who wouldn't dance or play cards or drive anywhere on Sundays. He'd escaped into his studies, but when he won his Rhodes scholarship no one but his sister back in Shanghai had believed it. When Knopf bought his first book, his father had asked, "Are you sure you're not putting any of your *own* money into this, John?" And on his forty-fifth birthday, John had received a letter from his missionary father reminding him that it was still not too late to "begin living a good and useful life."

Our lives changed. I bought a bigger house in Topanga and invited John to live with me. We created a bit of a stir at UCLA, and I got to experience being the world's oldest living floozy. I lost one of my best friends—Joan, the giddy, tortured girl I'd known since the seventh grade, the divorcée who, along with her three bundled-up kids and my two, would head off with me for a night of giggling at the China Palace. "I can't stand your happiness," she said. "I can't stand that you're with John."

Night after night we'd put our families together in varying combinations—with varying degrees of success. But at lunch just the two of us played hooky at a restaurant in Westwood, eating crabmeat and papaya salad, washed down with three martinis. Oh, happy, harmless daze!

My liver rebelled. I had to stop drinking for a while. We made up new rules: we drank only when we were over the county line (which

John Espey as a Rhodes Scholar at Merton College, Oxford, posing mighty hard.

made for a lot of nice road trips out of LA). We moved toward a compromise. We drank white wine; we drank champagne. But nowhere in the story of John and me is there ever going to turn up the bitter nighttime brawl that starts out: "The trouble with *you* is ...!" Because in twenty years that has never happened.

Our lives began to slide into sleepy routine, punctuated by simple, soothing treats.

Lisa had been out of the house for a few years. Her childhood had been extremely rigorous: she'd started as a happy kid who'd loved to imitate kittens, but my divorce from her father had knocked that sense of joy right out of her. She'd been happy with Clara when she was born, and unbelievably sweet to her, but my divorce from Tom had modulated her affection into hard responsibility. While I earned a living, Lisa got stuck with endless maternal chores.

As a teenager in Topanga in the sixties she must have had her share of high times, but she tells me now: "Just say I smoked my first joint with my grandfather and Mom, and I haven't touched the stuff for over twenty years!" Because of the circumstances of financial deprivation and divorce, she'd worked as hard as any of us just to keep afloat. She had a charming and natural ditzyness that had been crusted over by caution, control, dignity, and—I hate to even say it—a certain sadness. She'd found out, way too young, what can happen in a life. She was stunningly beautiful, fairy-tale beautiful, with translucent skin, delicate limbs, and flaming hair that hung to her knees, but she seemed careless about her beauty. She just blew it off. She was naturally *good:* once, carrying a rowdy Clara up the switchback path, she slipped and fell into the tramline bed. Instinctively, she twisted her body so that she landed on her back, saving Clara. And Lisa had a bad back ever afterward. She was the strongest of us all.

But after college she'd gone off to Greece with a nice guy named Roy. She'd put in years of grinding work. It was time for a good time—and she'd been studying demotic Greek for years.

Richard Kendall and Lisa See Kendall. I love the looks on their faces.

Lisa's parents and the newlyweds: Richard See, Carolyn See, Richard Kendall, Lisa See Kendall.

Somewhere in the year 1978 Lisa broke up with her boyfriend. She came home to live with us, and we—for fun—collaborated on two popular novels (where characters got to do what they *wanted* to do instead of what they had to do). Weekend after weekend we'd "play" *Lotus Land.* John, Lisa, and I, aided by plates of frozen waffles and caviar and bottles of champagne, either cheap or good, sat down to work. That champagne overcame the forty-two years that separated us—twenty-one between John and me, twenty-one between me and my older daughter. There were Sunday afternoons where we laughed so hard we fell off our couches. With enough Château Topanga in us we thought we were the funniest people in the world, and maybe we were.

Lisa married Richard Kendall, a wonderful man. It was a swell wedding, in the Lanai of the Polo Lounge at the Beverly Hills Hotel.

No one in our family that I could remember had actually done this the way my beautiful daughter did—walked down the aisle in a knock-'em-out dress—danced the afternoon away, looking more radiant than life itself. Her father had given up drinking years before and wasn't going to start again now. He was an ornament to his daughter, looking handsome in his tux, with the same goatee he'd always sported, but now it was silver.

In the next fifteen years or so, John Espey and I would travel—back to China, twice—where he would find the old mission, and the patch of grass where the Japanese had blasted his parents' home at the beginning of World War II. We traveled up the Rhine so I could write *Rhine Maidens*. We traveled to Paris for Christmas, and to Oxford for the Rhodes Scholars reunion. We *traveled*, as he'd said he wanted to. And we wrote. Some would say, big deal! But for us it was a big deal. When people would ask, "How's John?" I'd say, "Oh, fine," knowing that was a great conversation stopper, but he never did anything crazy, so what was there to report?

And John, after a certain amount of stalling, began to publish again, so much that one friend of ours remarked crabbily, "Who does he think he *is*, Grandma Moses?"

Then, finally, as we were flying to New York for a meeting of the National Book Critics Circle, John picked up a copy of Denis Wholey's *The Courage to Change*, an anthology that chronicled the many ways that Americans from Jerry Falwell to Pete Townshend had stopped drinking. As I remember (and I remember it fuzzily, because I was scared to death of flying, and pouring down Bloody Marys as fast as the stewardess could bring them), John remarked that he thought he might stop drinking.

Well if he was going to, I would too, not that day because I was five Bloody Marys in the bag, and the plane hadn't landed yet. But tomorrow, Sunday, before the NBCC convened on Monday, I would certainly stop with him, if that seemed to him like the right thing to do.

Sunday went by—we went to a matinee in Times Square and then came back to the Royalton, where I began to lose it. I thought about New York, and books, and all we wanted to do and hadn't done yet, and all those critics I'd be meeting the next day: Elizabeth Hardwick and the woman who'd sat between me and Elizabeth Hardwick the year before and snubbed me so badly that when I looked in her direction all I saw was a seething morass of frizzy hair, never her face, so intent was she on attending to Elizabeth Hardwick.

"I can't do it, John. I need a drink. Just a beer, OK?"

He took me across to the Algonquin and bought me a beer in the lobby—two beers. He had a club soda. It was a tense time for us. He wanted a drink, and I was waiting for reproaches, either plain or fancy. But he never reproached me in the years that followed. We were close enough together now that I guess he trusted me not to drive a car off the road or throw up on his shoes or say something astonishingly cruel. I went on drinking—only white wine and champagne, but isn't that what every alcoholic says, just as my stepdad Jim considered that he'd "stopped" drinking when he changed from scotch to vodka? I waited for the contemptuous look, or the rolled eye, or the zinging remark slung out at a party, but because John was so relentlessly good, none of those things ever happened. I believe John felt that you needed it as long as you needed it, and maybe his missionary parents had drummed it into him to judge not.

11. THE EMBARRASSING CALIFORNIANNESS OF IT ALL

Clara, Lisa, and me. We see abundance *everywhere* !

*G*oing back in time a couple of years—to 1976, when John and I moved into our new house in Topanga: it was kind of a jolt. The view was spectacular, celestial, but it was a new house, with nothing but scraped bare dirt around it. There were bourgeois things like a double garage and central heating and a scary yellow shag rug—wall to wall.

Clara didn't like it. Lisa hadn't come home yet, so just the three of us moved in. Tom and I went into one last screaming-and-hanging-up frenzy in a fight over a *cat*, who Tom insisted he wanted and wanted and then decided he didn't want. Clara tried to be brave.

Tom came into the kitchen a couple of times and opened the refrigerator looking for beer, but John took him to lunch and announced that if Tom did that again, John would hit him. Tom was enchanted. "Can you imagine? The guy said he'd hit me!" he told me on the phone, and then gave this match his limited blessing: "If anybody can live with you, *he* probably can."

But it was hard—the cooking, the cleaning, John's niceness—which could give you the heebie-jeebies sometimes. Mainly two things worried us: there was an eerie emptiness, even though we liked each other, loved each other. John's first allegiance had to be to his daughters and grandson, and I had my own daughters to think of. The other worry was more concrete and pressing. Money. That mortgage. That gas bill. Food. So one afternoon when a plucky single mother, Lisa Connolly, called up and asked me to go to an afternoon "money seminar" for only ten bucks, I agreed.

In someone's drab living room, a pleasant woman in a pink dress asked us all—about twenty dead-broke single moms—to please keep an open mind, and then began to talk to us about "scarcity consciousness" and "affirmations." She suggested that our belief systems contributed directly and indirectly to the amount of money we had.

She suggested we take turns around the circle and say "My income increases daily, whether I'm working, playing, or sleeping," or "My job is my pipeline by which I tap the infinite wealth of my United States economy." One woman objected strongly. "It's not *my* United States! And even if it were, the United States economy is going right into the toilet. What do you say to *that*?"

"I don't know," the woman replied hesitantly. "You want to say universal economy?" But the woman wanted her money back. The seminar leader, Susan Skye, displayed a small flash of temper. "What's the big deal? You say 'I'm broke, I'm going to lose this job, my boss hates me, I'll never find a decent man,' *all the time!* So what if you just say, 'I stay on purpose joyously?' Is that going to *kill* you or something? I mean, what do you want to do in your life?"

But this gaunt, gray, overworked mom didn't know. Nobody had ever asked her.

"Well," Susan said, "what if you went to a travel agent and said, 'Give me a ticket out of here!' And the guy said, 'Where to, Madam?' You couldn't go anywhere if you didn't know where you were going!"

When Susan suggested that we set up four bank accounts: one for daily life, one for "large purchases" like stereo equipment, one for investments, and one for permanent wealth, something you never spend but just look at and feel rich, about half the women looked as if they were going to throw up. "Put in a dollar a week," Susan said. "Put in a *quarter* a week. That'll be a quarter more than you have now!"

But some of us got pretty excited, and somewhere in the third hour of a four-hour seminar, Susan smiled. "You're beginning to get it. This isn't about money. Money is just the metaphor." She talked about her two mentors: Leonard Orr and Leo Sunshine. "Leonard is the serious one. He sees the dark side of things. Leo is still a kid. He's like a kid with a big new toy."

This was November of 1976. In January of 1977, *Money* magazine flew John and me to San Francisco to sit in on Leo's two-day, four-night seminar, to debunk this New Age Fraud. On the hotel stairs to the mezzanine, I heard some guy say to his date: "This is supposed to be the most fun of all of them!"

And here in this (actually rather small) hotel meeting room the atmosphere was charged with anticipation. A young man in a purple velvet suit zoomed out and advised us to take a good look at the world we saw now, this Thursday night, because the one we'd see next Monday morning would be a different world, then Leo Sunshine appeared, cute and in his early twenties.

Leo was Brian Murphy in his other, less magical life. As a youth, he told us during the weekend, he'd run drugs from San Francisco to Tokyo and back. He'd got caught and his girlfriend, as he'd languished in an Asian jail, had sent him the devastating telegram: SENDING NO MONEY, DON'T WRITE. Leo did time in a second jail in Northern California, when Werner Erhardt himself had run an est seminar for the convicts and had repeated to them at some length that "they were responsible for their own condition."

Leo bought the material, but he thought Werner was a glum kind of guy, and that he didn't cover all the bases. When Leo got out of jail he went into a frenzy of New Age self-improvement—taking classes in judo, aikido, rolling-and-falling. He got Rolfed (and said that where it got him the most was in his right arm, from the many times he'd wanted to bash his mom). That didn't keep him from taking a good backward glance at his mother and grandmother's religion, Unity, which had started in the Midwest during the middle of the nineteenth century, and set great store by "affirmations," "visualization," "outflowing," "treasure maps," and so on. Leo persevered: he got "cleared" by Scientologists; he took classes in Feldenkries. "So then I realized I was the only one around who had all of it to offer," he said modestly. "I thought I'd do a seminar of my own. Now we're going to do a game about passing, and what you get to do is pass. Take as much money out of your pocket as you can be accountable for and start passing. Go ahead, get up. Walk around! Start passing."

At the end of ten minutes, Leo stopped us. "How did that go?" John and I saw with relief that we had about as much money as we'd started with, but in the exchange of money—only ten minutes long!—a lot of drama had been generated. Little kids and men had tripled their investment, taking twenties as they were passed to them and handing out ones instead, and there was a strong contingent of near-hysterical women who demanded their money back: "That was my *cab* money! I need it to get home! That was my *rent* money, someone has to give it back to me!" But no one in the crowd felt like doing it.

"Didn't you hear me when I said, 'Take out as much money *as you can be accountable for?'* Don't you think you've been playing this game all your *lives?*"

In the middle of the ensuing pandemonium, I (and a lot of other people) considered that we might at least have had a hand in creating our own reality. To think of it! That my stepfather burned my baby pictures as part of some dopey game. That I mourned Tom Sturak for six years as part of a goddamn game. But Leo said that if we'd spent lifetimes creating disaster, we could take a turn and have a go at creating its opposite.

Oh, the embarrassing Californianness of it all! Do you think we didn't feel it, with our scholarly ways, our high IQs, our own morbidly glittering histories of suffering? Do you think we didn't feel *dumb* when we were forced to jump up and *dance,* singing inanely, "I deserve to be loved! Oh I deserve to be loved! Yes I deserve to be loved, loved all of the time!"

Leo might have been callow but he wasn't a sap. When, fifteen years later, *Time* and *Newsweek* ran stories about particle physics and chaos theory, we'd snort in disgust. "*Leo* knew that! He knew that *years* ago!" Leo would stretch out both his arms and wiggle first one set of fingers, then the other. "Move over here, it's going to shake over there. See? Think of it as cosmic Jell-O!"

At the end of the first night he sent us off to our hotel rooms with the injunction to repeat: "I'm a powerful, loving, and creative person, and I can handle it, and I can have anything I want." We thought it over.

Money was not the object in these four strange days. Leo thought—he *knew*—he had the universe aced. He was close to figuring out how it worked. But he had had no real education, he was an ex-con, and he spelled all right "alright." Because he was a kid, and a guy, he was interested in spiritual muscle building more than anything else. He dearly wanted to levitate. We spent time making each other light (lifting up burly guys with our little fingers) or making ourselves heavy. One young man totally stumped Leo, who couldn't lift him off the ground. Leo huffed and grunted and then walked around the guy. "How're you doing that?" he asked.

"I am an oak tree," the young guy panted. "I have roots all the way down to the very center of the earth!"

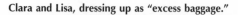

Clara and Lisa, dressing up as "excess baggage."

"Amazing," Leo said, and then lifted the guy up. "Because I am the *only* power," he said, "that can lift the roots of an oak tree out of the center of the earth."

We began to look at how people carried themselves—as victim or predator—and saw that each role was utterly silly. We got a forty-minute crash course in how marriages go wrong. We were sternly advised to give away 10 percent of our money to worthy causes. And life was a party, we were to remember that. A party where we were the guests of honor.

John and I flew home to LA and found Lisa and her boyfriend Roy, back from Greece. Roy was yellow as a lemon, half-dead from hepatitis. He'd already almost died in the Vietnam war, and had his face covered up in a helicopter by a tactless nurse. The poor guy had been through the wringer. Lisa was on the edge of tears.

But John and I responded with obnoxious New Age jolliness. "Surround your lives with a burst of golden light, and you'll get well again!"

Two weeks later Leo flew down to LA. John and I dragged Lisa, Roy, and Clara to see him. They were angry, and I didn't blame them. Money was tight and here I was throwing it away. The first night, when Leo suggested that we might have had a hand in creating our own reality, Roy, whose liver count was still high up in the dangerous thousands, got mad. "Now wait a minute!" he growled. "Are you telling me they left me for dead and I got maggots in my spine in Vietnam because I *wanted* to?"

Leo looked at Roy with a flicker of scorn. "You were in the Marines, weren't you?"

"Yes!"

"I don't believe you get drafted into the Marines. I believe you enlist in the Marines, right?"

Clara, at Leo's.

Lisa, at Leo's.

"Well, yes."

Clara absolutely wouldn't dance. But Leo said, "How can you expect to have any fun in life if you don't *dance?*" He pulled her twelve-year-old body up out of her chair. She stood frowning at him, her darkest Sturakian scowl. He blammed her with his own hip. "What's the point of being so *stuck?* Aren't you ever going to have any *fun?*"

Scowling, Clara began to move, just a little.

Later, Leo asked Lisa if she could have anything she wanted, what would it be? She didn't answer right away, and kept her aloof look, which, once you really examined it, was no more than the very thinnest porcelain mask over the dearest sweetest face in the world. I thought with a pang of shame that probably no one had ever asked her what she really wanted, not once.

"A house," she said finally.

"Then what?" Leo's idea was that we'd been culturally limited by the idea of "three wishes," that we could have all the wishes we wanted if we just asked for them.

"Another house."

Then what?

"Another *house!*"

And then?

"I'd like another house."

And then?

How could I have not allowed myself to see how yearning for simple nurturing and shelter Lisa was? She wanted five houses, before she got around to a car, or world peace, or whatever came next.

Thursday and Friday night, Lisa and Roy remained reserved. What a dubious procedure it was, after all, hanging out in a hotel room with a guy named Sunshine. But Saturday or Sunday, as Lisa sat in front of us, I saw what I still count as one of the sweetest sights in my whole life. Lisa laughed *so hard,* probably at Leo's monologue about bad marriage—the stupid Frederico ruining the life of the luckless Marylou by spilling mayonnaise on her freshly waxed floor and Marylou retaliating by stepping "accidentally" on Frederico's new fishing rod—that her long, rich, red hair began to shimmer and shake, and she laughed so hard she fell right off her folding chair.

And Roy laughed so hard that on Saturday night, at one in the morning, he ate more than he usually did, and said he felt better.

He felt so much better that the next Monday he went into Veterans' Hospital to be tested. His SGOT had gone down from 5,000-and-something to a measly thirty-five. The only bona-fide "miracle" any one of us had ever seen—although my first step-mother had prattled on about them at length to anyone who would listen.

All of us had an interesting time with Leo during the year 1977. What he said went to the very philosophical heart of the nature of suffering. What if you were just a little baby with your legs blown off? Leo dismissed that with an indifferent *tut tut*. You must have decided to get born into that situation, because children always chose their parents, for the lessons they'd get taught in this new life. He may have lost us right around there. But I thought, gee whiz! It's easier to believe *that* than in One God in Three Divine Persons. Lisa and Clara looked faintly ill that they might have actually chosen the hand they were dealt, but they were good sports about it. And Leo didn't pretend that he knew all the answers. He was just tinkering around with the universe, trying to figure out how it worked. He was obsessed with the shining frontier where art and physics and getting your own way met.

El Protecto, Leo's hand puppet, the physical embodiment of our

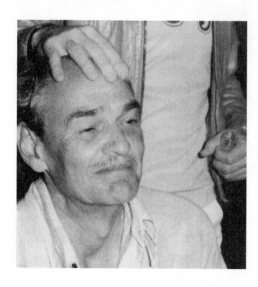

John getting glitter on his head.

elusive fears and most caustic self-criticism, told everybody all the bad things that could happen. Leo said repeatedly "If you get nothing else out of this, just get it about El Protecto! He means well. But what do you do when he tells you about breast cancer or your bank account or the next earthquake or the next war? Or just that you're too dumb to hold a job? Be polite to him! Just say *thank you*! Don't get mad. Just say *thank you*."

Leo went away at the end of 1977. He took a trip to Egypt, spent the night in one of the Pyramids, poured a whole bottle of Brut cologne around him to get rid of the stink of urine. When he came back he was as boring as anyone else who's been to the Pyramids. He said that he wanted to learn how to materialize wristwatches so that as they materialized they would exactly match the numbers on certain watches as they came off some Swiss assembly line. (The question was: *why?* Why not just go out and buy the watch?)

All this wasn't a game. It had to do with life, *was* life. When my father was diagnosed with lung cancer he had the chance to go with Dr. Simonton (stern taskmaster of visualization who has about a 50 percent death rate), or hike on down to the laetrile clinic in Tijuana, where, for twenty dollars a week, he could live with Lynda by the beach, eat yogurt, stop smoking, and probably live two years in relative suntanned, painless peace.

But he chose to check into Scripps Hospital, go through terrible and expensive agony, and put his family through it too. His supervising physician called me on Christmas Eve: "Merry Christmas! I called to tell you it's gone up into his brain!" Certainly some of this ghastly charade might have been avoided. But my father didn't want to avoid it. It would have been cowardly, in his eyes, not to suffer.

It was around this same time that Lisa and her friend Roy parted. A morning came when she sat outside at the top of our steep driveway, crying. "I'm not going inside there if I have to be your daughter and Clara's mother again! I'm *not* going to get stuck with all the dirty work while you write!" A half-hour later she was in the house, laying down her terms.

The years Lisa spent with us as a grown-up were some of the happiest in my life, and I think she had fun too. The three of us—she, John, and I, collaborated on those swashbuckling historical novels, and the three of *us,* at least, were crazy in love with our pseudonymous alter ego, Monica Highland. We were working out a whole new way of living. Taking endless television meetings, that led us into writing scripts that made us think we were in a bad Hollywood novel. We blabbed at women's clubs, arranged publication parties. When John published a book of poetry, Lisa introduced so many people to one another at his party that she said she thought of herself as a human infinity sign: "East, meet West!" "Black! Say hi to White!" "Evil, shake hands with Good," and captivated a man who would soon become her father-in-law. We were having some fun here. More fun than we'd ever had.

Lisa got up at five A.M. to catch a new TV evangelist—she was doing an assignment for *TV Guide*—and woke us up at five-fifteen to catch the rest of the half-hour show. We saw a blond woman wearing a linen blazer directly under the flight path of the San Diego airport. She was standing in Balboa Park, by a stream, with some ducks. Terry Cole Whittaker had to speak up from underneath all those planes. She talked about doing treasure maps to get what you want. She talked about generating energy—going out and *doing* something with your life. She'd had a flock of husbands and talked about them with loving scorn. She'd once entered the Mrs. America contest to prove she was a perfect wife. She'd always wanted to be a singer, but hadn't got around to it, not yet.

She'd gone to Cal State, LA, the same impoverished set of Quonset huts that I had. She couldn't stop laughing. The only places where she faltered were when she asked for money or when she quoted from Scripture. She always lost her place. She couldn't make her text match her homily.

Tagging along with Lisa down the coast while she interviewed Terry Cole W., we ended up at a small morning seminar of wealthy La Jolla matrons. "Every yacht has its barnacles," Terry cautioned. "When you get the yacht you get the barnacles. And very often a drunk captain as well. You want to be sure that you're up for *all* of it, not just the yacht." And later, at a hotel in San Diego, we saw that Terry had herself a new assistant, the prancing man in the velvet suit who used to open for Leo.

Because Leo was gone now. The story went that instead of leaving to learn to materialize wristwatches, Mr. Sunshine put together a cadre of his most devoted followers and went back to his old vocation, running drugs. They'd set up a semicircular route across half the world, from New Delhi to Montreal to upstate New York, to New York City and back. The run was successful until Leo himself was nabbed in upstate New York, where they didn't believe in men who thought they could make themselves invisible. Then the story was that Leo had escaped in a garbage truck, and been caught again. Trapped in a dank, miserable upstate New York jail cell, the small, spoiled, undereducated, overinformed young man had given it his all, and melted through a wall.

"I don't doubt it for a minute," my younger daughter, Clara, opined. "He próbably said *Baba Help Me Now!* And *went* for it!" The story was that he returned to New Delhi, where he was seen several times in a beautifully tailored white suit, and was finally killed in a shootout.

How could he have done that? How could he have taken away so much fun and put so much of what he said into moral jeopardy? But one of his more charitable followers said, "He was just a kid. He got loaded with too much information, and he shorted out."

But his material, his message, stayed around, considerably cleaned up by Marianne Williamson, who, despite her enormously successful best sellers, liked nothing more than to work a small obscure church on the West Side of LA like a late-night supper club: another inspired ditz, knocking herself out with her own jokes, talking about visualizations and affirmations and tithing and transforming the moment, dredging giggles from very sick men, because Marianne was and is into working with AIDS "victims," guys who have been knocked silly by the greatest plague of this generation. There's nothing wrong with helping people, she said often. "Why, *some* people, they'd call Mother Teresa an enabler!"

The same material. You can transform the moment simply by *transforming* it, in a millisecond. You can confound darkness by bringing light to bear on the subject. When religion runs out, you can reach around for a fistful of particle physics. You can unite the abyss and the golf course in one sweet cosmic spark.

—

Two whacked-out women and one sociopathic ex-con. The embarrassing *Californianness* of it all! If we wanted something to believe in, why couldn't we have just put on our Sunday clothes and hauled out to church? (When Terry Cole Whittaker threw an Easter service in a hotel down in San Diego, thousands of people showed up, with glitter on their cheeks and hair. The ushers wore bunny suits and squirting flowers on their lapels and zipped around on rollerskates, and the idea of skates had come from Leo, who loved to see his assistants zip around on skates.)

Why not go to regular church? Because the churches were run by affluent heterosexual men (at least they advertised themselves that way). They had nothing to gain by change. The bottom two thirds of the American population was drowning, drowning, and the guys in the big churches knew it, as did everyone in America who ever turned on a television set, but the guys in the big churches didn't give a vestment one way or another. It was just the embarrassing *Americanness* of it: all those people struggling with the social explosion that drugs, drink, depression, demoralization, and divorce had been detonating for over half a century like a nationwide string of firecrackers. All across the country, new ways of thinking and newly constructed belief systems were being chosen—systems that could possibly glue back millions of splintered lives.

In the South, people began being "born again," faster and faster, and a belief in a Satan as personable and charming as the young Christ himself also sprang up. All over the country, journalists wrote about Satan as if he was a Raiders' halfback, only a lot more interesting, and *why not?* How else could you explain PCP, gang warfare,

**Me, at Leo's.
I know it's not suitable,
but there it is.**

methamphetamines, the depletion of the ozone level, and the mass rape of nursery school kids?

And Blacks were taking up martial arts (said by some to be the one true cure for heroin addiction) and Oriental medicine (including acupuncture, said to *really* be the one true cure for heroin addiction) and homeopathy all united to be an alternative belief to big-hospital science which is just as dull and twice as scary as big-church religion.

If you squint your eyes a little, this search for a new belief system that will once again make us members of a meaningful family might be the thrust behind the Pro-Life movement. The Pro-Lifers, with their relative lack of formal education, have been metaphorically orphaned. They have been tricked; they have been laid off, short-changed, scorned. They know from their own lives what it is to have been *scraped off.* Maybe they think: there's going to be an end to all the scraping!

We *will* be a family again! A family like we seem to remember, with pigeons in the backyard, and a tree house and ballet lessons for the kids. And Mother in the kitchen or in the back bedroom, crying. We don't give a goddamn where she is as long as she's there. And Dad comes home at night.

But all along, through a good part of this century, there's been another belief system, perhaps the great modern religion of America today, where blind faith and high intelligence fit together with no problem; where it's a given that most families in America have been smashed to bits by drugs, drink, depression, divorce. They are the ones who have smashed their own families, but they are the ones who can put new families together again.

They do it by getting together, sometimes several times a day. They can do it by telling stories to pass the time, which everyone knows is the best way to comfort people, because everyone who's heard a story becomes part of it. They can be born again, in a way that's not embarrassing. Or not *too* embarrassing.

It's AA, of course. But you have to be a drunk or an addict to get in. Doesn't that frost you? Doesn't that *chap your ass?*

I'm stuck, in my own life, believing in a little guy looking at a dark jail wall in upstate New York. Maybe if I believe enough, it will have happened, and Leo Sunshine/Brian Murphy will have met the end he longed for, in a dusty Delhi thoroughfare redolent of spices, the air thick with danger and intrigue in the cosmic haze where art, science, and destiny sometimes meet.

Rose.

One rainy afternoon in November 1988, I passed the time with domestic chores and then more or less gave up on it, sitting on our flowered couch, watching the rain come down. The phone rang. A woman with a strong Mexican accent sobbed out, "Penny! Penny! Michael's dead, oh, he's *dead*!" I only knew two Michaels, bright and lively, wonderful kids. But had they been *Mexican*? I began feverishly thinking of any "Michael" who might be related to the frantic voice on the phone. But after a long moment, I could only say, "I'm sorry, but Michael who?"

"Oh, Penny! How quickly you forget!"

And it dawned on me, only my immediate family calls me Penny.

"Who are you? And who is Michael?"

"Rose's *husband,* Michael. Oh, you don't even remember your own *sister!*"

But I'd had social workers and even a private detective looking for Rose for years. And given up on it, taken it up again, decided all over it would be best never to find her.

"Wait. Wait! Don't get off the phone. Tell me about Michael!" I scrambled around for a pencil, some paper. "I . . . haven't seen or heard from Rose for years."

"Oh, really?" The Mexican lady had stopped crying. "Well, Michael was Rose's husband for about ten years, you know."

"I'm so sorry about your son. How did he . . . ?"

"Oh, honey, he was swimming in his swimming pool. It was about six o'clock at night, you know? And he got tired and he just died."

"That's terrible."

"Well, it was two years ago. But you know what Rose was doing? She was putting on her mascara. That girl was putting on her mascara! I said, 'Rose, you should have been out there with him! You *know* how tired he was getting.'"

"You're Rose's mother-in-law? Do you still see her?" The address, the phone number I've been waiting for, looking for—and avoiding—was a sentence or two away.

"Oh, honey, I've seen her a lot in these last two years. She's gone down, you know. She's gone down a lot since Michael died. But she'll always be like a daughter to me. I say that to her. 'Michael gave you a home. And as long as I'm alive, you have a home with me.' But she's real conceited, Rose. But I've seen her times when she's loaded or when she's drinking [she pronounced it "drinkeen"], that, oh, she looks so bad, and she feels so bad, she really *needs* somebody, you know? And kid, when she's drinking, her stomach bloats up, you know? And her face? She just loses all her looks."

"What happened to her after your son died?"

"She said she would stay in to Oakland because she had some friends up there. But she would get real lonesome and she would call us, and she'd be crying. She'd say, 'Sylvia, I miss Michael so much! He's the only one I'm ever going to love. He's my only *husband*.' Because that Hungarian man she was married to, he was really awful, you know? He was always going to jail, and finally he was deported."

"Ferenç," I say. "I remember."

"Well, so she'd cry and say she missed us all. So she came back and stayed with us for a few months, but she was always stealing things from us, and getting loaded, and selling drugs out of the house, and my other sons said, 'She's just taking advantage of you,' and so I finally said, 'Rose, I love you like a daughter, but you've got to go.' So she went back up north, and she had nothing, you know, no clothes, no anything, and she stayed with a Mexican man, he was married but he was good to her, but you know how she is, and finally he had to kick her out. Right out to the street! And she's not as young as she was. That life's not good for her."

"The drugs," I say. "I know she was into a lot of drugs."

"Oh yes, but by then she was using Southern Comfort, because she couldn't afford anything else. She'd go into a liquor store and take a half pint of Southern Comfort and drink it and go lie down in a park, and get up and do it again. And that's so dangerous up in Oakland! That's when we decided to go up and see her. We all got in the car and drove up to Oakland. And the address, where she lived with that married man? The house was boarded up. We got up and got out of the car and walked around the street, and we were shouting, *Rose!* It was real late at night, but we knew she was around there somewhere. We found her in another man's house across the street, and she was bad, real bad. So we took her down to the hospital. I thought, how can this be my little Rose? I thought we were going to lose her right then."

"And what happened?"

"Oh, she got better and we took her home with us again. She was real sweet, she can be real sweet. But then one day she went out, and we got a call, Rose's lying down in the park, and the cops were driving around the block and they were yelling at her to get up. So I got in the car with my sister and we went to get her, but we went to the wrong park. We went home and then the cops called us and said they'd booked her, and they found all her other tickets and warrants and they said she's going to have to go north to serve some time in jail. So she went."

I look around my darkening living room. Over the telephone, I heard Sylvia sigh.

"Sylvia? Do you know where she is now? Can you give me an address? Is she in jail or what?"

"Oh, I think she's out. And she's probably on that same street between that married guy and that black guy. She goes back and forth between them. I think I have their numbers some place." And after a long pause she read off two numbers but only gave me one name. The black guy was Charles. The married man, Al, was sensitive about his name getting out. He wants to keep his wife.

Then there really wasn't anything more to say.

"Why'd you call me today, Sylvia? When you had my number all this time?"

"I don't know. I guess because it was raining, and I got sad."

—

Twice during the last twenty years, my mother had tuned up to die. During both these medical crises, the question of trying to find Rose had come up. If my mother was checking out, shouldn't she have the opportunity to say good-bye to her younger daughter?

But the truth was, she couldn't stand her younger daughter, and she didn't like the rest of us, either. My idealized vision of finding Rose faded.

Until this phone call from the mysterious Sylvia. She had left me with two phone numbers: the day after the phone call, I called both.

Al almost perished when he found out who I was. He told me never to call that number, and gave me another number, and then called back later in the day to tell me never to call him at the second number, and gave me a third one. "I haven't seen Rose in weeks," he said, not very reassuringly, "but I know she's out there on the streets. I'll ask around. But don't call unless you have to. I'll call you, OK?"

Charles was a different breed of cat. He was drunk and overwhelmingly genial: "You Rose's sister? You Rose's *sister*? I know Rose for a long time. I didn't know she had a sister. No, I did know that. I *did* know that. So, you Rose's sister!"

Was there a place where I could find her?

"Do *I* know where Rose is? My house is open to her. I don't have much. The Lord knows I don't have much." He started to weep energetically. "But whatever I have goes out to Rose. I have esteem for that girl. I have respect for that girl." He thought about it. "Even though she steal me blind every time she come here."

"Well . . . Charles? Does she come over to your house a lot? Is there any other place I could find her?"

"She come here when she need something. She come here when

she sick. She come around and steal from poor old Charles. She sleep in Charles's bed when she don't got another one. That what she *do*."

"But . . ."

"You're her sister, right? Oh, she speak to me often about her sister. She say, 'I got a sister, Charles. You never going to meet my sister.' But here I *am*, Rose, talking to your sister. Oh, you never think of *that*, Rose!"

Old Charles was pretty far gone.

"Here's what I'm going to do," I said. "I'm going to give you my phone number. And you're going to write it down. The next time you see Rose, you tell her I'm looking for her, and give her my number."

"What if she don't want your number?" He pronounced it *yoah numbah*. "She don't like her sister very much."

"That can't be right," I told him. "She doesn't like her *mother*."

During the next two months, Charles called once or twice a day, once or twice a night.

"I seen Rose today," he'd say. "Oh, she in terrible shape."

"Did you give her my number?"

"Oh, you don't want to see her. She in terrible shape."

"What did she *say*, Charles?"

"Oh, I didn't talk to her. You can't talk to that girl! *You* try talking to Rose. *You* see how far it get you!"

"You didn't even give her my message?"

"She five, six blocks *away*. I ain't going to run five or six blocks just to talk to *Rose*. I got a life to live, I got my dream, you live down in LA?"

"Huh?"

"Doan give me none of your sass. You heard what Charles said. You live down in LA or *not*? I got to *know* before I go forward."

Pretty soon it got so Charles would just call up to say hi. "Hi, it's Charles, how you doin?"

Every time he would call, he'd call collect. Every time the operator would tell me Charles was calling, I'd think he'd found Rose. Sometimes he wanted to talk about what he was watching on television, or about the nature of love. "Does it work better if the man love the woman too much, or if the woman love the man too much? You tell *me*!"

When I suggested that John and I come up to Oakland to look for Rose, Charles said no. "People like you be *killed* on these mean streets."

Finally, at 3:30 one morning, I was jangled out of sleep by Charles. The operator said it was urgent. When Charles came on the line, he was irate. "I can't stand it any more. You be jivin me, Carol! You been trodding on Charles. I can't stand it."

My daughter Clara stormed into the room.

"Give the goddamned phone to me," she shouted, and yelled into it as loud as she knew how. *"Goddamn it, Charles!* You may stay up all night drinking and God knows what else, but there are people in this house who HAVE TO WORK FOR A LIVING! We're HONEST PEOPLE! And don't call us at all if you can't find Rose. GOT THAT?"

She stormed back into her room, slamming the door so hard that dust whirled around in the lamplight.

We didn't hear from Charles again for a few weeks, and when he called this time, he was businesslike. "Have you heard from Al?"

"No."

"He gonna call you soon. Stay by the phone. Don't leave now!"

Less than an hour later, Al did call. "I've got her here."

"Can I talk to her?"

"She's in pretty bad shape."

"We'll be right up."

"I can't keep her here."

I thought of Rose at seventeen, wearing a feather boa, proclaiming to one and all that she was going on "The True Diet." I wished my dad was alive, even though he wasn't her dad. He'd know what to do.

"What I could do," Al said, "is try to get her into a rehab program. She usually says no. But I think I could do it. She hasn't got anything else right now."

That evening, he called back. "We did it. We got her into a place."

"We're coming up, then. We're going to see her."

"You can do that. You can check into the Oakland Hyatt."

"What's the name of the place you put her in?"

"I don't remember. But you wait at the hotel. I'll be in the lobby tomorrow at noon. I remember the way to the place. You can follow me over there."

"How will we know you?"

"I'll know you. I'll give you a signal."

The next morning we flew to Oakland, rented a car, stopped and started our way across slums where, because of the recent earthquake, two-story frame houses from the turn of the century had been tipped off their foundations. House after house sported "condemned" signs, but people were living in them anyway, Blacks who looked curiously cheerful and carefree. The ground where the double-decker freeway had squashed all those drivers had been scraped absolutely clean.

We checked into the Hyatt, sat on the bed, looked at each other. It was about eleven A.M. We hadn't thought too much about this. For instance, how would Al know us? Rose and I hadn't seen each other, except for occasional glimpses, in twenty years. And she'd never seen John. How could she have told Al what to look for, who to look for?

We spent a silly three or four hours in which John and I took turns staying in the lobby or staying upstairs by the phone, or leaning in the hotel doorway. I went up to every vaguely Latino guy I saw and whispered, *Al?* As we waited, the lobby filled up with African-American families. Huge groups came streaming in, mothers and grandmoms and a zillion young men in expensive sports clothes and uncles and dads, all of them earnest and harried, carrying every kind of luggage. The girls (or their moms) hauled what looked like big wads of fluff in plastic garment bags.

Finally, I was paged in the lobby. It was John, calling from our room. "He's phoned. He doesn't want to see us, and he doesn't want us to see him. But he drove over to the halfway house this morning. He gave us directions."

We hauled out the car and chugged up to Berkeley. A quarter of a block from the university campus, we found the house. Vines covered the front wall. Wrought-iron latticework stood patiently under tangled honeysuckle vines. Inside, the place gave way to the look of a bare and scary institution, filled with haggard, blank-eyed dope fiends.

Half an hour later, I'd gotten the word. Yes, a Rose had been remanded to them, just that morning. But didn't I know that they never let their clients see, write, or talk to their family for at least six months, probably a year? If I'd cared about her so much, why hadn't I thought to take care of her during all the years she'd been outside? I asked if I could at least leave her a note, to tell her I'd been to see her. The man in charge said yes. Then, as I reached the door of his office, he threw the note in his wastebasket and gave me a big smile.

That night, John and I ate in the sandwich bar of the Oakland Hyatt, which jutted out from a mezzanine on the south side of a two-story space. The north side of the space was taken up with escalators that zoomed up and down from another whole mezzanine that connected to the hotel rooms. A grand ballroom abutted the lobby.

Tonight, hundreds of black debutantes were coming out in Oakland. John and I ordered salads. He ordered Perrier and I drank white wine as we watched an enormous and wonderful party begin to take shape.

A zillion little kids, dressed in hotshot evening clothes, raced around the mezzanine balcony, then swung on over on the *down* escalator, just so they could zoom back on the *up* escalator. Every five minutes or so, a stately grandma sheathed in a wonderful corset and a gown of bronze or steel-gray bugle beads would step on the escalator and sail downward.

On the north mezzanine, handsome men shot their cuffs, leaned their elbows on the fretwork, joked, kept watchful eyes out for their womenfolk.

They came soon enough, the mothers slim and elegant in bright sequined reds and blues, bedecked with jewels and flowers and peachy makeup. Each mom or aunt or cousin seemed to have her hands plunged into the twinkling tulle of a beautiful young girl—smoothing net, yanking up a luminous white bodice. Once the female groomers finished, the families came down; father first, debutante daughter next, beautiful beyond words, coffee-colored shoulders catching the light against perfect white gown, and then, proudly, just behind, slender, bright aunts, cousins, moms.

The escorts waited for the debs at the foot of the escalator. They took the arms of the beautiful girls and turned them left, where they walked down the hall and over to the Grand Ballroom, where the music had already started.

Everyone knew each other, it went without saying. Everyone was having the best possible time.

After we finished dinner we went upstairs, got undressed, turned on the television. John went right to sleep. I figured what the hell, and called up room service for another glass of white wine.

———

Almost a year went by until John and I flew north again and this time we protected ourselves with a cover story—I had a reading at Black Oak Books in Berkeley for an anthology, *Sex, Death and God in LA*. We would try to visit, and then I would read. We didn't know if we'd be able to see her.

Rose had been having love troubles, baby troubles. She was clean and sober, living with someone named Carl, a house painter she'd met in rehab. He was sixteen years her junior, a devout Catholic, and wanted a "family." Rose had gotten pregnant, been ecstatically happy, and had a miscarriage at Carl's mother's house. They had baptized the fetus under the kitchen tap. Then Rose was pregnant again, and lost that one too.

As I talked to her on the phone, I heard sadness in her voice. They had found an apartment on the island of Alameda in San Francisco Bay, and lived across the street from a nursery school.

"Every day I see these women in their suits, with their briefcases, coming by in the morning with these little kids, and I think, how can the mothers *do* that? Just have them like they were some BMW or a toaster and then walk away and leave? And I can see them, the little kids, crying? It's like they're saying I'll take one of these for my perfect little life, and another one of *these* for my perfect little life, and then they walk off and leave. And then on the bus, when I go to work"—she was taking care of a woman with Alzheimer's four hours a day—"I see all these—excuse me!—*niggers,* and all of them are high on crack and they have more kids on the bus with them than they know what to do with. So I ask myself, how can some nigger bitch have a baby and I can't do it? Do you think there's anything wrong with my medical history?"

It was conversations like this that had pretty much kept me from going up there. I didn't know anybody, except my mother, who talked like that, and even my mother had given it up in public. But another time, when I'd call and leave a message on the answering machine, Rose would call me back with the greatest sympathy and concern: "What is it? What is it? Are you worried about the kids? Don't you feel well?" And three out of four times she'd be right on the money.

We landed at the Oakland airport and drove north to downtown Berkeley. That night we'd rest; the next day drive over to visit Rose, then do the reading, then the next day fly on home.

Alameda. A sweet little island! Maybe half of it still given over to a naval base. The other half a maze of side streets and California cottages. A fire station. An elementary school. A crowded main street with grocery stores and clothing stores and hardware stores, but no coffeehouses, no boutiques, nobody selling ethnic art: we could have been in Wichita.

We were just on time. We got out of the car and saw that the apartments had no numbers or letters, but the manager knew Rose and pointed us up upstairs.

How could one little girl wear so much makeup? (Except she was forty-one.) She wore perfectly fitting jeans, a spotless white T-shirt, a tiny gold crucifix. The apartment, small, was wildly clean. (Except that on the coffee table there were two cups, two saucers from break-fast, and a portable makeup mirror with an opened bag of all Rose's cosmetics.) She'd neglected the trip to the kitchen in favor of her eyelashes. (To say that my mother had hated her when she'd got up at five in the morning to put on her makeup to get ready for school is to misstate the facts. If my mother could have laced Rose's cos-metics with a deadly poison and gotten away clean from the murder she would have, without a millisecond's hesitation.) There was also a curling iron on the coffee table. Rose's long brown hair had been coaxed to curl out, away from her face, in Valley Girl style.

Rose sprinted to the coffee table, picked up the cups and saucers. "The time got away from me! I thought you'd be late!" We stood there stock-still, helpless in the living room. Rose seemed so ener-getic we couldn't seem to live up to it. We couldn't think of what to say. "This is the bathroom!" And it was, yellow and spotless. "This is the bedroom!" A small room with a low-to-the-floor kingsize waterbed, perfectly made up, except for one lump. "The cat!"

In the living room, the furnishings were meager. One black leather couch. One black leather chair. One coffee table. One televi-sion set. One stereo. One big picture of a sailboat.

Rose couldn't seem to sit down. She put John in the chair, and me on one end of the couch. She sat down at the other end, got up, went out to the kitchen, checked the bathroom, got up again, offered us Diet Cokes, sat down, got up, sat down.

Rose displayed her left hand in such a way that I saw an enormous engagement ring, a diamond maybe a carat and a half, maybe more.

"Some ring!" I said.

"I went out yesterday and got it cleaned. Because you were coming."

If I ever wanted a drink in my life, it was then.

"You've got some great diamonds in your ears," she said. "What would they be, about a carat apiece? Did John buy them for you?"

But I said no, I'd bought them for myself, to celebrate when one of my novels came out. I was about to say that a lady in that book had stuck a boxful of loose jewels into her blistered hands after an atomic bomb fell in her neighborhood, but it was going to sound too dumb.

Rose leaned forward, examined those stones in my ears, and then leaned back again. "It was so sad, right after Christmas? Carl couldn't get any work because his work is seasonal. He can't work in the rain. So we just sat on this couch. Then we took the earrings he gave me for Christmas down to the pawnshop and paid the rent for that month. They're still down there. I think we can get them back pretty soon. They're very good quality.

"In fact," she went on, "the best investment you can make now is in jewelry, especially with the recession and the way the S&L's are going. Because if you get good stones—rubies are good, diamonds are good—they always keep their value, and sometimes they even go up."

"Rose! How'd you figure all this out?"

"From Michael, when he was dealing. Lots of times his customers didn't have money, and so they'd pay him with a handful of rubies or emeralds. It's a real good form of currency. And that carried over, you know? Like all the money that the dealers made? Probably the best place to put it is in jewelry stores. So if you look around now, the jewelry stores that are *new* in the country? The ones that aren't, like, some old family business from the Netherlands? The new businesses are mostly from dope money."

"Tell me about what you've been doing, Rose. Tell me about Carl."

Rose twisted around on the couch. She arched her back. She touched her neck. She patted her long hair, making sure it was still in place. "I've been wanting to ask your advice. Carl really wants to get married, and he really wants a family. But don't you think I'm too old for him? I mean, it's all right *now*, but when he's forty, I'll be fifty-six. When he's sixty, I'll be . . ."

"Careful!" I said, because John, sitting in his chair looking bemused, was seventy-nine.

"Yes, but it's different for a man."

"What does Carl's mother think?"

"Oh, she's real nice. Carl says, 'How come she's turning into such a good mom now when I don't need a good mom anymore?' All she ever used to do was work and sleep. So that's the only way Carl ever saw her. But he must have been a handful!"

"Like how?"

"Well!" she said, and smiled. "*Besides* the dope, he was always getting into accidents. He had this other wife . . . And one night when he was real young, he and his wife were going home from a party and they'd been drinking and everything else, and they had an argument about who was going to drive, so she ended up driving, and she ran into a tree, and Carl was in a coma for six weeks. He's *real* handsome! But his whole skull was bashed in and if you look at his eye and along his cheekbones, you'll see this line of stitches, and there's another thing. His eyelashes burned off and they'll never come back. They don't have plastic surgery for it. He had to learn to walk and talk all over again, and his memory is still pretty bad. Sometimes he'll ask me things like, 'How did Robert Kennedy die again? Can you remind me about that?' "

"Well," I said. "It sounds like he made a pretty good recovery."

"But right after he was getting better from all that? He went out to a biker bar, and he must have said something to get on somebody's nerves, because during the middle of a dart game a stranger shot him five times in the chest. They really thought he was dead that time! He's got this tremendous scar from here to here." She draws a line from her collarbone to her pubic bone. "That's when he thought God must be trying to tell him something, and so he got into the program."

"Is that how you met Carl? In New Bridge?"

"That was another guy, Ted. Don't you remember?"

"Do you ever see Ted?"

"I haven't seen him since they kicked me out." She shifted around, she didn't look me in the eye. Something about her puffy little cheeks reminded me . . . reminded me of me.

"They caught us fooling around, but they had to keep Ted in New Bridge because they had more of an investment in him. They were getting about five times more money for keeping him than for keeping me. Because I was off the streets, and the city was paying the minimum for me, but the Feds were paying a *lot* of money to keep Ted in the program."

"Why is that?"

"Because Ted was, what do you call it? Federated? He had owned such a big spread up north, he did such a huge business, that he was the first man in America to commit this new crime they figured out . . . they invented it for him. He wasn't just growing marijuana, he was *manufacturing* it. So he made a lot of money. And he put a lot of it away. What happened was—the government confiscated all his property and his house and cars and everything. And then he bought it all back with cash. So that's why they wanted to keep him there. He was like a feather in their cap. But Penny, Carolyn, this is what

I want to ask you: should I marry Carl or not? Because he really, really loves me. And he really wants a family."

Wordless disorientation came over me then. I could look past Rose and see the open window and leafy green trees and hear birds singing. It was about 3:30 in the afternoon. It was the regular world. The cat in the bed was a cat, the television playing with the sound down was regular Oprah. John lounging in his chair was regular John. But Rose was asking me if she should marry a twenty-four-year-old guy who couldn't remember how Robert Kennedy was killed.

I took a cowardly way out. "What does the rest of his family think?"

"His mom thinks it's fine. And his dad isn't there. And his brother—his brother is going through what I guess we all go through. He was going to be this great actor, but he's a waiter now, and he's got a job and an apartment. He's making a living and every-thing, but he's dealing with these feelings. Is this *it*? This is the life I'm going to have? Carl's been trying to help him with it. Because Carl realizes. You get up, you go to work, you come home. You buy a car. You go out. That's it. That's life. And you have to come to terms with that. But, what do you think? Should I marry Carl? Or am I just setting myself up for heartbreak? Because when he's forty, I'll be fifty-six."

I told her about Clara's coming marriage, and the bridesmaids' dresses, strapless and shocking pink. And mentioned Clara's dress, with a hundred thousand yards of tulle.

"Little Clara," she said, absently. "Can you imagine? But what should I do about Carl? Because no one has ever loved me the way he does."

"Well, what the hell," I said. "Go for it. Nobody knows what's going to happen in five years, anyway."

"Do you think so?" She twisted around to look at John and I saw her small waist, her perky breasts under the white T. "John, what do you think?"

"You should do whatever you think is best for you," he said mildly.

"So, are you coming tonight?" I asked my sister. All of a sudden, I felt jumpy as hell.

"What is it exactly?"

"A reading at Black Oak Books. Just a few blocks from New Bridge, down on Shattuck."

"I know where it is. But what's going to happen?"

"There's this new book. It's an anthology. Some of the writers are going to read from it." I felt helpless and sad, like I used to with my mother, trying to explain what it is that I do. There wasn't one book in this apartment, I realized. Not one.

"Will there be a lot of people there?"

"Not many. Maybe thirty. And there'll be a little party afterward. It would be great if you could come."

Back at the French Hotel, putting on panty hose, trying to get at the snap at the top of my black dress, pulling on a Chinese silk coat—all these were like magic gestures, grounding me back down into a familiar world. In the hall, I saw Lynell George, a beautiful girl who'd done a chapter in *Sex, Death and God in LA*. She seemed thrilled and excited and vigorous and young. And, with a couple of other writers, we walked two blocks to Black Oak.

Like life, the reading had its ups and down. Yes, there were about thirty people here, from our Los Angeles point of view a little too refined. Five people would be reading, three too many. Friends and strangers, some of them going gray, filled up the folding chairs.

The first joe who read, read his whole essay. Something happens to people when they get behind a microphone, especially to writers, lonely as they are. Beautiful Lynell got up and was great. Rubén Martinez, a Latino activist who saw the emotional energy was close to comatose in this well-intentioned room, knew he had to keep it short and loud. He didn't read, but shouted out some poems instead. His Spanish was jam packed with the most outrageous insults to the white community, but this particular white community was either too well-mannered or too bone-bored to react. Then another man, fond of his own voice, elected to read his entire chapter.

So, at the last, I read only two pages. But they were good pages. Because of my silk coat, and because I chose to be "optimistic" about the dying city, the activist took me on afterward in a moderately spirited debate about how West-Side rich people don't know their ass from a hole in the ground. Rubén, if you only knew. At the party later, another writer—when we bitched to each other about how, on a tour, you have to sometimes put up your own money and go broke—blurted out, "I thought you were rich!" My feeling was: you can get a lot of mileage out of a silk coat.

People kept drifting in all through the reading, so it ended up a standing-room-only crowd. I kept looking for a heavily madeup lady with a twenty-two inch waist and a perky chest, and a guy with no eyelashes on his left eye.

But my sister that night had to be Lynell George, black, young, and beautiful. And my raffish brother-in-law, Rubén, personable and loud, sporting his trademark flashy tie.

I thought of the embrace that Rose had given me when we'd left.

You know how, sometimes, arms go around you and hold you, but you can feel somebody's solar plexus move away at the same time, unintentionally, maybe, but it moves away? Maybe I had done the same thing. Partly, I was relieved that she hadn't shown up tonight. Because now that we had found each other, what in the world were we going to do with each other?

Maybe forgetting would become the order of the day. Maybe soon we too would be going around, plucking on sleeves, asking, "Could you just fill me in again, on what happened to those Kennedy boys? There were bullets involved, right?"

Mother, hamming it up at the zoo.

After Rose left home when she was sixteen, Mother seemed to have gotten what she wanted, or at least what she said she wanted: a life free from the responsibility of bringing up children. But the catch was—since she hated men more than cockroaches—she found herself living alone.

In a terrible irony, she went through much the same sense of abandonment when Rose left as when my father had gone. During my visits I'd see signs and bills and a "will" posted all over the little house in Victorville where she lived now—no more than ten blocks from the bungalow court where Aunt Helen and Uncle Bob had lived during the Great Depression. The "will" went like this: "To my daughter, Penny, I leave everything and to my other daughter, Rose, I leave the sum of one dollar. Because not only did she steal my car, and pull the fire alarm at her junior high school three times in one day, and act up in church, and steal my credit cards, and force me to call the police, but she also . . ."

Convinced she was going to be abandoned, Mother did everything she could to facilitate the process. Every time it happened she went through hell again, but every time it happened she proved once again she was right: "family" was a bitter charade. Friends were the only ones you could rely on.

A space of charged air surrounded her. When you reached over to hug her, her body shivered with revulsion. Still I hung around, the moron-daughter who couldn't take a hint. But what's the ultimate torture for a masochist? *Not* to hit him. What's the ultimate torture for my mother? *Not* to leave her. So even though she's said a zillion times that I'm "just like my father," I will be like my father in that I'll drink too much and have dubious dates after my divorce and develop a paunch from eating too much and tell silly jokes, but I won't leave my mother. Even more irritating—as she insists that "in life you've got to take *shit*, take *shit*, take *shit*!"—I counter by plastering a vacant smile on my face and remark that life is very nice. Toward the end of this twenty-year period, when, by luck, I end up with a little money and respect, she'll say to me, drawing her lips back over her teeth, "Well, you worked like a dog to get where you are today." But I know what will drive her the most nuts, and so I always say, again with the most cretinous smile I can muster, "No, Mother, I just love what I do. And I only work a couple of hours a day. I really don't believe in work! I think life should be fun, don't you?"

My father couldn't have said it better, and I can see it's all my mother can do to keep from beaning me with a two-by-four. There's more to it than that. I have in my mind that a person doesn't leave her mother. Also, I guess I love her.

—

The characters in her own life changed. Uncle Bob, who'd been looking peaked, was taken to the Victorville hospital. Before he got into the car he stopped in the driveway on Forest Street and took a long look at the two-bedroom house with the garage turned into a den, and a little rose garden surviving along the side of the house, carefully tended plants in desert sand. He stood in the street-baking heat and looked at the house. He was silver-haired, stooped, the silver plate still sizzled in his head. He still told people that other people sometimes thought he "came from the British Isles."

Aunt Helen's disposition did not improve, sitting as she was in the driver's seat in the broiling sun. She shouted to him to for God's sake, *come on*! Get in the car! Shimmying a little, for he drank constantly from morning to night, he finally did. But he got in with dignity, because his family had, for as long as he could remember, owned this town—two or three blocks of property along the railroad tracks, and for many years, that's all there was to Victorville.

Aunt Helen drove him over to the hospital where, in a couple of weeks, he died. He'd had cancer for over two years, and hadn't told her. She wasn't exactly grief-stricken. She'd collected some boyfriends in town over the long years, but she found a new one named Mr. Pratt and married him. I took the bus up from LA to visit my mother. (This is something I did three or four times a year for decades; I can't justify it.) I'd bought a new white blouse and my friend Judy made me a tweed jumper. My hair was blond then, with bangs. Aunt Helen and her new husband, Mr. Pratt, and my mother and two human logs who worked for the postal service were there in the living room. They made enormous fun of my hair because my ears stuck out, they made fun of my absent husband, and also of my jumper, because it didn't have a waist. They drove me to tears and I went out on the front porch, asking myself, for the zillionth, zillionth time, why I'd come up here. Mr. Pratt came out on the porch to pat my shoulder. "They don't mean half of what they say," he said. "They don't really mean it."

You poor insane boob, I thought. What planet did *you* come in from? He died a few months later. So there were Kate and Helen, alone now in their respective houses, perversely loyal to each other, always making fun of each other, and between the two of them, keeping Hill and Hill in business.

You could always tell what was going on with my mother when she'd make up some barefaced lie, and lay it on you out of the blue. Thus, when she said about her marriage (in the church) to Jim Daly, "Anyone who asks, did he pay some money to get his first marriage annulled so he could marry me in the church? I say it's none of their goddamn business. People say you have to pay money for that? We're married in the church and it's nobody's goddamn business!" By this I deduced that Jim Daly had paid somebody some money to get his first marriage annulled. Like I cared.

During one visit, my mother said, "If anybody says Helen was drinking a little more than she should when she was driving? And somebody might have gotten hurt? *I* tell them it's none of their god-damn business!" I deduced that Helen must have plastered some-body pretty good on a desert highway. She left Victorville soon after, in a flurry of costume jewelry and rouge, and went to live "down below" in a beach town.

So Helen was finally out of the way. Rose was out of the way.

Except for maybe four visits a year, I was out of the way. Mother could begin to put together the kind of life she wanted, and, little by little, she did. She was secretary to the principal at the local junior high. That man and his wife were kind, and they loved Kate. There were two other teachers at that school, one of them named Carolyn, one, Rose. They became Mother's friends, the daughters she should have had.

Above all, she was able to begin to act out what she had defined years ago as the perfect life. More than anything on earth she wanted to "drink and play cards." She joined bridge club after bridge club. She played poker on the weekends. She put together a circle of friends, including Edna, with whom she shared a house for a few years, and they had a pretty good time. Edna, a counselor at school, drank more white wine than I did, but she loved to hike and play the violin. She and Mother had some nice days up in the mountains; Edna took a violin, Mother took a book, and the afternoons passed quietly, filled with the smell of pine. Her only companions were women, the kind of women who had been so long without men that they looked like men.

Through the years, my mother's friends cohered. A wild bunch at the school got together every weekend to drink and party and compare notes about the general rowdiness of the kids. I never saw one of these parties, but I heard about them. They started out with jokes but ended up with one or two people crying inconsolably in somebody's bathtub, sobbing, asking, "What's the use? Is this all life holds out? Is this all there is? The Green Tree Inn, the Hilton across the street, the Happy Hours that are never, never happy, the sand, the boredom?" The friends console him or her. It isn't that bad. We're having some fun, aren't we?

Victorville, Barstow, Baker, Adelanto, aren't like other towns.

Sure, there are plenty of churchgoing folks, and now plenty of ethnic minorities making a new life out in the desert, but since the
towns are on the Vegas Road, there are roadhouses and prostitutes
and cowboys and people who haven't paid their taxes and don't plan
to, and people whose personal lives leave a little something to be
desired. There are plenty of secrets about killings and rapes and
beatings. If you really want to devote your life to drinking and playing cards, this is the place to do it.

—

One night in a Western dance bar in Victorville, old cowboys and
waitresses whose faces look like road maps are doing the two-step,
and some of these desert rats have neon lights on their behinds that
flash on and off, *start me, start me.* We're sitting up against the wall,
seven or eight of us, and my mother is down at the other end of the
party. One of her kindest friends, a sweet woman, is getting more
and more shit-faced.

"Penny," she yells, "there's something I have to tell you."

"Yeah?" I scream, "what is it?"

She puts her mouth close to my ear. "I'm a lesbian," she yells.
She's very drunk, but who isn't in this place?

"Tell me something I *don't* know."

"I could lose my job."

"I don't *think* so!"

"I've tried to tell your mother. She hates that stuff."

I could say a lot of things. Be careful what you say to my mother.

"You *really* knew?" she asks, screaming again. "I didn't think anybody knew. I did try to tell your mom. But she just won't hear of it."

Sure enough, six months later, I'm driving my mother home from
a trying excursion to Santa Barbara, where she's driven me to near

matricide by insisting over a game of Trivial Pursuit that the Sea of Cortés and the Gulf of California are not the same body of water.

Mother speaks up: "You know what makes me sick? You know what I find repulsive? So disgusting I can't even find words for it? *Lesbians!* They're foul! They're *disgusting.* They're worse than anything I can think of. I can't stand it. I can't stand to *think* of it."

"Then don't think of it," I snap.

"No, really. I can't think of anything worse. There is nothing *worse.*"

"What about ax murderers?" I inquire. "What about Hiroshima? What about Vietnam?"

Mother won't be moved. "There's nothing worse on the face of the earth than a stinking, disgusting lesbian," she insists, and manages, in the next few months, to lose perhaps the sweetest friend she ever had.

—

As the seventies rolled away and the eighties came into view, I began to get another take on my mother. She was always hopping on a bus and zipping off to Laughlin, to gamble. She called it "Going to the River": "I went over to the river last week and won twenty-eight dollars. When I was over at the river I was on a Exercycle and woke up—boom!—on the floor. I passed out. They took me to the hospital and said I was all right."

Sometimes, when I went up there, we zipped through the desert; I was the passenger. Mother drove like a fiend, and her car was filled with stuff. It looked like a Mexican car, with beverage holders and sheepskin and chenille and God knows what all. We'd be driving along and she'd say, "See that power station?" Well, of *course* I'd see the power station! Standing fenced and menacing by the road, poking up out of an endless stretch of sand, covered with signs that say HIGH VOLTAGE, DANGER, PELIGRO, KEEP OUT!!

"We were out driving and drinking one night and we stopped and went in and played tag. It was a hell of a lot of fun."

Or, "See that stretch of sand right there?"

Of course I saw that stretch of sand right there.

"We were out driving one night and Eileen was drunk and somebody said something she didn't like, and she *threw herself out of the car* and went stumping into the sand. She's got a wooden leg, you remember. She must have gone a half a mile before we caught up with her. Old Eileen."

Another time, Mother got mad at her violin-playing friend, Edna: "We all went out to the ranch in the afternoon and, the deal was, we were all going to ride *horses,* but I'm not going to ride any goddamn horse! But you know Edna, she thinks she can do anything. She'd had about two gallons of white wine before we even got to the ranch, and I *told* her it was a dumb thing to do, but of course she got up on the goddamn horse, and then the horse starts to move and Edna falls right off and breaks a couple of ribs and has to have surgery. She's damn lucky to be alive and I *told* her that, but she had to spend two weeks in the hospital, and she had to have a transfusion, and she got jaundice and hepatitis, her liver wasn't in the best shape to begin with. So I guess she won't do any more drinking for a couple of months . . ." I can see it. The ramshackle ranch, the leathery old drunks, the lethargic horses, poor old Edna, a decent person, lying on her back with broken bones, while someone trots back to the house to phone for an ambulance.

I remember back to a pretty iffy chapter in my own life as a divorcée, when once again I thought I might ride out from under the constraints of my own life and drive across the country with my daughters in our Volkswagen to live with a handsome black man in a loft on the Lower East Side of Manhattan. I would have flown to Mars with a Martian (if I could have taken the kids) to get away from my own life in those days. Our first stop on our trip across the country was Victorville. Mother was fully repelled by me. She usually began to drink at six but today, at four o'clock, she was so drunk she could barely form her words. "You're ruining your life," she said. It came out, "Ya rooonin ya laf."

We decided to go out to the park in Victorville. We poked around on different rides, taking the fresh afternoon air, giving Clara a chance to play, giving depressed Lisa some space, giving Mother a chance to sober up. But it wasn't going to happen. We all got on a little manually operated merry-go-round, where you sat on metal animals and faced each other and propelled the contraption with your feet. We did that for about four minutes until Mother passed out. She was only about eighteen inches from the green grass of the park, and in a millionth of a second she'd hit that grass, all of her, flat against it. She fell so fast! It was an astonishing sight. Because we all came from the same murky gene pool, we began to snicker.

Drinking was the dead center of my mother's life at that time, the whole reason she lived. The highest compliment she could pay to anyone was: he/she likes to drink. "You'll like old Edna. She likes to drink." The most encompassing apology was its opposite: "Maureen and Louis have been really good to me. They don't like to drink, but they're always ready to help out when you need something."

Every Easter for years and years we'd go with Mother to Las Vegas, spending the night in Victorville, then hopping in the car and making the four-hour desert drive, always stopping halfway at the little town of Baker, where they have two motels, about a dozen trailers, and a restaurant that has the best Bloody Marys on earth.

The drive to Vegas would not be too bad. Sometimes it would be just Lisa, Clara, Mother, and me, but after John Espey came into our lives, he was often the driver.

So it is that when my children go to their therapists, they not only have multiple divorce, a history of suicide on all sides of the family, nagging worries about alcoholic or drug-prone genes (although each of them appears to be a one-woman temperance union), *but* they also have to come to terms with the fact that for eight or nine crucial years during their childhood and adolescence, instead of being taken to church or at the very least an Easter-egg hunt, the children cele-brated the appearance of the risen Christ by sitting through a mandatory performance of *Spice on Ice,* in which topless dancers skated around sadly on a nine-by-twelve rink, because that was the continuous and ongoing show at the Hacienda, on the Vegas strip, where we stayed.

Mother enjoyed the first days of these visits tremendously. As soon as we unpacked and the kids went out to the pool, Mother would grin and pull out her Bible, which didn't have any pages but held instead a pint of whiskey and two shot glasses. Then we'd prowl out, find the nearest liquor store, stock up on vodka, whiskey, white wine, soft drinks, salted nuts, get on the phone, make some reserva-tions for the bigger shows, go on out to the pool, and get blasted while the girls swam.

Mother played the slots. I think she was too shy to try anything else. Clara hit the second story of Circus Circus just for kids, where you could put fifty cents in a slot and watch a real chicken play the piano. We saw Leslie Uggams in *Guys and Dolls,* and Liberace, and Juliet Prowse, and a lot of shows I don't remember. I remember sit-ting through Bob Newhart wowing the audience while I watched an exit sign with double vision, and tried through the show—without success—to make the two exit signs into one.

The days were like a furnace. As we trooped glumly from one casino to another we got to see all the rest of the Americans who had thought it might be cool to celebrate Easter by coming to Vegas: whole sad enormously fat families lining up at the Hacienda buffet eating withered sausage and watery eggs and sickening sweet waffles with butter and muskmelon that had seen better days. Most of the adults nursed colossal hangovers. Their hands trembled, their faces were puffed and white.

After the first day, Mother would point out our flaws to us: Lisa thought she was God on a rock, Clara might be mentally ill. Why didn't I get a *real* job? (Writing didn't count.) And did John look like he was going to die soon?

The drive home was always a nightmare. We played Geography—Geography, the game where I say Argentina, and you say Aegean, and the next person says Nantucket and the next person says Texas and I say Stockholm and so on. One taxing day, my mother got one *A* too many from Clara and said, with all her regular malice, "You disgusting little girl," but Clara rapped right back: *"You disgusting old lady!"*

And those were our Easters, for years.

There were other vacations: a summer in Catalina, where I went with my divorced friend Joan and her three kids and I and my kids. John flew in, and the weather was beautiful and the beach was only a block away, but Mother came over with some of her friends and drank so much that she pulled up a chair one night when we'd just gotten dinner on the table and *plunk!* there went her head, facedown in her plate of baked ham. Do you laugh? Do you react with scorn,

Mother, giving John a Christmas dirty look.

as a visiting teenager with his own problems did, muttering "She's drunk," and turning his head away, in a gesture I'll remember until I die?

I had verbally, or not verbally, made it clear I wouldn't bail out on her. That must have meant, in her eyes, that she had a permanent license to behave as badly as she could. And she was a master at this pastime! In Denver, where I was to speak at a writers' lunch, I asked Mother along. I always did this! I always thought there would be a day when she'd say, "Gosh, I'm proud of you!" In the hotel elevator, we descended to the literary lunch, but two others crowded in, a young man in a tuxedo and a girl in a bouffant bridal dress. Riding down to their wedding.

Mother looked her up and down and asked, "What are you, *going to a Halloween party?*"

The bride looked as if she'd been shot.

Mother grinned.

So was it the meanness, or was it the drinking, or was it both?

I only knew that every fall I tended to get anxious and ill because it meant that Christmas was coming in two months. And as I tended to get more happy in my own life, Mother upped the ante. Lisa married. Kate asked if she'd ever get invited to "the house of the princess." Clara took up with a nice guy still working his way through college. Mother asked what was in it for him. She repeatedly said John was going to die soon.

On one of our last holiday outings we decided to fly down to Yucatán for Christmas and come back on New Year's Day. It was not a pleasant week. For our expensive, festive, New Year's dinner, six women and the long-suffering John Espey watched dimly as my mother, that ever-feisty Kate, staged four separate walkouts, pushing herself away from the table and storming out onto the street because she was so displeased with our behavior. By the third or fourth walkout, none of us even looked up from our plates, or our tired talk.

After dinner we wandered the streets of Mérida, looking for a party. Finally we found a decorated bar and headed in. My mother went back to the hotel in a rage. The rest of us stayed and danced, and drank. I talked to Edna and the dear woman who'd told me she was a lesbian. I felt that, without breaking any confidence, since God knew it was obvious, that I could say what I said. I was so drunk I felt as though I spoke from another dimension: "My mother and I can't stand each other, you know? But we're both too stubborn to stop trying."

Against the Christmas lights, backlit, Edna nodded pensively. "You're right about that," she said.

And the young woman who would become the object of so much of my mother's hate tilted her head back. "God, I'm shitfaced," she said. "Happy New Year."

In 1980, John Espey and I traveled to China for a month, and then to Bali. We went with some trepidation, because both my parents were ill. My father was recovering from a lung-cancer operation. He begged us not to go, but we figured he'd be OK for the time we were gone.

My mother had been very sick for about a year. Whatever she ate, she couldn't keep down. We'd watch her order "a seafood salad without the shrimp" and a Manhattan with dry vermouth. As always, she picked through the salad until she found what she thought was a shrimp, and then gagged, gagged so much she had to throw up the Manhattan she'd just chugalugged. She'd order another, ignore her salad, and throw up her second Manhattan. "It's terrible to be so sick," she'd say. "It's terrible."

She looked so bad that I ended up asking *her* if she wanted us to stay home, but she said no. She'd wait until we came home to have her operation. The week that we came back, she did have it—a routine gallbladder procedure. Lisa and Clara and I went up to be with her; Clara was fifteen, Lisa, twenty-five. We played cards in the hospital room the night before the surgery. Clara won, as usual. Mother accused her of cheating. The next morning I saw Mother as they brought her back from the recovery room. She was trying to sit up in her moving bed. She was in terror and great pain. I wish I hadn't seen her face that day.

We stayed for three more days and then went home. Three nights later the doctor called me late at night. Mother had gone into a coma and wasn't expected to live. I got back to Victorville around five in the morning, and went in to see my mother. She was on a respirator.

Nobody could figure it out. Her Filipina internist was furious at her surgeon brother-in-law, who wore gold chains and played tennis. "It was a clean incision," he told me, and shrugged. I had my mother taken off the respirator, since that had been her wish. By the middle of the day Lisa and Clara were back in town. We took turns being with Mother, talking to her. Fastidious Lisa even climbed into bed with her to whisper in her ear that she'd be all right.

She only had three days to live. We went out funeral shopping for my mom. We tried to explain to the undertaker that my mother was a hell-raiser, that if she had ever been afraid of anything, she'd shoot first and ask questions later. That all she'd ever wanted was to drink and play cards. So instead of praying hands on that little memorial folder, could we have a poker hand instead? He got excited. "I've got a cannon around here some place," he said. "Do you think she might like it if we shot off a cannon?"

We said we knew she'd like it.

That evening, late, Lisa and Clara went out for a snack. There was nobody around in intensive care except me and one tired nurse. She came to turn Mother over and give her a shot in the behind. She let her hand stay on Mother and pushed. Pushed again.

"Does your mom drink?" she asked.

"You bet."

"I think she'll come around tomorrow. She's sort of pushing *back*, you know?"

"I'm sorry?"

"This is probably alcohol poisoning. It's pretty common after an operation. You can't have a drink, so you suffer alcohol withdrawal. We get them all the time up here. People drink hard in the desert."

By the time the kids came back for me, I was in that state that only my mother can put me: *Suckered Once Again!* We were irate. All our grief, worry, for a case of *alcohol poisoning*!

But this is how we celebrated—having received a diagnosis that actually meant something, rather than the confused ditherings of a pair of immigrants (who might have been just trying to be tactful): we drove to the county fair, which was going full blast just outside of town. We found a steakhouse and chewed our way through great big steaks. Then we went back to The Green Tree Inn, where the air-conditioning had conked out. We put a fan on a chair, opened the door, turned on the TV, and drank canned margaritas. It was, I guess, the first time Clara had ever drunk in front of her family. Her face turned red as a tomato and she laughed so hard her knees buckled. We were giddy with relief. It was Grandma Kate, you know? We didn't want her to die.

The next morning, after three days in a coma, Mother woke up in a roaring temper. Someone had stolen her purse, she was sure of it. She'd been at a stadium, and gone down a long hall toward a bright light. There'd been a doctor down at the end and she'd asked him, "Is this where they bring the banged-up athletes?"

"You had a real death experience, Ma!" I said, "Going down a long corridor like that. Seeing that bright light. That's amazing."

"Somebody stole my purse, goddamnit! I want it found right away!"

My mother would literally hover between life and death for the next thirty days. Her bowels wouldn't move. The internist and the surgeon held heated arguments right in front of me. They were both so small that I, only five feet four myself, looked straight down on to the tops of their heads as they bickered.

"You wan' her to die onna table?"

"*Fine!* You wan' her to die inna *bed*?"

My mother compounded all this by telling everyone to hold a pillow over her face and kill her because life wasn't worth living. She wanted me to do it, which I said would be perfect for her, since she'd get to die, and I'd have to spend the rest of my life in jail. She'd give me the fish-eye and ask me who stole her purse.

Still, an atmosphere of mild festivity prevailed. Clara's and Lisa's boyfriends and girlfriends kept making the 100-mile drive up to the High Desert. Lisa and Clara spent hours in the emergency room, playing cards and keeping track of the appalling carnage that kept coming down in Victorville, Apple Valley, Hesperia, Adelanto. Motorcycle accidents, battered wives, stomach cancer, knife wounds. Violence and chaos!

Clara and Lisa were there, playing gin rummy, when Aunt Helen turned up. She blew into the waiting room looking truly scary. Instead of dusting her face with powder, she'd used rouge. She still knew a lot of these people. Hadn't she carried for half a century the sobriquet "Mrs. Victorville," or, alternately, "Mrs. Liquorville"?

When Helen found that her sister was in ICU, still between life and death, she demanded a wheelchair. No way was she going to be

Mother, in a temper in Yucatán.

upstaged by Kate. I saw her in the hall. *"Hi, Hi!* Penny!" she wheezed, but didn't linger, knowing I wasn't a fan. She wheeled past me into ICU. I followed, and got to see my mother recognize her, and groan, and turn her face away. If Helen's feelings were hurt, she didn't show it. She wheeled back out to the waiting room, engaged Lisa and Clara in perfunctory conversation, then turned to her elderly buddy Wilma, with the old enthusiasm. "Well, Wilma! Time for a short snort!"

Aunt Helen wouldn't come back. She said it was too "upsetting" to see her sister like this.

During these thirty days, my mother gradually came to herself. She displayed tremendous bravery. When they threaded a wire straight to her heart she held my hand, but not very hard, and looked patiently at the ceiling. Once she asked me, "Am I going to die?" and I answered as truthfully as I could, "I don't think so." She took it in, and thought about it.

Somebody got the idea to have her swallow a ball of mercury on a string. The idea was that the volatile mercury, rolling its way down through her digestive system, would hit her intestines, and by nudging, falling, leaning, might wake up her lower digestive tract. The danger of death by toxic infection was present every second, the way things were. The down side of using the mercury was that if the ball broke, she was a dead person. Every day the tennis-playing surgeon shouted at the internist that he had to operate. "You wan' her to die inna *bed?*" Every day Mother swallowed about another foot of string. The mercury wasn't working.

Lisa and Clara went home. John and I moved into a cheap motel with a Western motif—a neon horse out front. Every night I took a couple of canned margaritas to the room and John opened a book. (There was no TV here.) We were in the desert, waiting. Finally, even the internist had to admit that her brother-in-law had to do something. She couldn't let Kate die. That night my mother's friends came and went, and John and I stayed with her until around midnight. She asked us not to come in early the next day. She didn't want any demonstration, she hated that stuff. But she was sad, looking death in the face.

The next morning, I went to the hospital to hear the bad news. The surgeon sidled up to me with an uneasy grin on his face: "We decided not to do the operation after all . . ." I raised my arm to hit him, and he cringed.

At dawn that morning as they'd wheeled Mother into X-ray, she'd surprised them all by defecating over everything. And again. And again. So many times that it came to them they didn't need an operation.

So she was better. Her internist told her *no more drinking*, and she never did take another drink. Her friend Edna told me that Kate, before her operation, had put away half a gallon of vodka a day, and still kept up her bridge schedule.

Just after this crisis, my father sickened and died in a way almost diametrically opposed to how my mother had faced death. He was terrified. When I visited him on the cancer floor at Scripps, he sat, petrified, in a wheelchair, convinced that a Chinese gang headed up by a man named Ching Chang Phouie was after him. (What a cruel reward for a lifetime of making up silly stories.) I told him there definitely wasn't any Ching Chang Phouie after him, and wheeled him out for a lap around the eighth floor of this gruesome monument to Western science, so different from the slapdash coziness of the little hospital in Victorville. As we wheeled past his bathroom, he couldn't resist a sidelong glance, looking for Ching Chang Phouie.

Every test they could do on my dying dad, they did. They put him through a CAT scan to see if he had a brain tumor. He did. *What a surprise!* They loaded him with chemicals and radiation, they maximized the bottom line. As soon as his insurance stopped, they pitched him out of the hospital. Lynda, with a young child to take care of, had to put him in a nursing home. He lasted there three weeks, calling home every day, begging to come back. He took dying very badly.

But Mother was getting better. And getting her old disposition back. She came down for Christmas and wouldn't speak to us during Christmas dinner. (Clara passed me a note on which she'd scribbled *No More! No More!*)

As a gesture to end all gestures, at a Christmas during the late eighties everyone pitched in to give Mother a magic gift—she and I would spend a week in Cuernavaca the week before her birthday. The family thought I'd gone completely nuts, taken my martyr role far far beyond any reasonable limits. Because it would be just my mother and me, and I wasn't drinking at the time.

I did take a bottle of Valium though, and every time I got even a twinge of the old panic, I took another Valium. I took so many Valium that, in a filial echo of my mother's old ailment, my bowels didn't move for a week. We saw the Diego Rivera murals, we saw Malinché's residence, we spent a wonderful afternoon in the town square watching a Red Cross drive. One night, Mother accused me of thinking I was too good for her, but I just took two more Valium.

On our last day in Cuernavaca we went to a fancy gringo restaurant with rolling lawns and squealing peacocks. We had a swell lunch, and, after dessert, they brought us complimentary Kahlúas. Mother drained it off. "It isn't alcohol," she said. "It's just flavoring. Go ahead! Drink up."

I did. I was dying for a drink, to put it mildly. Mother looked at me and smiled the Devil's smile. "I knew you couldn't stay with it," she said.

With my mind, I still saw my mother as admirably strong. Or as a "victim of society," trained to be beautiful and nothing else. I remembered that she squeezed fresh orange juice for every last one of us. With my heart, I remembered the terrible three weeks when she gave in to grief after my father left. And I remembered her incredibly brave days in the hospital forty years later.

You can't get on with your life unless you forgive and forget. But what if you can't forgive and forget? I applied a double standard to my mother. It was easy to forgive Richard, or hot-tempered Tom—and ask them to forgive me—or even, when I thought about it, to forgive my sewn-up stepdad. God knows I made their lives as hard as they made mine. I made it a point to apologize as often as I could to my own daughters, and I hoped they forgave me. But I came up against a blank wall with my mother.

In the spring of 1989, John and I drove out to a community college in San Bernardino—at the far eastern end of what they call the Inland Empire. Fifty miles more over the Cajon Pass, and you'd be up in the High Desert, in Victorville. We harangued four hundred hardworking high school teachers at eight in the morning. They wanted to hear the words we told them. We told them they could write if they wanted to; that they were so lucky to be teaching young minds; that we were all having a lot of fun here; that, relatively speaking, we were living in heaven on earth.

Afterward, as I was signing books, I looked up to see my mother, who had come uninvited. She was mightily pissed. She came up to me and said, "You're bullshit, you're bullshit. Everything you do or say is bullshit." Later, as I stood shaking hands with teachers, she engaged them in conversation. "When she got lippy when she was little, I beat her up pretty good. I guess they could put me in jail for that now."

The next day, I composed ten separate postcards, each with the topic sentence: "Funny how people's ideas of bullshit can differ. Here is one of mine." I mailed three before I came to my senses. I told Mother I'd never see her again except in a public place or in the company of a therapist. She chose a Christian therapist up in the High Desert, whom we saw twice for a two-hour session, and nearly drove one more person to madness.

Two years after that, in 1991, as we were packing to go to the Miami Book Fair, the Filipina internist called to say that if we wanted to see my mother alive we'd better come right away. Swearing bitterly, I put away the resort dresses I'd bought and pulled out my Victorville clothes.

It was after midnight when we hit that same old hospital. Everyone was, as always, exceedingly kind. I worried that when Mother saw us she'd die of rage. She had congestive heart failure and a clot on her lung. She looked so small when we saw her! Up in her eighties now, and weighing about eighty-five pounds. I shook her shoulder very lightly. She turned over, recognized us, and gave us a friendly smile. "Oh, hi!" she said. "How *about* that Magic Johnson! Doesn't he make you want to *throw up?*"

We saw Mother in 1992, for what I personally hope is our last Christmas together. We drove up to Victorville to give her some presents. The deal was, we'd meet only in a restaurant, since in a public place she'd go easy on saying awful things. We met in the evening, and she had her friends with her. Such nice people! It seemed we'd stay in The Green Tree Inn and give her those presents at breakfast.

At seven in the morning, Mother called and said she was too sick to go out. We'd have to drop the stuff off where she lived. *Suckered once again!* She wasn't sick at all, just in another rage. Two hours later, I watched a gingerbread loaf skitter end over end along the length of her trailer, as she gave it one last desperate, underhanded pitch, trying once again to express hatred that stayed pristine, unchanged, and inexpressibly strong.

That could be my last memory of her, or the memory of her hanging up on Rose when she called during that second terrible illness to see how her mother was. But the most entrancing one I have is of both of us, nervous as cats, sitting in the parlor of the Christian therapist (the kind of woman who has ceramics all over her tables, and macramé hangings on the wall).

The therapist is looking over two questionnaires she's had us fill out. "Carolyn, I see you've been married twice, have two children, and consider that it's possible you might have a drinking problem, is that right?"

I nod solemnly, on my best behavior.

"And, Kate, you're widowed, have one daughter, and don't drink at all?"

"That's right," my mother says sweetly, "I have one daughter, and I don't drink at all."

The thing is, you have to admire my mother. Mom stands pat.

Clara Sturak marries Chris Chandler.
A very happy day.

*E*arly in 1992, Clara decided it was about time to get married to her boyfriend, Chris Chandler. They'd been together for over five years, and living together for one of those years. Chris was still an undergraduate at UCLA, working at Dutton's Bookstore in Brentwood. Clara worked full time in Santa Monica at a shelter for women who were homeless and mentally ill. It was Clara's job to save young women—fifteen at a time—who had been living on the streets, messed up from drugs, often alcoholic, repeatedly raped and beaten, abandoned with stony unconcern by their own families. She and her staff would clean them up, feed them great meals, find them some clothes, get them on a set of drugs that might make them sane again, find them a job, an apartment, then start in with another batch. Hard work, and dangerous. Clara's most endearing client had beaned her husband with a dresser drawer to keep him from beating her anymore, and done time for murder.

In spite of her spartan, almost saintly lifestyle, Clara decided she wanted a magnificent wedding.

It was going to be a challenge. You could see it shaping up to be a challenge from the very first day. Because of divorce, guess who said that fancy weddings were a bourgeois sellout? Her dad might not have said it. He might have been joking. She might not have heard him correctly. But it was more or less inevitable that they would disagree. Besides, he might not be able to come.

Clara approached the latter problem with breezy cheer. She showed her father an open calendar: "You pick the date," she told him. "I won't get married without you!" She also said that she wanted both of us to walk her down the aisle. She wanted the wedding to be in her dear friend Gretchen's garden, a lush and perfect forest out of a fairy tale. Clara wanted John to write a poem and read it.

While Lisa's husband's family was an exemplum of "stability," Chris's family was a mirror image of our own. Meanwhile, Chris wanted a friend and all his brothers to be groomsmen. Since each of his brothers had a different mother, this looked like it might be a problem. Chris didn't care. He wanted everybody. He wanted his mother and father to walk him down the aisle and was mightily bummed when he realized *he* didn't even get to go down the aisle.

An afternoon wedding, with white dinner jackets. But Clara began to get depressed. Her father said he had never worn a tuxedo; never had, never would, and wasn't going to start now. Her young half brother, Michael Sturak, a spookily beautiful photocopy of his dad, and slated to be one of the groomsmen, said if his dad wasn't wearing one, he wasn't wearing one. Even Clara's stepmother, Tom's third wife, usually a cool peacemaker, opined that tuxedos might seem a little extreme. Clara gnashed her teeth.

She called up one afternoon from a store in Brentwood and said she had found her wedding dress. Would we like to come by and check it out? John, Lisa, her friend Gretchen, and I went over to the store. It sold fake hippie dresses, "flowerdy" prints, things with wrinkled ribbons coming off. Nothing here on the racks even looked vaguely like a wedding. Clara was a little late and she clomped in, the way she does when she's already made up her mind, when she expects an argument.

She grabbed a dress off the rack, went into the dressing room, came right back out. Her face was pale with stress. "I figure this is it," she said stubbornly. "All I need is a hat." She grabbed a hat with flowers and plunked it flat down on her head. "What do you think? This is fine, isn't it?" She was so grim that all we could do was stare, unable to say yes, afraid to say no.

An up-and-down white frock of crinkled white organdy hung straight from her shoulders to mid-calf. Two shepherdess panniers draped in front.

"You might want to look around a little bit," her sister said.

"It does look better with the hat," I said.

"Fine, fine," John said gamely.

Gretchen just looked.

"Why don't I put a deposit on it?" I said. (That was easy, because it came in under two hundred dollars.)

Clara changed into a sweatshirt and baggy pants and clomped off.

Heartbreak time. What had we—or life—done to Clara, that she thought her net worth came to under two hundred dollars?

Was it that *father* of hers? Or was it the car accident she'd been in, which might have left her feeling not pretty enough? Where *was* that drunk-driving Guatemalan! We'd kill him.

"I'm not saying anything," Gretchen said, and drove away, sad and quiet.

I was scared to say anything either, because I knew from hard experience that whatever your mother tells you to do, you will try as hard as you can to do something else.

In the end it was Lisa who talked to Clara with some heat, explaining that Clara had to be the most beautiful woman at her own wedding, no matter how much money it took. It was Lisa who marshaled us all at the bride store, the one where they serve the relatives coffee and stick the bride up on a pedestal and pin $2,000 creations on her. Clara began to object. "I cannot stand the infantilization of the bride," she cried. "I'm not a doll, I'm a human being!" Underneath her socialist harangue, and not very well hidden, I thought I heard the scathing phrase: *bourgeois sellout.* But hadn't I tortured her poor father for years with "You can take the house, the books, blah blah, but YOU'LL NEVER HAVE MY GOOD OPINION"? Might not this be Karmuppance for us all?

What was it in our family that made us impostors in our own eyes? Why was it, with all the education in the world and all the therapy and all the training, we still felt, or would at least occasionally succumb to the feeling, that we weren't "good" enough to dress up, have a party, be beautiful, stand up for a marriage—and have children, and friendships, and grandmas, and cookies, and nobody throwing up in the living room?

Part of Clara's objection was that to pay two thousand dollars for a dress and parade around in it for one day was *criminal,* the way the economy was. Every day she struggled to find clean underwear for her homeless ladies. How could she do it? And how could she cross her father?

OK, well, then things started to happen. The sales girls stuck a dress on her that made her breasts look like cream and her waist something like Miss America's, and the skirt a fluff of tulle. Of course she wouldn't buy it at this flossy store but found a discount warehouse that carried it. The happy couple picked out invitations and when a friend of Chris's criticized the quality of the printing, Clara threw him out of her house, just like some crazy Sturak Slovak of old. Every one of Chris's brothers was coming, and every one of their mothers was coming. Then Chris's own dad said he couldn't/ wouldn't come. Too many wives! But Clara and Chris would make him do it.

Clara wanted Richard, my first husband, to come, along with his mom and his wife and nice daughter from his second marriage. He would be marrying a third time about a month after Clara, finally hooking up with a fabled "beautiful black woman," Anne Jennings. Anne would be out of town, but Clara wanted his second wife, Pat, to come, because she was family by now.

Because they were related to Lisa, and weren't we all family now, and didn't *family mean everything* to Lisa, Clara, Carolyn, Tom, Richard, John, Dick Kendall and his dear sister Nan and her husband, Pat, and John's daughter, Alice, and her husband, Ralph, and John's younger daughter, Susan, and her son, Jordan, and Chris Junior, Chris Senior, and Chris's mom, and stepmoms and everyone by now? Clara invited my mother. She invited Rose, who was still brooding on the teasing subject of marriage.

Invitations. How come people don't RSVP anymore? *What's wrong with this country?!* Lisa threw a shower in her garden for a flock of pretty ladies in country dresses. Clara wore her first choice for her wedding dress, the crinkly organdy one, and the hat full of flowers. It looked great, and she started collecting juicers, lasagna pans. Chris's dad called to say he'd be coming after all. How could he miss the occasion?

Clara found bridesmaids' dresses. Cake-box pink with artificial pearls over the shoulders like sundresses. Cocktail length. The thick-headed mother of the bride took cocktail length to mean somewhere down around the ankles, but cocktail length meant somewhere above the thigh. You could crumple a dress in one hand and still have room left over for a sandwich. "No infantilization of women!"

Mexican food! A mariachi! All of Chris's family put up in one hotel. John got up at five one morning and bounded back to bed at seven. "I've done it," he said triumphantly. "I wrote them a sestina, a difficult form that first came into existence in the year 1190. Nobody writes a sestina anymore!"

During a series of frank discussions with his daughter, in which

Clara and her bridesmaids. "No infantilization of women!"

Tom Sturak reportedly made as many moves as an octopus trying to get out of a handbag, he finally shifted gears, toned down, allowed as how he might wear a tuxedo *down the aisle* (and allow his son to do so as well) on the strict condition that he be able to change into a high-fashion black T-shirt as soon as the ceremony was performed. I guess you might say he and Clara came to a bourgeois draw.

—

The night before the wedding, John and I, Clara and Chris, were going to have dinner with Chris's mother, Marthe, a brilliant professor of philosophy. The first of Chris Chandler, Sr.'s, wives and mother of two of his children, she would be flying in alone to California. We were going to meet at *I Cugini* (the cousins, in Italian), and we would get to know each other. Clara thought her new mother-in-law might have some nervousness about seeing her ex-husband in this whole wedding context, and—God!—probably some general nervousness about the whole thing.

John and I waited in the early evening California beach sunlight. You got to see the whole world here in *I Cugini,* how the better part of the California almost-rich had made it through the past thirty years. Girls swirled by in long, sheer Janis Joplin dresses, hard-working females in suits and carrying briefcases came in, sat down, and sighed. Big, beautiful, tanned men came in to cruise: it was a good bet they hadn't done a day's work in years. Carefree, careless, careworn. This was a big restaurant and it was filling up quick. John and I began to worry. It was the kind of place where you couldn't sit down until the rest of the party showed up. So, where was the rest of the party?

Then we saw Clara, outside, striding along, swinging her purse. Smiling. She went straight to the hostess. "Instead of a party of five, we'll be a party of eight." Then, to us, "Chris found one of his stepmoms in the hall of the hotel. Denise, you met her, didn't you? And her husband, and Chris's brother, Travis. They'll be joining us for dinner. They're waiting for Trav to get ready. Sixteen-year-old boys. You know how long *they* take!"

Then they all came barreling in. Denise de Clue, successful screenwriter, with a handsome, affable husband, Bob; Travis, a lanky, blushing version of his older brother; and Marthe, holding onto Chris, looking exactly like Chris, and looking a little like me. Because our families really did mirror each other.

We went for it! Found a corner table, and then ordered champagne, and then went for the good white wine, trying to cram eight life stories into a three-hour span. "The mothers want another," Marthe and I would say, or "The mothers need a drink." We drank toasts to the future and the wedding and the present. I remember Marthe telling me about how terrible she felt when she had to take a teaching job, after she worked so hard for her PhD; how she felt she was shortchanging the boys: "But I had to," she said, and her face came into close and perfect focus, "I had to do it *then*, or else I'd never do it."

I told her about going off on magazine assignments, leaving the kids to fend for themselves. "But I had to," I said. The sentence had two meanings. One was that we had to support the kids, because our cute husbands (who looked uncannily alike, it would turn out) were devoting their lives to heedless pleasure, and we had to support the kids! But the true "I had to" was *"I had to."* I had to make a meaningful life, follow my calling, or I would have died or killed somebody. Or made another whole set of people achingly unhappy, which—be fair—might have happened anyway.

"I wanted you to come out here," Chris said steadily to his

mother, "so that you could see what I've made of my life. I'm not the same person I was five years ago."

Chris was right. He had come from that familiar metaphorical nothing our family knew so much about, out from Chicago to live in LA in an apartment supplied by one of his dad's girlfriends', worked as a busboy in one of his dad's girlfriends' restaurants, found the charming and beautiful hostess, my Clara, worked in a print shop, found friends, gone back to school, invented an honorable life. All on his own. Chris was a hero.

After dinner we split. Denise, her husband, and Travis wandered off to the Santa Monica Pier. Clara and Chris took his mother back to the hotel. John and I drove home and went to bed early to be up in time for the wedding.

So ordinary! So extremely pleasant! During the last six months of planning, there had been no slithering storm of vicious insults that stuck and stung like poisonous jellyfish. No hard drugs. Not even a real raised voice. And the tuxedo question, which might have occupied us earlier for from five to ten years of acrimony, was already beginning to fade from memory. It was not impossible to put a dozen divorced wives and husbands together, along with two hundred of everybody's closest friends. It was going to be ordinary. We had, knock wood, gotten into the habit of being happy.

—

The wedding was held—*held,* what a great word—in Gretchen's backyard. Gretchen was Clara's friend since the seventh grade—part of her extended family now, since Gretchen's parents had taken Clara in during a Topanga flood. Some backyard! A sylvan glade on two levels, with a meadow and a winding creek and dappled light all over everything. Trees twined overhead to frame the wedding party.

In the back bedroom five beautiful women struggled mightily with control-top panty hose and underwear they weren't used to, and when they were dressed, four girls were in cake-box pink cocktail dresses (and you could see Clara's point: no infantilization. She wanted *babes, women,* out there), but there was one missing dress—one missing scrap of cake-box crepe. Consternation.

I took a look in the mirror. The mother of the bride, all right. I'd gained some righteous weight after the last wedding. I looked like one of those Helen Hokinson ladies in the old *New Yorker* cartoons. And there was that same old birthmark, hanging around like a boring party guest who won't go home. (But of course it was home.) Without it, I might have taken typing, married a dull man, and lived my life asleep. I was certainly in no position, now, to complain.

Clara, composed and dignified, swished out to have her picture taken. Tom's wife, Jacqueline, was at the ready, by the guestbook, looking swell in lace and flowered cotton. "I went for comfort," she said demurely.

We were nervous! Nervous in nineteen ways. Please, I prayed, don't let me lose it here, don't let me confide some strong-minded *opinion* about somebody, or if someone does the same to me, let me be silent. Lisa, in her size two cake-box pink outfit, kept zipping her lip, pulling her fingers across her firmly closed mouth. She'd have her own dad, Richard, her former stepdad, Tom, a surrogate stepdad (jolly Harvard) and another surrogate stepdad (dear John). Besides her half sister Clara, she had another half sister, Ariana, from her dad and her former stepmother, Pat. "I'm keeping my lip zipped," Lisa said a hundred times, and then went off to get her picture taken. The lost dress got found.

The Mariachi UCLATLÁN strolled in, ranged themselves along a raft of greenery, and began to tune up. Time had gone by! We'd listened to them, critically, since they'd been weedy undergraduates at UCLA. Now the lead musician had a long gray beard. I stood beside Tom—he'd turned away from me, what else was new!—but we both watched the mariachi. A few tentative notes, and they began to play. *"Escaleras de la Carcel,"* the steps of the jail. Tom's best friend, Jim Andrews, dead now, had played that on a scratchy record when he got married in Topanga, the night I'd found out about Jennifer. *"Escaleras de la Carcel."* What a way to think about marriage. But now it was just beautiful music. "Reminds me of Jim," Tom said.

If you were a guest, you strolled into the garden, checked out the beautiful green world, let the violins and the *guiteron* vibrate through your skin and into your bones. You signed the book, surveyed the folding chairs, but between them was a bartender serving white wine and frozen margaritas. It seemed the most natural thing in the world to reach for a refreshing drink, swallow a margarita imprudently, so that the roof of your mouth began to ache and, gasping, begin to call out to friends. There were Cousin Jerry and Cousin Jack! Because of the cruel dynamics of divorce, I hadn't seen those cousins of Tom since Jerry had model airplanes hanging from his ceiling.

It was wonderful to see them. There was the graduate student who'd lied to me about Tom, covering for him when he was off with Jennifer. Ah, that graduate student was sixty now, with white hair. And I'd covered for Judy when she ran off to the Island of Yap. Judy was there, absolute reassurance locked in a human body.

And up where the groom and his men were flocked, cool and urbane, with white wine in their hands, Chris—who'd died a hundred deaths of worry about his family and whether they'd make it here and be OK—seemed happy and serene. His father, equally urbane and killingly handsome, chatted amicably with all his wives and girlfriends. Well, didn't Muslims do it all the time?

The judge joked about those smashing bridesmaids' dresses. (He came in a seersucker suit, on the way to see his mother.) John read his sestina, a work of sheer elegance that nobody could understand, but it knocked the poets in the place right out of their folding chairs.

Continuity. Stability. Civility. How do you even describe these things? What are the telling details?

After the mariachi went away, a DJ played golden oldies. Everybody danced. This was no Philip Roth wedding, where aging uncles grumbled because they hadn't had enough blow jobs and life had passed them by. Every grown-up danced because they'd lived through years of drugs and drink and divorce and other people's dying awful deaths. Because of the envelope of time they'd lived through, they'd probably had too *much* pleasure, if such a thing is possible, but now it was time to calm down, rest up, buy some Wedgwood china, cash in on all those years and years of therapy, come back down to the ground.

My grandson Alexander led a conga line across the lawn and over the dance floor and all around the meadow. He was nine, and he loved his tuxedo. "How'd you learn how to do this?" a hard-boiled journalist asked him. "Oh, it was spontaneous," Alexander coolly replied. His little brother danced too. My stepmother, still a beautiful woman, regarded my little brother, six feet tall and twenty-three, as he rocked out. What am I trying to say here? That in some places, some times, this is a beautiful world.

Lisa, as the afternoon wore on, danced more, receding to an age when she had once been a go-anywhere, do-anything beauty of Topanga. Her husband, Dick, danced along with her. After ten years of marriage, they were still the perfect couple, and would remain forever young.

During the toasts, I mentioned that this really *was* the triumph of hope over experience, and that everyone in our "overextended family" was a sport. Tom saluted Clara's sturdy and relentless determination to change the world. She was so much more than one of a thousand points of light! She was an Old Testament miracle, she'd make those patriarchs sorry they'd tried to take advantage of innocent homeless women and children.

Chris's father, celebrated rakehell, the one who outscored all of us—in terms of drugs, drink, and serial marriage, from two thousand miles away—had written out his toast. His hands shook when he read it. "Clara and Chris," he said, "don't do as we did. Do what it was we wanted to do when we started our lives. Adhere to *those* high ideals. We were part of our times, we were part of a larger social explosion. Learn from our mistakes . . ." I thought I heard him say: "Who knows, you might make it!"

In the house and out in the shrubbery you could catch a whiff of a little pot-smoking from the younger generation, but there was a lot of Perrier being imbibed too, because many of the married ladies there were pregnant, or were going to be. And inside the house Lisa had brought videos for the grandkids, so that when Alexander and his little brother, Chris, got sick of the conga line they could catch up on *Terminator II*. Their new uncle by marriage, Travis, so cool and sixteen, got tired of the party and went in to loll with the kids, to snuggle, even, checking out the video. Clara's little brother Michael liked his new brothers-in-law from Chicago and showed his affection in such a sweet Sturakian way: he slammed into them repeatedly; they picked him up and turned him upside down.

Then it began to end (although neighbors would complain good-naturedly that the loud music went on way too long). We finally stopped dancing. Clara and Chris were among the last to leave. "Whatever else," Clara said contentedly, "this has shown me that I can exert my will, and things will go my way." John said later, "Everyone came in to the wedding as though they had just met that very day. There was no past, only the present." I thought that I had seen my family—like so many other ordinary families in America—stretched right to the breaking point, stretched and pulled by drugs, drink, and divorce until it had to break, and in fact it had exploded. But what explodes implodes. What blows up can come back down. Another dialectic had been brought to bear.

"It was the strangest thing," Chris Chandler, Sr., said. "Peace broke out."

Two people hadn't come to the wedding: my mother, who said that "under the circumstances" she would not attend, and Rose, who never RSVPed, but admitted on the phone the next week that she'd been scared to come. "You don't even see it," she cried. "We still live in separate worlds."

And within the year, that guy Carl, who'd been going to marry her in the church, drifted off.

SESTINA COMPOSED IN CELEBRATION

OF THE MARRIAGE OF CLARA STURAK

AND CHRISTOPHER CHANDLER

13 June 1992

Love knows no laws, and yet each age commands
Tribute to Erato, of marriage vows the muse.
And who are we here gathered on this green
To risk the breaking of an ancient law?
For sweeter tongues than mine have gladly lent
Their music to her service, gladly sung.

Sappho has burned, Theocritus has sung,
Each answering an age's strict commands;
And after them Catullus' passion lent
His playful singing to evoke that muse.
Each voice its own, yet each obeyed the law,
And we still answer them, they are still green

In ageless youth, and we too on this green
Have gladly gathered, spoken more than sung,
Our sanction, our obeisance to that law,
Our wishes answering the stern commands,
Our hopes together asking of the muse
That all her blessings to this pair be lent.

For once the power of her gift is lent
To bless this couple here upon the green,
No earthling can deny the granting muse
Her wishes, but, her praises sung,

Gladly will answer all that she commands,
Gladly obey her great, yet gentle, law.

To Clara, beam of light, indeed a law
Unto herself, now let my voice be lent
To celebrate her beauty, her commands,
Her spirit ever young, forever green,
Her glowing talents ever to be sung,
Herself a magic figure, her own muse.

To Christopher, who finds in her his muse,
Wisely obeying most of her soft law,
Knowing the song is best when it is sung
In harmony, his wit and kindness lent
To keep this union flourishing and green,
Answering to her and to his own commands.

Now I have sung, my voice have gladly lent
To woo for them the muse, and give them on this green
To our own man of law, to answer his commands.

—John Espey

Lisa, John, and me as "Monica Highland." We've
had a lot of good luck.

I'm almost the only one around here who drinks anymore. But I
like to sit out back and look at the steep walls of Topanga and sometimes—after or during a third glass of chardonnay—I dream a little
bit about my family. I think of hot days and nights in Victorville,
with scorpions and centipedes in the corners of the room. My Aunt
Helen, frisky after work, tucking her legs up underneath her, waiting in the evening heat for Uncle Bob to bring her a drink. "It's
Toddy Time!" Or I think of Uncle Bob, watching television with
Tom, shyly remarking, as Godzilla smashes an aircraft carrier to bits
and sends it to the bottom of the sea, "I guess this reminds you of the

old days." Because Tom has been in the Navy. *I suppose this reminds you of the old days!* I dream of Aunt Helen: "Hi, Hi! Let's have a short snort!" For forty years she said it, never flagging.

My mother loved her sister, just loved her, and sometimes, when they stopped being hell on wheels, they'd sit down at the piano with much giggling and nudging, and play a duet—"Nola," or "Kitten on the Keys." Having fun, repeating fun that they must have dreamed up long ago.

My mother, before her divorce, was a beautiful woman, and sometimes she'd look through the kitchen window and sing as she did the dishes. "That old black magic has me in its spell, that old black magic that you weave so well . . ." When I was six or seven or eight, spending the night at a schoolfriend's house, I'd get so homesick, thinking of mother singing that song, I'd cry myself to sleep. Once, later, when I was in my teens, driving in the car with my dad, and he was on his same old welcome litany about what a nice kid I was, what a wonderful kid I was, and I was dreaming, dreaming, taking it in, soaking it up, taking it as it came and for what it was—just comforting talk—his conversation took an unexpected direction. "I really don't know why you turned out so well, except that Kate used to get you down on the floor when you were six months old or so, and play with you for hours."

What? What? *What? Play with me for hours?* Well, it must be true, because my dad would never tell a lie.

Something must be getting to me. Maybe it's the skyline of Topanga, where I look when I'm dreaming. There's not a rock, a star, an indentation in those mountains everyone in this family hasn't wished on, hasn't thanked. Thank you, God! Thanks for Charlie, who came out of nowhere and brought groceries for my broke and brokenhearted mom, and did that until he couldn't do it anymore. Thanks for Harvard, who did the same thing for me and my kids, so that one year when I was doing my taxes, it looked as though my total income was $2,800. Add on the hundred a month from Tom, that brought it up to $4,000. Not enough to live on! But the invisible part of the equation was Harvard, trudging up the hill with great food and great wine for seven, eight years, and he wouldn't *have* heartbreak! He wouldn't stand for it.

And I think of poor old sewn-up Jim, a desperate man. He threw shoes, he burned up my baby pictures. Such timid crimes! How lonely he must have been, with no one to love him, no one to laugh at his jokes—if he ever made a joke.

That loneliness! I remember Richard—who's still here, sober as a judge, right here in the present, married to his Beautiful Black Woman. He's handsome as ever. Sometimes, at some garden party at our daughter's house, I want to ask him, *What was the story, Richard?* Why couldn't we pull it off?

And I want to ask Tom the same thing, but he couldn't answer, any more than I could answer him. He said, "Ah, Carolyn," at Clara's wedding. Gave me a one-sided hug. Maybe that *is* the story. Absolutely enough of the story.

How did we get so lucky? I think of Rose, back in the seventies, stubbornly telling her story only to me, while Mother seethed, unnoticed, in a corner of Nate 'n' Al's. Rose told me about living in Kauai, in that cave, swimming all the way out, two miles, and floating in the ocean on acid, looking back at clouds and mountains, surveying the entire known world. "So that's what I've done," she said that day. Does she miss that world, clean and sober now in her little apartment? Does she miss her own majestic dreaming?

How did we get so lucky? John Espey, when he came up to see his old graduate student, must have been lonely. When I went to his apartment, it didn't have a couch in it. When tough little Clara spit in his Coke, trying to run him off, he drank that Coke right down. He hung in, wanting a family as much as we did. And drank, and stopped.

How did we get so lucky? When I think of my children I can only think I don't deserve them, and then I think, "Get a grip." *We all deserve the very best and now is the time for it!* I think of Lisa, beautiful and sixteen, vulnerable and wild, burdened unbearably with responsibility, having to carry our family as much as any mom, and Clara, six, laughing as much as she cried, yelling that any marijuana we smoked could get us arrested, standing on her head having a tantrum, her tears sliding from her eyes across her forehead and down into her hairline. She was my Rock of Gibraltar. They were both my lifelines.

I think of the weekends in the summer, when the girls and I would all drink coffee in the old Topanga cabin and the sun would pour in and we'd get under the same quilt and talk until we got so hungry we had to fix breakfast. Or those times when Harvard had made up his mind to cook Indian food, so when we did get up and forage in the morning we'd find his vegetable curry in the refrigerator, one of those magic foods, so much more than the sum of its parts that you had to eat it until it was gone.

How did we get so lucky? My stepdaughter, Katharine, Tom's kind girl who discovered that rattlesnake in the patio so many years ago, learning we were coming to Australia for a visit, turned her house upside down for us. Her message, so sweet: *See? I turned out OK.* See my beautiful and accomplished French husband, my three gorgeous kids, Eloise, Yara, Marius—bilingual, well-cared for?

Jean-Pierre made us one of the great French Sunday dinners; a roast with a billion vegetables, and quantities of red wine. Katharine's mom was there, and we tried out a little conversation about Tom, the husband we once shared. Carman got up, actually stood up, and made a speech: "I was only married to Tom for five years. And we were barely in our twenties. I hardly remember him. But if not for him, I wouldn't have Katharine. So I thank him, always."

Jean-Pierre, beaming, filled all our glasses. What a devil! The story they tell is: he turned my mother-in-law, Tom's mother, on to marijuana, she all the while maintaining she couldn't feel a thing, until she got the giggles and the munchies.

Penny, are you strong? I don't know, but the people around me are, and have come to live lives of moderation and temperance. My daughter, Lisa, has constructed an existence as complex as Sara

My baby half brother, Dad's son with Lynda, Robert Headsperth Laws III.

Murphy's, a life of fine accomplishment and perfect beauty, with a husband devoted to public service, and her two boys, so elegant and funny.

My daughter Clara, married now, in an airy apartment with a dedicated student, and they love each other! If you stand in the center of their place, and turn slowly, you see light flooding into every room. Light means everything.

I talk on the phone to my friend Jackie late one Saturday afternoon. We used to sleep under newspapers at her house when we were in the seventh grade; now we're both looking at sixty. We're chatting along and she says, "Wait a minute! Someone just crossed my lawn! It's your brother, in white boxer shorts, hiding his face with newspaper, so nobody will see him! Oh my gosh. What a sight!"

Brother Bob, my dad's son, only twenty-five, boards with Jackie now, in her ex-husband's dance studio. My stepmother worries that he has an "addictive personality." He loves to drink and he goes to the track, but he's in graduate film school, he stays away from hard drugs, and he's wonderful to his mom. My father would be so proud. Maybe, of all of us, Bob will make it in the movies. To look at him is to love him: his sweetness shines out, direct from his mom and dad.

The next day Bob turns up cheerful, with a bruise on his face. "I was out doing my laundry at Jackie's house, behind the pool," he says. "I must have been sleepy because I slipped and fell. Can you believe it?"

As his big sister I want to believe it, believe that respectability has come so far in our family that on a Saturday night my brother Bob is filled with nothing so much as a burning desire to do his own laundry. But on behalf of our granddad, who killed a man in a gunfight and drank himself to death, and our own dad, party doll until almost the very end, I hope—I can't help hoping—that Bob hasn't hung it up so soon. I hope he got that little bruise from hard living and the heedless pursuit of pleasure. Most of us have found the way to get out of the abyss and onto the calm and placid golf course. But there's something to be said for free fall, the wild life. It's ruined us, but it's helped to save us too. It's given us our stories; and made us who we are. It has to do with dreaming, inventing, imagining, yearning, and there's more of it—like blue smoke—in the American Dream than we're ever, ever, going to be able to acknowledge or admit.

CAROLYN SEE is professor of English
at UCLA and a book reviewer for
The Washington Post. She has two
daughters and lives with John Espey
in Topanga Canyon, California.

ABOUT THE TYPE

The text of this book was set in Janson,
a misnamed typeface designed in about
1690 by Nicholas Kis, a Hungarian in
Amsterdam. In 1919 the matrices became
the property of the Stempel Foundry in
Frankfurt. It is an old-style book face of
excellent clarity and sharpness. Janson
serifs are concave and splayed; the
contrast between thick and thin
strokes is marked.